Patterns of Middle Class Consumption in India and China

Patterns of Middle Class Consumption in India and China

Edited by

Christophe Jaffrelot
Peter van der Veer

SAGE   Los Angeles • London • New Delhi • Singapore
www.sagepublications.com

First published in 2008 by

SAGE Publications India Pvt Ltd
B 1/I-1, Mohan Cooperative Industrial Area
Mathura Road, New Delhi 110 044, India
www.sagepub.in

SAGE Publications Inc
2455 Teller Road
Thousand Oaks, California 91320, USA

SAGE Publications Ltd
1 Oliver's Yard, 55 City Road
London EC1Y 1SP, United Kingdom

SAGE Publications Asia-Pacific Pte Ltd
33 Pekin Street
#02-01 Far East Square
Singapore 048763

Published by Vivek Mehra for SAGE Publications India Pvt Ltd, typeset in 10.5/12.7 Minion by Excellent Laser Typesetters, Delhi and printed at Chaman Enterprises, New Delhi.

Library of Congress Cataloging-in-Publication Data

Patterns of middle class consumption in India and China/edited by Christophe Jeffrelot and Peter van der Veer.
    p. cm.
Includes bibliographical references and index.
    1. Middle class—India. 2. Middle class—China. 3. Consumer behaviour—India. 4. Consumer behaviour—China. I. Jeffrelot, Christophe. II. Veer, Peter van der.
HT690.I4P364   305.5'50951—dc22   2008   2008002198

ISBN: 978-0-7619-3623-7 (HB)   978-81-7829-787-3 (India-HB)

The SAGE Team: Sugata Ghosh, Samprati Pani, Sanjeev Sharma and
                 Trinankur Banerjee
Photo Credit: Jakob Montrasio, Mckay Savage

Contents

List of Tables

List of Figures

Acknowledgements

This book is the result of a conference that was put together by the International Institute for Asian Studies (IIAS) in the Netherlands, the Centre d' Etudes et de Recherches Internationales (CSH) in France, Centre de Sciences Humaines (CSH) and the Institute of Chinese Studies (ICS)/Centre for the Study of Developing Societies (CSDS) in New Delhi, India. It was funded by these institutions and by the India–China Program at Utrecht University, and was held at India International Centre in Delhi, 7–9 November. We are very grateful to Shoma Munshi who did the main organizational work and follow-up for the conference. Our warm thanks also go to Patricia Uberoi, Veronique Dupont, Bertrand Lefebvre and Ravni Thakur for their efforts. Special thanks to Angmo Bhotia of the ICS and Mallika Hanif of CSH for taking care of logistical details on the days of the conference. We also thank the India International Centre for the use of their facilities; and Neville Tuli, who, when contacted by Shoma Munshi, very kindly loaned us film posters from his personal collection and Osian's, which adorned the walls of the conference room, adding a touch of glamour and colour. We thank Jairam Ramesh for his incisive talk in opening the conference. Sugata Ghosh at SAGE immediately saw the importance of this project and has been immensely supportive. The conference and the book that has resulted from it are a step in the direction of more scholarly interaction between Europe, India and China.

Christophe Jaffrelot
Peter van der Veer

1

Introduction

CHRISTOPHE JAFFRELOT
PETER VAN DER VEER

The middle class is a notoriously elusive social category. It is defined, almost by default, as 'what-is-in-the-middle', between the upper layers of society and the plebeian masses. Thus defined, this group would not fit in a pre-modern, feudal order. For instance, what would it be in pre-revolutionary France? Not the third estate which comprised the bourgeois as well as labourers. The 'middle class' is a phenomenon of the capitalist era. Indeed, the phrase was used for the first time in Great Britain, by the end of the 18th century, to designate those 'who have some education, who have some property and some character to preserve'.[1] But situating the birth of the middle classes in its context does not make their definition much easier. Though Marxism—the main sociological school associated with the rise of capitalism—is the pioneering doxa so far as class is concerned, it was rather badly equipped for deciphering whether this collective being was on the side of the exploiters or on that of the exploited?[2] In the West, it has always been on both sides because of its composite nature.

The other classical theorist of class, Max Weber, has also emphasised this complexity. For Weber, class situation is largely determined by the material resources and skills one brings to the market. Certainly,

Weber differentiates the propertied-class from the non-propertied one, but within the former he distinguishes the large proprietors from the 'petty bourgeoisie' and among the latter, the working class from the 'intelligentsia', which does not own any property but has skills (1978: 302–05). In the Weberian reading of the class structure, the 'petty bourgeoisie' and the 'intelligentsia' are certainly the mainstays of the middle classes—the plural seems more relevant than the singular given the dual nature of this intermediary stratum. Weber's views were certainly more heuristic than the Marxist ones for analysing the situation of the middle classes in India, especially during the colonial era.

But in India as elsewhere, the social scene became more and more complicated as societies modernised. In the West, the middle classes gradually included entrepreneurs and traders (ranging from the small shopkeepers to middle merchants) who exerted control over labour, on the one hand, and salaried people ranging from managers to journalists, on the other. The industrialization process and the bureaucratization of the state led to the emergence of a new brand of middle class, the white collar salariat, which was studied by C. Wright Mills (1951) after World War II in the United States. This group gained momentum along with the growth of the third sector, the services, which developed at the expense of industry and agriculture. The more it developed, the more it got differentiated and stratified, so much so that one felt the need to qualify this category as comprising an upper layer—the 'upper middle class' —and a lower strata—'the lower middle class'.[3] The classification of these social groupings was primarily based on socio-economic criteria such as occupation and the standard of living. But other parameters such as patterns of consumption are often taken into account too. Gradually, the latter became a kind of focal point to which the middle classes started to converge, so much so that today, the middle class may recover its singular designation because of its rather homogeneous consumption pattern.

SEARCHING FOR THE MIDDLE CLASS IN INDIA AND CHINA

In India, scholars maintain that there are very few studies on the character of the middle classes. In his seminal work on the subject, B.B. Mishra

(1961) lamented, in the first sentence of his preface, that it 'remained virtually unexplored'. Forty years later, Sanjay Joshi (2001: 4) regretted that 'Indian historiography ha[d] more or less ignored the middle class in recent years. Scholars of the 1950s and 1960s did use the term extensively but for most part assumed the middle class to be a self evident sociological category which did not need further explanation.'

In fact, Indian and western scholars have made stimulating attempts at analysing the Indian middle class(es) in the last decades. In this body of work, we can even distinguish two types of interpretation, reflecting the heterogeneity of this social category. The first adopted a political economy point of view, drawing its inspiration from the notion of 'intermediate regimes' developed by the Polish economist, Kalecki (1972). The economists and historians who applied this concept to the Indian situation, usually in a Marxist perspective, considered that India was an intermediary regime due to its incomplete transition to capitalism before the colonial era. Burton Stein (1991), for instance, argued that India was on the verge of a capitalist revolution, which was arrested by British colonialism. As a result, the country was left with a strong 'petty bourgeoisie', which represented the Indian variant of the middle class.[4] More orthodox Marxists have highlighted the role of the petty bourgeoisie in Indian society either by considering that it was bound to disappear because of the polarisation between the capitalists and the proletariat (Dutt 1940) or by regarding it as simply one segment of the ruling bourgeoisie (Kosambi 1964). The issue remains undecided among historians even today. Claude Markovits (2001: 46), for instance, argues that 'merchants, traders, and medium or small scale industrialists... obviously account for a significant chunk of the overall middle classes in terms of numbers, but there remains a big question as to whether they constitute a separate social group or can be seen as part of a broader sociological category', that is, the bourgeoisie.

The Indian economy has undoubtedly created niches for middle class entrepreneurs right from the British era. If the factories of Lancashire and elsewhere submitted Indian artisans to unfair competition in many ways, local economic agents managed to corner large chunks of the domestic market and benefit from the modernisation impact of new means of communication and the import of new technologies. Post-Independence, India was even more favourable to the interests of these small- and medium-size entrepreneurs because of its protectionist overtone (the import of manufactured consumer goods was almost banned in 1957) and because of the 'licence raj', which reserved large sectors of the economy to cottage industries (officially known as small scale industries) in a Gandhian cum social democratic attitude. In 1960, there were 36,460 small factories registered under the Factories Act as having a fixed capital of less than Rs 5,00,000. They employed 38 per cent of the registered factory employment, that is, 1,338, 000 people. They represented 17.5 per cent of the fixed capital of all registered factories and contributed to about one-third of the total production (Ministry of Industry 1963: 16).[5] Contemporary India is, indeed, a country of entrepreneurs—mostly small and inter-mediary in size.

Yet, when historians and sociologists search for the origins of the middle class(es), they do not look primarily in this direction. For most of them, everything started with the British Raj. B.B. Misra (1961: v) argues along these lines in the preface of his book:

> In the West, especially in England, for example, the middle classes emerged basically as a result of economic and technological change; they were for the most part engaged in trade and industry. In India, on the contrary, they emerged more in consequence of changes in the system of law and public administration than in economic de-velopment, and they mainly belonged to the learned professions. India's traditional emphasis on literary education combined with Britain's rule and her imperialist economy to make the intelligen-tsia the dominant strand in the composition of the Indian middle classes.

The main impact of the colonial policy implemented by the British lay in their decision to resort to local intermediaries for ruling India. There had never been more than 1,40,000 people to administer a terri-tory larger than Europe; therefore, in addition to the Maharajahs they had left at the helm of the princely states, they needed indigenous bureaucrats. They trained them in an 'Anglicist' perspective,[6] to quote the famous 1835 'Minute on Indian education' by Lord Macaulay, in order to 'raise up an English-educated middle class [*sic*] who may be interpreters between us and the millions whom we govern—a class of persons Indian in colour, in blood, but English in tastes, in opinions, in morals, and in intellect' (Stokes 1989 [1959]: 46). Members of the

Indian elite were sent to Britain to pursue their studies, and subsequently universities were open in India to train an ever larger number of bureaucrats, lawyers, accountants, and so on. A class was taking shape as a result of a public policy decision. B.B. Misra (1961: 11) concludes from this process that:

> These ideas and institutions of a middle class social order were imported into India. They did not grow from within. They were implanted in the country without comparable development in its economy and social institutions. The middle class which the British aimed at creating was to be a class of imitators, not the originators of new values and methods.

This assessment is symptomatic of the love–hate relation that Indian scholars have with the middle class despite belonging to that class. More importantly, this assessment is wrong. Certainly, the British made the initial impact, but the graft was so successful because the men (and women in much less numbers) they had shaped, fashioned their own culture and identity and even invented new values out of the old materials they had at their disposal.

The middle class Macaulay envisaged, turned out to be an intelligentsia in the true sense of the word, that is, a group of individuals socialized in their parents' tradition but western educated and equipped with the litteratis' skills. In the early 19th century, the best exemplary of this synthesis was probably Rammohan Roy, known as 'the father of modern India' (Robertson 1995). According to Sanjay Joshi (2001: 2), this figure fully illustrates one of the defining features of the middle class, that is, its adoption of modern ways of life:

> Much of the power of this group of men, and later women, who fashioned themselves as the middle class, came from their claim to emulate an ideal-typical modernity first appropriated by their counterparts in the West. But the Indian modernity they constructed had also to be different.

Indeed, Roy was a reformist more than an 'occidentalist'; he tried to adapt aspects of western modernity to Indian conditions (for instance, see his plea for women's welfare and education) rather than imitate the

West in each and everything. In fact he was very proud of the mainstay of Hindu civilization—including the vedic scriptures that he publicized for the first time—and developed a form of ethnic nationalism. The socio-religious movement he created in 1928, the Brahmo Samaj, therefore, was both a modernization force and a proto-political society prefiguring the Congress, which was to be created in 1885 by reformists from the intelligentsia.

If the reformist attitude of the intelligentsia was a major characteristic of this sub-group of the middle classes, the other sub-group we have described before, the petty bourgeoisie, was more attached to traditions. This judgement needs to be qualified because some of its members like G.D. Birla displayed a great deal of reformism, but they were in a minority (Timberg 1978). Naturally, this state of things harked back to the lack of interest in western education that this socio-economic milieu displayed, in contrast to the emphasis the intelligentsia put on it. Such a difference of behaviour regarding social customs is a good indication of the radical heterogeneity of the middle classes in terms of ethos and 'mentalité'.

There is a criterion, however, which both sub-groups have in common and that is caste—the petty-bourgeoisie and the intelligentsia both came from upper castes.[7] Claude Markovits (2001: 53) stresses the 'fairly narrow base of recruitment in terms of caste' of the merchants and entrepreneurs and the fact that, because of this common sense of belongingness, even today, they 'continue to give preference in employment in their firms to members of their family, kin, caste and community, even if they are less competent than "outsiders" (although probably to a lesser extent, now, than in earlier periods)'. Andre Béteille (2001: 84) makes the same remark about the intelligentsia of the 'babus' (bureaucrats, literati).

Here, we reach the point where the Weberian theory loses much of its relevance. For Weber (1958), class and status groups, like castes and tribes, are two separate realities:

> In contrast to classes, status groups are normally communities. They are, however, often of an amorphous kind. In contrast to the purely economically determined 'class situation' we wish to designate as 'status situation' every typical component of the life fate of men that is determined by a specific, positive or negative, social estimation of

honour... status honour need not necessarily be linked with a 'class situation'. On the contrary it stands in sharp oppositions to the pretensions of sheer property.

Certainly, status groups and classes do not coincide, but they cannot be de-linked to that extent. Critics of Weber have convincingly argued that the social and the economic cannot be dichotomised but form two faces of the same coin. Prandy (1998: 361), for instance, argues that:

we need an integrated conceptualisation of stratification, which allows both for their resources associated with work and employment that typically figure in class schemas and for those associated with social interaction and evaluation that inform ideas of status. The two are simply aspects of a unified social reality.

As early as 1958, Lockwood has experimented this approach in his study of the Blackcoated workers where he showed that 'the position of clerks had to be considered in terms of three aspects—their market situation, work situation and status situation' . For Lockwood, 'status situation' refers to 'the position of the individual in the hierarchy of prestige in the society' (1989 [1958]: 15).

The relationship between class and status group is a key issue in India because of the strength of caste, a status group par excellence. In contrast with the Weberian assumption mentioned earlier, we shall hypothesize in this volume that caste and class cannot be considered separately but need to be analyzed together. Though they do not coincide, they closely interact in the social life of India and exert a strong influence over the identity of the middle classes.

The consideration of caste as an additional variable defining the middle classes allows us to reduce their heterogeneity since their two mainstays, the 'petty bourgeoisie' and the 'intelligentsia', and most of their other components as well come from the upper castes. While there is an inevitable tension between the value system associated with class, which is based on individualistic values, and the one associated with caste, which is based on hierarchical, collective values, the caste background of the middle classes made them more cohesive in terms of shared values.

The growing homogeneity of the middle classes—which meant that, by the turn of the 21st century, the plural came to be replaced by the singular in a spontaneous and natural way, like in the title of Pawan Varma's book, *The Great Indian Middle Class* (1998)—stems from other factors too. First, the differences related to caste eroded. Sons (and even daughters) of the economic bourgeoisie paid more attention to education and followed the same kind of curricula as sons and daughters of the old 'babus'—MBAs became a must, instead of humanities or the Indian Administrative Service (IAS). This change was due to the liberalization policy the Indian government adopted in 1991, which opened avenues for new opportunities. Second, the upper castes among the middle class tended to share the same concern vis-à-vis positive discrimination programmes, which reduced their prospects in the high administration. In 1990, the implementation of the Mandal report introduced a new employment quota of 27 per cent of the jobs in the central administration for members of low castes—the Other Backward Classes (OBCs). As a result, upper caste youth, be they brahmins or banyas, protested that merit was not given its due. Merit, in fact, became a keystone of the discourse and of the identity of the upper caste middle class. Last but not least, the liberalization process gave birth to new patterns of consumption that all segments of the middle class valued equally. New western consumer goods made their appearance on the Indian markets and the middle class, the first target of the importers, developed more Americanized tastes and habits. This new pattern became *an ethos* based on uninhibited consumption. Varma (1998) argues that for the first time, state policies legitimized a materialistic worldview whereas Gandhism and Nehru's socialism had emphasized other ideals. The worst part of this new socio-political agenda was the reinforcement of the natural inclination towards selfishness of 'a class which was already morally rudderless, obsessively materialistic, and socially insensitive to the point of being unconcerned with anything but its narrow self-interest' (ibid.: 174).[8] This assessment is supported by the enormous popularity of the show broadcast by Star TV, *Kaun Banega Crorepati* (Who wants to Become a Millionaire) and, less anecdotally, by social scientists' surveys, which show that what the middle class values most in the new economic policy is the accessibility of consumer goods that it hitherto had to import from abroad through expatriate relatives (see Fernandes 2000).

More than ever before, Indian society looks at itself as middle class-centred. Certainly, this social group has increased. The 1998 National Council for Applied Economic Research (NCAER) Report on Indian market demographics classified the consumer groups into three categories: the very rich, the consuming class and the climbers (Natarajan 1999). These three groups increased from 77.6 million households in 1994–95 to 87.8 million in 1995–96! Even if this impressive growth rate has remained unchanged, the most optimistic assessment regarding the size of the Indian middle class cannot put the tally beyond 200 million people, which means that this class would represent one-fifth of society. In spite of this minority status, the middle class sets the terms of reference of Indian society, not only because of its development, but also because it is the darling of the official discourse and policy makers.

All the caveats for using the concept of the 'middle class' in the Indian case are also applicable to the Chinese case. In late imperial China, in the second half of the 19th century, we might understand the middle class in the first place in terms of the imperial encounter as a class of traders that developed brokerage between the imperial powers and the Qing imperial system. After the Opium Wars it had become clear to some Chinese that China had to modernize quickly by developing relations with western nations. The modern sector of the Chinese economy was still marginal as compared to agriculture and this continued to be so till far into the 20th century. The traders and middlemen who occupied positions within the emerging economy of industry and foreign trade remained dependent on the bureaucratic complex that led the modernization efforts of the Qing Empire (Bergere 1989). The important group of bureaucratic officials, largely emerging from the educated gentry, can be seen as the other part of the middle class. This structure of a middle class consisting of merchants or entrepreneurs and officials continues in present day China. What also continues is that the middle class is connected to the West, combining notions of brokerage with notions of selling out to the West. The conceptual problem of the definition of a middle class in China is, therefore, immediately connected with the issues of imperialism and globalization. In the Marxist view that became central in Communist China, the middle class was accordingly conceptualized as a comprador class that can only exist in dependence of imperialist interests.

Incidentally, this was also the Marxist analysis of the middle class in India that was important for the Communist Party in India (Ghosh 1985).

It is only in the 1910s and 1920s that in places like Shanghai, an urban middle class with greater consumption needs emerged. Shanghai not only became a financial centre for banking but also a centre of consumption with big department stores. Leo Ou-fan Lee (2000) shows in his work how Shanghai became the centre of producing a new culture (xin wenhua) with emphasis on *new*. That new middle class culture could be found in advertising in new newspapers and magazines and it showed significant changes in gender relations in the domestic sphere and in leisure activities. However, it is important to understand that this new middle class never became the self-assured carrier of a bourgeois nationalism in China. It was an isolated class living in some big cities, emerging in a period of incredibly violent conflicts, led by different warlords, and great economic turmoil.

This period ended in 1949 with the victory of the Communists in their struggle with the Nationalists. The Communists organized one campaign after the other to eradicate feudal landlords and bourgeois capitalists. Their attempts to create a classless society led to the destruction of patterns of private production and consumption. Shanghai was singled out as a 'city of vice', an un-Chinese city that had surrendered to western imperialism. Its middle class was chased away to Taiwan and Hong Kong. To be called 'middle class' or bourgeois was to ensure great difficulties in getting a decent life for oneself and one's children. For instance, in 1957 over 3,00,000 intellectuals were branded 'bourgeois rightists', a label that destroyed their prospects in society (Spence 1990: 572). Even sociologists who had written critical reports on societal issues, such as Fei Xiaotong, repudiated their reports, with the result that our independent knowledge on China is limited (Mcgough 1979). Such 'anti-rightist' campaigns were launched all the time, culminating in the Great Cultural Revolution that urged children to accuse their parents of bourgeois leanings if the latter would just as much like to listen to classical music (Krauss 1989). At the same time, however, there is clear evidence from the 1950s that a salariat, a professional, bureaucratic class, connected to an expanding state sector emerged (Davis 2000). This class of managers of state industries was part of the entrepreneurial groups that developed after Deng

Xiaoping's economic reforms of 1978. Deng's decision to develop Shanghai again as a financial and commercial centre is a telling illustration of the turn towards globalization, led by the Party leadership. These economic reforms that are central to China's spectacular economic growth over the last three decades have not been coupled with political reforms. Attempts by students and others to force political democratization have been answered by attacks on 'bourgeois liberalization'. While, on one hand, political liberalization continues to be branded as 'bourgeois' and 'anti-Chinese', consumerism, on the other hand, has become fully accepted. The 'Four Musts' (bicycle, radio, watch, sewing machine) of the Maoist era have, under Deng and his successors, been replaced by the 'Eight Bigs' (colour television, refrigerator, stereo, camera, motorcycle, furniture, washing machine and electric fan). As in the Indian case, consumption patterns have become the way to understand the middle class.

The criteria used for identifying the middle class are changing today. For long, its definition was based on occupations, revenues and education. But scholars from different schools of thought have stressed that 'social class' was as much an objective as a subjective reality (see Bourdieu 1979, Elias 1983 and Castoriadis 1987)—the 'ranking' of individuals was largely overdetermined by social imaginaires. As a result, there are often obvious discrepancies between self-perceptions and objective indices like income and occupation. In India, this subjective dimension has not been taken into account for long. Instead, the standard parameters accommodated status-based ones, like caste in India. But today, a new variable has to be emphasized— the pattern of consumption, which has given birth, as argued in India by D.L. Sheth, to a *new* middle class in which the imaginary dimension is more significant.

New because its emergence is directly traceable to the disintegration of the caste system, this has made it socially much more diversified compared to the old, upper caste oriented middle class that existed at the time of independence.... Membership of today's middle class is associated with new lifestyles (modern consumption patterns), ownership of certain economic assets and the self consciousness of belonging to the middle class. As such it is open to members of different castes—which have acquired modern education, taken to non-traditional occupations and/or command higher incomes and the political power—to enter this middle class (1999:11).

Indeed, in a recent survey, the Delhi-based Centre for the Study of Developing Societies (CSDS) considered as members of the middle class the respondents who said they were part of it and who possessed two of the four characteristics: (*i*) ten years or more of schooling, (*ii*) ownership of at least three assets out of four, that is, motor vehicle, TV, electric pumping-set and non-agricultural land, (*iii*) residence in a *pucca* house—built of brick and cement, (*iv*) white-collar job. Consumption patterns had obviously made their entry among the criteria of social classification, at the expense of traditional considerations like caste. The CSDS findings indicate that on the basis of such parameters, about 20 per cent of the sample population could be identified as belonging to the middle class and, interestingly, while the upper castes accounted for a quarter of the sample, they represented half of this 'new' middle class—a clear indication that old categories like caste might lose their strength, but display some resilience anyway.

CONSUMPTION IN INDIA AND CHINA

While it is undoubtedly true that the IT revolution and other forms of globalization have drastically transformed our life-world and its patterns of production and consumption in recent decades, we are still largely heirs to the Great Transformation of the 19th century. A major aspect of that transformation is an increased rate of urbanization. The rural–urban divide and the divide between the urban poor and the urban middle class are thus important in our discussion of changing consumption patterns of the middle classes today. Many of the consumption patterns that now define our lives originated in the global urban centres in the 19th and early 20th centuries, and in Europe they are captured in the literary imagination of Baudelaire in Paris, Henry James in London and Robert Musil in Vienna. Cities emerge as 'sites of dreadful delight' as Henry James put it (1922) and that is not only true for European and American cities, but also for Shanghai and

Mumbai. The department store, global fashion, photography and leisure are all signs of becoming modern, a seemingly never-ending process. The question always remains what is more 'with the times', more advanced and what lags behind, seems backward, old-fashioned. That advancement is always in some ways related to notions of greater personal freedom and brings with it the complexities and contradictions of liberty and surveillance. In societies in which the majority of the population lives in rural areas, the city is a place that disrupts feudal arrangements and well-established obstacles to self-expression and is foremost a place of unlimited visibility of consumption. This is even true, to an extent, for an economy of fantasy in which the urban poor participate.

While urbanization is one aspect of the Great Transformation, a more foundational one is the ascendancy of the economy as a primary source of value. It is perhaps best characterized by Adam Smith's notion of the 'invisible hand'. What economists and political scientists today call the 'rational choice of individuals', but what Smith calls 'the individual pursuit of happiness', leads in the economist's view to general welfare in a mechanical way. While this is the foundation of liberal capitalism, Marx's dialectical materialism is not different in its selection of the economy as the prime mover. In this way the economy becomes the most important purpose of society.

This secular framework is just as metaphysical as the religious one that preceded it in Europe and in Asia. The secular metaphysics of the economy is not only basic to modern social science and policy making, but also to its rejection as gross materialism. Charles Taylor has pointed out that in the ancient regime, the excessive pursuit of individual wealth was seen as a corruption that threatened the order of society, while in the modern social imaginary the order of society is created by it (Taylor 2004). However, the notion that the economic perspective on society is corrupt continues in a modern form as the rejection of materialism. This rejection particularly concerns the consumption side of the economy. The rejection of limitless consumption becomes as central as consumption itself in the modern social imaginary.

While the Great Transformation is deeply connected with the rise of European empires, the rise of a new consumer culture has been crucial to the development of American hegemony in the world.

According to Woodrow Wilson, in 1916, America's 'democracy of business' had to lead in 'the struggle for the peaceful conquest of the world'. Wilson argued that 'the great barrier in this world is not the barrier of principles, but the barrier of taste' and connected states-manship and salesmanship in his advice to his countrymen to 'go out and sell goods' and 'convert the world to the principles of America' (cited in de Grazia 2005: 1–3). This indeed has been successful. America has become the 'Market Empire', as Victoria de Grazia has called it in her recent book (2005) on the way American consumer culture has conquered Europe. This conquest became really successful in the aftermath of World War II. The Atlantic alliance between Western Europe and the United States was accompanied with the enormous popularity of American music and products. The older cultural resis-tances against it, especially in France, continued, but they came to look more and more like a lost battle. After decolonization, both India and China tried to develop into modern industrial societies without becoming part of the capitalist world under American hegemony. Till the late 1980s, India and China were remarkably resistant to American consumer culture, a resistance that basically took two forms. In China it took the form of Maoist secular utopianism, while in India it took the form of Gandhian religious utopianism. Foundational to both forms is an anti-imperialist nationalism.

Basic to the anti-colonial imaginary in India is the opposition be-tween eastern spirituality and western materialism. This opposition is part of the exceptionality on both sides of the equation. It explains the exceptional material success of western modernity and the mate-rial defeat of the colonized societies in the East as well as the philo-sophical shallowness of that success in the face of the exceptional richness of eastern traditions. Gandhi is the best example of this line of thought.

The response to imperialism in China is quite different. Chinese nationalism embraces material progress and scientific materialism. In China, both in the Republican period and in the Communist regime that followed it, science was the sign under which the nation and mo-dernity were conceived. At the same time, one notices the emergence of a new urban consumer culture, for example, in Shanghai in the 1920s and 1930s. After the victory of the Communists, however, consumer culture, especially in Shanghai, was violently repressed till 1980.

What we see in China from 1950 to 1990 is a long period of invoking the revolutionary spirit of the people against feudalism, against individualism and against the capitalist enemy, most clearly USA. This invocation was necessary for a number of ill-fated campaigns such as the Great Leap Forward and the Cultural Revolution. This was the period of socialist frugality and uniform appearance in Mao costumes as well as the patriarchal repression of sexual liberty, as described in Ha Jin's novel *Waiting*. A city like Shanghai with its pre-war cosmopolitanism, a city of dreadful delight, was seen as un-Chinese and had to be repressed till the death of Mao and the rise of Deng Xiaoping (a former leader of Shanghai). It is interesting to see that the Chinese often see the Mao period as a period without religion and consumption but full of enchantment and collective illusion. Clearly, Mao became the ultimate leader with something that resembled a heavenly mandate, but one who focused on mobilizing the peasants and celebrating the peasant. The bourgeoisie and the landlords were targeted as counter-revolutionaries. Peasants were the pure source of revolutionary spirits and during the Great Cultural Revolution urban people had to be re-educated by going to the countryside and learning from the peasants. It is this period of repression that is crucial for our understanding of the rise of consumption and the emergence of an urban middle class in China since the declaration of 'socialism with Chinese characteristics' by Deng Xiaoping in 1978. What happened in China can perhaps be best understood as a socialist transition comparable to what happened in Eastern Europe after the collapse of communism. The anxiety about the rise of class differences, loss of solidarity and of the state's 'iron rice bowl' mixes with the joy of consumerism in the cities. The disillusion with Maoist collective effervescence has promoted a world of great opportunism or 'grasping one's fate' (bawo sizide mingyun), of magical belief in 'good luck' (yuan fen) and cynicism. This is perhaps clearest in the generation that participated in the idealism of the Tiananmen student revolt and is now totally devoted to making money.

In contrast to the Chinese case, where we find a form of extreme secularism, that is at the same time an enchanted materialism, in India we find a spiritual rejection of materialism in Gandhi's contribution to the struggle for Independence. Gandhi was as charismatic as Mao in mobilizing the masses for his vision. He was deeply aware of the connection between materialism and anti-imperialism in British intellectual circles when he started writing about India's struggle for Independence in his book *Hind Swaraj* in 1910. He himself saw that struggle as primarily a spiritual one. The sources of that spiritual perspective were multiple: Hindu tradition, Tolstoy's understanding of Christian spirituality, Ruskin's thoughts about industry and Nordau's views on civilization. His anti-consumerism came from banya frugality and asceticism that came to be linked with Ruskin's critique of industrial products. Furthermore, he was strongly influenced by R.K. Dutt's argument that Britain had de-industrialized and underdeveloped India. These thoughts came together in Gandhi's decision to discard English dress and wear only homespun cloth (khadi) and ultimately go as far to wear merely a loincloth, signifying asceticism as well as solidarity with the toiling poor. This was a radical rejection of both European production and consumption as deeply embedded in imperialism. The Gandhian dress comes to be as symbolic for political service to the nation as the Maoist peasant dress in China and both signify a resistance against urbanity and consumerism.

Gandhi's 'experiments with truth' were attempts to strive for moral truth through disciplines of the body such as fasting, celibacy and frugality. All this implied a strong anti-consumerism, an economic autarchy and a celebration of simple rural life. Gandhi wanted economic progress for India and saw the materialism of imperial power as one of the causes of India's decline. Gandhian philosophy deeply influenced even Nehru's secular modernism that was strongly geared at creating economic self-sufficiency and led the state away from violent modernization, such as Mao's Great Leap Forward, but also left society's deeply ingrained hierarchies intact. Nevertheless, it is striking how much both India and China sought to secure their national Independence in anti-consumerism with an emphasis on heavy industry rather than on creating a consumer's market.

A major element in economic policy in both India and China between 1950 and 1980 has been great restrictions on foreign trade and foreign investments with a strong emphasis on self-reliance. This put great obstacles on the development of a consumer's market which could be legitimized by Maoist and Gandhian ideologies. However, since the 1980s, both India and China have been opening up their economies to the world market. This has had wide-ranging effects on these societies including rising income levels for the middle classes and a change in consumption patterns. What does the consumer revolution after the 1980s mean for India and China, politically and socially? First, we may see the new confidence and assertion of the middle class. In India, this has been clearest in the connection between the middle class and an aggressive religious nationalism. In China this is much less clear because of political repression, but perhaps the violently suppressed Falun Gong with its messianic nationalism shows some of the tensions inherent in the rise of the middle class. Second, we see a kind of youth revolution, signified in the middle class by the new professions taken by young people and the different lifestyles enabled by the higher salaries they acquire. Parents often complain about the selfishness of these new generations, but are also bewildered by the new money and conspicuous consumption of these youngsters. Third, we may see new gender relations. This is quite clear in some parts of the Far East, such as Taiwan, where young, professional women prefer not to marry men who seem old-fashioned and patriarchal. This trend is visible to some extent in China, but hardly in India. Nevertheless, in India also, one finds the 'modern woman' with new demands on career possibilities and gender equality.

Obviously, the developments described in this book are not part of a global process of westernization or Americanization, but are part of a global modernity that is experienced in significantly different ways in China and India (Breckenridge 1995). Sometimes we may suggest that forms of conspicuous consumption seem to have survived the onslaught of Gandhian and Maoist anti-consumerism even at the height of their influence. In India, it is marriage with its dowry system that seems to not have been controlled by a spirit of anti-consumerism. Deeply embedded in hierarchical thinking, it has spurred competitive spending and indebtedness in a nation devoted to a saving glut. In China, it is the creation of guanxi relations in banquets that seems to have escaped the Maoist onslaught (Yang 1994). The extent to which men are involved in dining out in large groups and today also go to Karaoke bars is remarkable and explains the existence of an elaborate restaurant culture.

This book is precisely intended to analyze the specificity of today's middle class in India and China—to what extent it follows a similar route in both countries and to what extent it is really new. The first five

chapters after the 'Introduction' constitute an interdisciplinary reflection on the reliance of traditional sociological notions on which definitions of the middle class were based so far in India and China. These
chapters analyze the intermingling of these old notions and new attitudes or *mentalités*. To begin with, Christophe Jaffrelot proposes an
explanation of the declining electoral participation of the Indian middle
class by revisiting the role of caste in politics. He shows that the middle
class citizens who abstain from voting are mostly from the upper castes:
the low caste middle class people do vote *en masse*. Certainly, the upper caste middle class boycotts the polling booth not only because of
an overt rejection of opportunist and corrupt politicians, but also
because they are losing out to the lower castes—Dalits and OBCs—a
clear indication that caste matters a lot in the politics of the middle
class. However, depoliticization of the upper caste middle class needs
to be qualified. Carol Upadhya very convincingly argues in her chapter
that the IT professionals she has interviewed combine a deep sense
of globalization and a strong attachment to their Indian roots. This
hybrid 'global Indian' identity, fostered by the diasporic relationship
India entertains with the US, is certainly not cutting off this new
social group from its past. Thus, concludes Upadhya, 'the identity of
transnational Indian IT professionals is produced more through
consumption of *ideologies* of the family and nation, and of the *idea* of
Indian culture, than through consumption of new consumer goods
and lifestyles'. From a purely political point of view, the inclination of
the upper caste middle class towards Hindu nationalism substantiates
this interpretation. Betrand Lefebvre makes a similar argument when
he shows that the development of corporate hospitals in metropolitan
cities like New Delhi is partly overdetermined by the seeking of national pride: not only do the rich need not go abroad any more for
getting the best healthcare, but also westerners come to India for their
own medical treatment! However, Lefebvre rightly emphasises that,
above all, 'the corporate hospital can be read as an enacted utopia for
the Indian middle class, as a monument dedicated to consumerism in
the realm of healthcare'. Hence its promotion, in the advertisements
he scrutinizes, as a five star hotel and the inclusion of shopping centres
as well as IT offices in its premises—incidentally the corporate hospitals concentrate in the new frontiers of the Indian cities, like in south
Delhi, where they cohabit with shopping malls of a new kind.

Zhou Xiaohong shows in his chapter that in China too, the middle class is not a taken for granted notion. In mainland China, it is still assessed by the people according to 'the amount of assets owned'. His study suggests, however, that about one-tenth of the big cities form a rather homogeneous middle class today. This group, which is the direct outcome of the reforms initiated in the late 1970s, is defined according to canonic criteria such as occupation, education and income. It is made of the owners of newly-born private and township enterprises, other self-employed people like petty proprietors and small traders and, of course, the bureaucrats and intellectuals, be they part of the administration, the Party or the university system. Jean-Louis Rocca adds that besides the objective criteria there are other subjective ones which need to be taken into account. He makes a point that lifestyles are especially important in any social hierarchy based on class. According to him, the Chinese middle class distinguishes itself—in Bourdieu's sense—by their professional ethos and their consumption pattern: they 'have a tendency to work more than other groups, to strive continuously to climb the social and professional ladder', 'they consume a lot and mainly sophisticated products', 'they plan for buying, they save money before spending', and so on. It is precisely from the point of view of consumption that the middle classes of India and China present the most striking affinities.

The second part of the book describes significant elements of the new consumer culture in India and China. Pál Nyíri and Xun Zhou examine the consumption of experience in what has become one of the most important global economies: tourism. Nyíri describes the way Chinese middle class tourism has totally transformed the town of Songpan in Sichuan Province. Interestingly, the Chinese authorities want to use planned tourism as a way to promote the 'material and spiritual aspects' of Chinese civilization. In that way, tourism plays an important role in the incorporation of minority ethnicity in Chinese nationalism. The transformation of cities not only happens in relation to tourism but also to other leisure activities of the middle class, as discussed in Anand V. Taneja's essay on Delhi. Taneja discusses the arena in which overlapping claims on a piece of land in Delhi are debated and decided. It is not simply a case of local interests that are marginalized by national politics, but various conflicting claims on history and heritage that are fought over in relation to new patterns of middle class consumption, such as playing golf.

Another aspect of the new consumer culture in India and China that is discussed in this volume is the entertainment industry. Chua discusses what he calls an 'East Asia pop culture sphere', consisting of an ethnically Chinese sub-region (the PRC, Hong Kong, Taiwan, Macau and Singapore) as well as Korea and Japan. Consumers are aware of the integration of this culture sphere by watching the border crossings of major actors and actresses. Very popular are Korean TV dramas and especially their lead actors who have huge fan followings in this region. One can perhaps speak of virtual communities of shared taste supported by lifestyle magazines.

Munshi moves us away a bit from our exclusive focus on the middle class. She discusses the way the working class of Delhi consumes media images through television. Her study shows the extent to which consumer options are influenced by television even for people who have a low income. They do not want to appear 'out of fashion' and they want to get more out of life. This desire bridges the gap between lower and middle class consumption patterns. Elfick looks again at a high-income earning group in industrial Shenzen, China, and discusses the ways in which sexual behaviour is influenced by American television dramas, like *Sex and the City*. Again it is the consumption of experiences, like in the tourism industry, that guides these young conspicuous spenders. It is as if the sexual revolution of the 1960s has finally hit China and with a vengeance. The flip side of this is the continuing importance of marriage and the romance of it. Patricia Uberoi examines a number of bridal magazines and argues that just as interesting as the emphasis on the aspirational modernity of marriage, is the erasure of the continuing existence of traditional forms of matchmaking and the giving of dowry. Uberoi's analysis of the Indian imagery is informed by the existing literature on wedding photography in Taiwan which is a booming industry of conspicuous consumption. Finally, Xun Zhou discusses the remarkable spread of Karaoke entertainment from Japan to the rest of the world, including China. She shows how much Karaoke has become part of today's male work culture. The increased uncertainties of employment and working conditions have made Chinese men more vulnerable and Karaoke allows them to relieve these tensions somewhat. It also recreates an egalitarian ethos that is increasingly lost in the new management styles that stress differences in performance. At the same time Karaoke is also part of the dining culture of China, part of the efforts to create guanxi business relations. Karaoke thus signifies several levels of the development of new consumption patterns in relation to significant changes in the conditions of labour and business.

At the highest level of consumption, we find a new acceptance of real wealth and the display of it in China. Art dealers have discovered a willingness to pay a high price for homegrown artists. Ho describes in some detail this new market of consumption as well as the growing interest in residential developments with avant-garde architectural styles. In this and other essays, we find that a certain pride in the national ability to consume is at least as important as the desire to distinguish oneself from others through conspicuous consumption. Consumerism is thus not only class-oriented but also nation-oriented. There is a great interest in buying Chinese art and that is not only for aesthetic reasons but also for nationalist reasons. Something similar can be found among Indian art buyers who show a preference for Husain or the Bengal school. Obviously, this is right now an elitist possibility but gradually it will widen to a larger middle class audience and, ultimately, become connected to tourism as a mass phenomenon.

Finally, when comparing India and China, it is interesting to note that India seems to be more resistant in many ways to global consumer culture in the fields of sexuality and music despite its long colonial past. This confirms to the theory that under colonial conditions Indian culture became a site of resistance against foreign oppression. While China has suffered from imperialism too, it has never been colonized. Its modernization project was in the hands of native leaders. Since the demise of international communism as the focus of society, it is nationalism and national culture that has to replace it despite the decades of attacks on traditional culture.

Notes

1. To quote Rev. Christopher Wyvill, the North Riding-based founder of the Yorkshire Association for parliamentary reform (cited in Warhman 1995: 443).
2. Indeed, the rise of the middle class has provided the critics of Marxism with some of their most effective ammunition against this class theory.
3. On the middle class in the West, see Stearns (1979), Pilbeam (1990) and Mayer (1975).

4. See also, among those who applied the Kaleckian notion of 'intermediate regimes' to India, Raj (1973) and Fox (1984).
5. In 1965, a new survey showed that the 1960 one had underestimated the strength of the small scale industry sector—it enumerated 1,00,000 units (Planning Commission 1966: 238).
6. In the early 19th century, the advocates of 'Anglicism' argued against the 'Orientalists' that the culture of India was of no worth compared to the science of the West, and more especially of Great Britain, which needed to be taught to the local literati.
7. This element of homogeneity needs to be qualified, however, because both sub-groups, in the 19th and 20th centuries, have been largely equated with two clusters of castes—while merchants and entrepreneurs came from the third varna, the vaishyas (or banyas), in large numbers, the intelligentsia was primarily a product of the literati castes, brahmins and kayasths. This rather clear-cut division explains their diverging views of education, the latter being used to relying on their traditional skills, whereas the former never put any such emphasis.
8. Interestingly, the critical overtone of this assessment is also found among the Hindu nationalists. In 2005, the English mouthpiece of the RSS, *The Organiser*, published a similar indictment of the middle class: 'The middle class is that it wants many things—money, comforts, entertainment, prestige and, above all, a clean environment and good government—all at once on a platter. But anything in return? Probably none. It negates the ever true "demand and duty" relationship which holds the mankind together...' (Saxena 2005: 15).

References

Bergere, Marie-Claire. 1989. *The Golden Age of the Chinese Bourgeoisie*. Cambridge: Cambridge University Press.
Béteille, Andre. 2001. 'The Social Character of the Indian Middle Class', in I. Ahmad and H. Reifeld (eds), *Middle Class Values in India and Western Europe*. New Delhi: Social Science Press.
Bourdieu, P. 1979. *La Distinction*. Paris: Editions de Minuit.
Breckenridge, Carol A. 1995. *Consuming Modernity: Public Culture in a South Asian World*. Minneapolis: University of Minnesota Press.
Castoriadis, C. 1987. *The Imaginary Institution of Society*. Cambridge: Cambridge University Press.
Davis, Deborah S. 2000. 'Social Class Formation in Urban China: Training, Hiring and Promoting Urban Professionals and Managers after 1949', *Modern China*, 26(3): 251–75.
de Grazia, Victoria. 2005. *Irresistible Empire: America's Advance through 20th Century Europe*. Cambridge, MA: Harvard University Press.
Dutt, R.P. 1940. *India Today*, London: Victor Gallancz.
Elias, N. 1983. *The Court Society*. Oxford: Blackwell.
Fernandes, L. 2000. '"Nationalising the Global": Media Images, Economic Reform and the Middle Class in India', *Culture and Society*, 22(5): 611–28.

Fox, Richard G. 1984. 'Urban Class and Communal Consciousness in Colonial Punjab: The Genesis of India's Intermediate Regime', *Modern Asian Studies*, 18(3): 459–89.

Ghosh, Suniti Kumar. *The Indian Big Bourgeoisie: Its Genesis, Growth and Character*. Calcutta: Subarnarekha.

James, Henry. 1922. 'London', in *Essays in London and Elsewhere*. Freeport: Books for Libraries.

Joshi, Sanjay. 2001. *Fractured Modernity: Making of a Middle Class in Colonial North India*. Delhi: Oxford University Press.

Kalecki, M. 1972. 'Social and Economic Aspects of "Intermediate Regimes"', in M. Kalecki, *Selected Essays on the Economic Growth of the Socialist and Mixed Economy*. Cambridge: Cambridge University Press.

Kosambi, D.D. 1964. *The Culture and Civilisation of Ancient India in Historical Outline*. London: Routledge and Kegan Paul.

Krauss, Richard. 1989. *Pianos and Politics in China: Middle-Class Ambitions and the Struggle over Western Music*. Oxford: Oxford University Press.

Leo Ou-fan Lee. 2000. 'The Cultural Construction of Modernity in Urban Shanghai: Some Preliminary Explorations', in Wen-Hsin Yen (ed.), *Becoming Chinese: Passages to Modernity and Beyond*, pp. 31–62. Berkeley: University of California Press.

Lockwood, D. 1958/1989. *The Blackcoated Worker: A Study in Class Consciousness*. Oxford: Clarendon Press.

Markovits, C. 2001. 'Merchants, Entrepreneurs and the Middle Class in Twentieth Century India', in I. Ahmed and H. Reifeld (eds), *Middle Class Values in India and Western Europe*. New Delhi: Social Science Press.

Mayer, A. 1975. 'The Lower Middle Class as a Historical Problem', *Journal of Modern History*, 47(3): 425–52.

McGough, James. 1979. *Fei Hsiao-t'ung: The Dilemma of a Chinese Intellectual*. White Plains, New York: M.E. Sharpe.

Mills, C. Wright. 1951. *White Collar: The American Middle Class*. New York: Oxford University Press.

Ministry of Industry. 1963. *Development of Small Scale Industries in India: Prospects, Problems and Policies*. New Delhi: Government of India.

Mishra, B.B. 1961. *The Indian Middle Classes. Their Growth in Modern Times*. London: Oxford University Press.

Natarajan, I. 1999. 'India Market Demographic Report, 1998'. New Delhi: NCAER.

Pilbeam, P.M. 1990. *The Middle Classes in Europe 1789–1914: France, Germany, Italy and Russia*. Basingstoke: Macmillan.

Planning Commission. 1966. *Fourth Five Year Plan: A Draft Outline*. New Delhi: Government of India.

Prandy, K. 1998. Class and Continuity in Social Reproduction: An Empirical Investigation, *Sociological Bulletin*, 27(2): 361.

Raj, K.N. 1973. 'The Politics and Economics of 'Intermediate Regimes', *Economic and Political Weekly*, 8(27): 1189–98.

Robertson, B.C. 1995. *Raja Rammohan Ray: The Father of Modern India*. Delhi: Oxford University Press.

Saxena, S.N. 2005. 'A Role for Middle Class', *The Organiser*, 24 April.

Sheth, D.L. 'Secularisation of Caste and Making of New Middle Class', *Economic and Political Weekly*, 21–28 August 1999. Available at http://jan.ucc.nau.edu/~sj6/epwshethmclass1.htm, accessed on 5 September 2006.

Spence, Jonathan D. 1990. *The Search for Modern China*. New York: Norton.

Stearns, P.N. 1979. 'The Middle Class: Towards a Precise Definition', *Comparative Studies and History*, 21(3): 377–96.

Stein, Burton. 1991. 'Towards an Indian Petty Bourgeoisie: Outline of an Approach', *Economic and Political Weekly*, 26(4): PE 9–20.

Stokes, E. 1959/1989. *The English Utilitarians and India*. Delhi: Oxford University Press.

Taylor, Charles. 2004. *Social Imaginaries*. Durham: Duke University.

Timberg, T.A. 1978. *The Marwaris: From Traders to Industrialists*. Delhi: Vikas.

Varma, P.K. 1998. *The Great Indian Middle Class*. Delhi: Penguin.

Warhman, D. 1995. *Imagining the Middle Class: The Political Representation of Class in Britain, c. 1780–1840*. Cambridge: Cambridge University Press.

Weber, Max. 1958. *The Religion of India: The Sociology of Hinduism and Buddhism*. Glencoe (Illinois.): Free Press.

————. 1978. *Economy and Society: An Outline of Interpretative Sociology*. Berkeley: University of California Press.

Yang, Mayfair Mei-hui. 1994. *Gifts, Favors and Banquets: The Art of Social Relationships in China*. Ithaca: Cornell University Press.

2

'Why Should We Vote?': The Indian Middle Class and the Functioning of the World's Largest Democracy*

CHRISTOPHE JAFFRELOT

The political culture of the Indian middle class has often been analyzed in terms of partisan orientations. From its inception till the 1950s,
the Congress party was looked at as a creation of the middle classes,
resulting from the process of 'macaulayisation' already mentioned in
the introduction of this volume (see Seal 1968; Broomfield 1968).[1] In
the 1960s, the Jana Sangh appeared as 'the party of small industry and
commerce' (Graham 1990: 158), largely because its traditionalist—even
corporatist—ideology led its leaders to defend family-based economics. Twenty years later, the 'middle-classes were keen supporters of
Rajiv Gandhi' (Hasan 2002: 159) who then embodied a promising form
of modernity epitomized by his motto 'to prepare India's entry into
the 21st century' (Weiner 1989). Then in the 1990s, the Indian middle
class was attracted by Hindu nationalism once again. They contributed to the Bharatiya Janata Party's (BJP) rise to power in 1998 and the

* I am grateful to the CSDS Data Unit and more, especially, to Sanjay Kumar for
providing me with many of the survey data on which this paper is based.

re-election of its coalition, the National Democratic Alliance (NDA), in 1999.

While the party got 19.7 per cent of the valid votes in 1999, it received 23.8 per cent of middle class votes, according to the figures of the CSDS Data Unit. They became the cornerstone of what Yogendra Yadav, Sanjay Kumar and Oliver Heath (1999) called the 'BJP's new social bloc'. In the BJP, writes Suhas Palshikar (2002: 172):

> the middle classes could find almost everything they dreamt of: a frankly market-oriented economic policy, a foreign policy striving to befriend the Americans, a suave middle-of-the-road prime minister (A.B. Vajpayee) along with a strong home minister (L.K. Advani); all coupled with an appropriate dosage of chauvinistic cultural-nationalist assertion.

In the BJP, the middle classes also found an undeclared hostility to positive discrimination on behalf of individual merit and strong reservations vis-à-vis parliamentarianism. Hindu nationalism was never fully reconciled with parliamentarian democracy, a regime borrowed from the West (see Jaffrelot 2000). The party believed more in a presidential system with authoritarian overtones. Its leader, A.B. Vajpayee, declared in the 1996 'Desraj Chowdhary Annual Memorial Lecture' that 'the present system of parliamentary democracy has failed to deliver the goods' and that his first choice was a presidential system. In his view, such a system would emancipate India from the rule of parties and enable the country to replace politicians by bureaucrats and technicians.[2] This anti-parliamentarianism was well in tune with the political culture of the middle classes. In 1993, an opinion poll conducted by MARG in Bombay, Delhi, Calcutta, Madras and Bangalore revealed that 58 per cent of the interviewees agreed with the proposition: 'If the country is to progress it needs a dictator' (Sunday 1994: 59).

The anti-parliamentarian inclination of the Indian middle classes not only results in their proximity vis-à-vis the BJP, but also explains the distancing of this social milieu from the institutional functioning of the world's largest democracy. The most obvious symptom of this alienation—that may amount to a real depoliticization—lay in the declining electoral participation of the middle classes. Yet, this notion needs to be qualified because such an assessment applies only to the upper caste segment of these classes.

The Declining Electoral Participation of the Urban Middle Classes in India

At first glance, electoral participation is on the rise in India. From a meagre 45.7 per cent in 1952, the turnout rate has increased steadily to peak in 1984 at 64.1 per cent. This was an exceptional achievement due to the tragic circumstances of the assassination of Indira Gandhi. But since then, turnout has never dropped below 58 per cent at the time of general elections. However, this general picture dissimulates important geographical and social disparities. North and west India do not vote as much as south and east; the turnout rate of women remains much below that of men; voter turnout is higher in villages than in cities and towns.

This is a new development, as evident from Table 2.1, which shows that in 1977, rural constituencies had a lower turnout rate than urban ones (57.2 per cent as against 61.4 per cent), whereas this order was reversed in 1991 when the rural constituency turnout remained at 56.1 per cent while the urban turnout fell to 53.8 per cent.

This trend has continued since then, so much so that the difference between the rural and the urban turnout rate has never been less than

Table 2.1 Turnout according to the constituency categories

Year of election	Urban	Rural
1977	61.4	57.2
1980	58.3	53.9
1984	64.0	63.0
1989	61.3	60.8
1991	53.8	56.1
1996	54.6	57.8
1998	57.7	61.5
1999	53.7	60.7
2004	53.1	58.9

Source: For 1977–99, *Journal of Indian School of Political Economy* (2003). For 2004, CSDS Data Unit.

3 percentage points and has increased as much as 6/7 percentage points, with rural constituencies registering a rate of almost 59 per cent in 2004 whereas urban constituencies fell to almost 53 per cent, the lowest ever. The cities of India vote less because the urban middle class votes less.

The Exceptional Indian Pattern of Absenteeism

In most democracies—if not all—electoral absenteeism is positively correlated with social and educational backwardness (to use terms the Indian Constitution is familiar with). Hence the popular expression, 'the disenfranchised' which is used to designate those who had no right to vote in the past—because of their low income—and who continue not to vote today because of their socio-economic condition. In the United States, the correlation is perfectly linear: in November 2002, for the mid-term elections, 78 per cent of those who earned less than US$ 5,000 a year did not vote, compared to 43.4 per cent of those who earn more than US$ 75,000 a year. Those who voted less were the un-employed (abstention rate: 72.8 per cent), whereas those who voted the most were government workers (40.9 per cent) and the self-employed (51 per cent) (US Census Bureau 2004). Similarly, 63.5 per cent of those who earned US$ 10,000 did not vote in 2004 for the presidential elec-tions, while only 21.7 of those who earned more than US$ 150,000 abstained, the correlation being perfectly linear too—the richer you were, the more you voted (US Census Bureau 2004). In Britain also, the proportion of those who voted was higher for self-employed people (71 per cent) during the 2001 general elections than for employed people (66 per cent); unemployed people were the least likely to vote—only 48 per cent voted (see http://www.statistics.gov.uk/cci nugget_print.asp?ID=1008). In France, only 40.4 per cent of unem-ployed people and 40.2 per cent of the workers voted in the 2002 elec-tions, whereas 58.8 per cent of the 'Cadres et professions intellectuelles supérieures' (executives and higher intellectual professions) did so (Octant 2005: 5).

In stark contrast with this dominant pattern, in the world's largest democracy, the poorer one is, the more one votes and the richer one is, the less one votes. This is evident from Table 2.2, which shows that during the last Lok Sabha elections, 59.3 per cent of the very poor people

Table 2.2 Turnout according to class during the 2004 Lok Sabha elections (CSDS post poll survey weighted by actual turnout)

Social class	Voters (percentage)	Non-voters (percentage)
Very poor	59.3	40.7
Rich	56.7	43.3
Average	58.1	41.9

Source: CSDS Data Unit.

the CSDS agents interviewed in the exit poll survey said that they had voted, whereas only 56.7 per cent of the rich said the same.

This unusual pattern is especially pronounced in big cities. Delhi is a case in point. During the 2003 state elections, the gap between the turnout of the 'rich' and the turnout of the 'very poor' was almost 32 percentage points, even though the difference was not so great so far as the 'poor' were concerned (see Table 2.3).

If one aggregates the 'very rich' and the 'rich' into a single category, it is quite clear that this class is the only one where those who do not vote are more numerous than those who do.

Table 2.3 Turnout according to class during the 2003 state elections in Delhi (CSDS post poll survey weighted by actual turnout)

Social class	Voters (percentage)		Non-voters (percentage)	
Very poor	77.5	60	22.5	40
Poor	57		43	
Lower middle	53.5	53.6	46.5	46.4
Middle	53.8		46.3	
Rich	45.8	48.3	54.2	51.7
Very rich	57.5		42.5	
Average	53.4		46.6	

Source: CSDS Data Unit.

Why do the Urban Rich Vote Less?

To answer this question, one must explore several hypotheses which reflect—each in its own way—the multi-faceted identity of this category that we call the middle classes.

The most trivial explanations have much to do with the materiality of the voting process: voting is painful because one has to stand in the queue and wait for hours under the sun or the rain—something rich people are not used to. This is an excuse I have heard repeatedly, but it is not as convincing as it might have been in the past because the Electronic Voting Machines have substantially reduced the queues in front of the booth.[3]

Another aspect of the voting process invoked by the middle class to explain why they do not go to the polling booth concerns the voters list. These lists are criticized because many names are missing from them, an anomaly that is generally attributed to the ruling party's malpractices. Impersonation is another related issue. A university lecturer protests: 'Many a times when you go to the polling booth, you find that your vote has already been cast.' Though this is hard to believe given the computerization of voter lists and the checking of IDs as well as the marking of one finger of every voter with indelible ink, this phenomenon may have reached massive proportions in some towns and cities. But then the question is: why has it dissuaded middle class people to vote and not others?

Middle class people are not so easy to reach during the election campaigns. In India, more than in any western democracy, party activists canvass by going door to door. This method cannot be really effective in the case of an urban middle class, which is eager to protect its privacy. In contrast, the plebeians are more accessible and some political activists may even take them to the booth collectively (in trucks or buses), though this is strictly forbidden by the law. The Representation of the People Act of 1951 stipulates that 'the hiring or procuring, whether on payment or otherwise, of any vehicle or vessel by a candidate or his agent or by any other person for the conveyance of any elector (other than the candidate himself, the members of his family or his agent) to or from any polling station is a corrupt practice' (cited in Viraraghavan 1956: 129). But, these are rather common practices in the countryside till today, which may partly explain the gap between the turnout rates of urban India and rural India. While these parameters and the 'gifts' (saris, alcohol, and so on) offered to the poor may explain why they go to the polling booths, they do not explain why the rich do not go.

In fact, most of the arguments based on the materiality of the voting process are allegedly for justifying attitudes which are not legitimate in a democracy where voting is a duty as well as a right. Obviously, one must look for more profound explanations.[4] One of them lies in a strong rejection of the political personnel—there is no need to vote because MPs and MLAs form a political class known for its corruption and its unethical arrangements. One of the faculty members I interviewed in Jammu University in March 2005 says it plainly:

> Well firstly, I would quote the definition of democracy which is 'Of the people, by the people, for the people'. In the context of the Indian democratic system, I will quote that it is a democracy which is 'OFF the people, FAR the people and BUY the people'.... As far as the Indian polity is concerned, it is totally dominated by money and commercial elements. So, as far as the politics of Indian politics is concerned, it is a politicization of criminals, corruption, the caste system and communalism. So where is this political system going? Only a few politicians are deciding the future of the country. According to their vested interests, they are misguiding the people. Now we have the coalition politics. They have contested the elections separately, and they formed the coalition without uniting in principle and ideology. So this is a democracy decided by the polity. In the Indian context, that is why I say that democracy is not working properly as far as the masses are concerned.

The era of coalition which India entered in the 1990s has apparently aggravated the discredit of the political personnel because the outcome of the elections regarding who will form the government has not been decided by the voters but through behind-the-scenes negotiations. This happened in 1996 and 1998. Since then, however, *pre-electoral* alliances have been able to take over power—in 1999, the BJP-led NDA and in 2004, the Congress-led UPA.

In addition to their lack of morality, politicians are rejected because of their ineffectiveness. This argument is recurrently made by executives who are used to the rules of management applied in the corporate sector. A Bhopal-born senior executive at Indian Oil who works seven days a week and does not even find the time to visit his parents 800 km away declares in this vein:

> This is an opportunistic democracy. In the name of democracy we have lost all sense of discipline. The army and, to some extent, the

judiciary are the only disciplined institutions in this country. Corruption is everywhere. People have no sense of public interest. Nobody pays taxes—except we, the salaried people. In the name of democracy we have let rural India escape all taxes. They don't even pay for electricity. This is the bane of democracy. The party which makes the peasants pay taxes and electricity bills will be out of power for ten years.

This corporate executive targets the populist dimension of Indian democracy, which results in demagogic, anti-economic and inequitable decisions. Interestingly, he praises a more disciplined brand of polity. Such an attitude, which originates from the booming private sector, has become very common among the new middle class. These people are not so much calling for a military regime as for a more managerial democracy on behalf of efficiency. One remembers the heading of the homepage of the website of N. Chandrababu Naidu, the then Chief Minister of Andhra Pradesh who tried to make Hyderabad a high tech city but was voted out by the peasants he had thoroughly neglected—'Chandrababu Naidu: CEO, Andhra Pradesh', showing him typing on his laptop (see http://members.tripod.com/chandrababu/).

The 'State of Democracy in South Asia' survey that the CSDS coordinated in 2005 shows converging results. When asked whether 'We should have a strong leader who does not have to bother about elections', 38 per cent of the interviewees from the 'elite' agreed and 30 per cent of the interviewees from the masses agreed. However, only 15 per cent of the interviewees from the 'elite' felt 'The country should be governed by the Army' whereas 80 per cent felt that 'All major decisions about the country should be taken by experts rather than politicians' (CSDS 2008). This is a clear indication of the development of a new political culture that believes more in managers than in parliamentarians. This shift is not unrelated to economic liberalization and the growth rate of the economy, which is attributed to a more managerial style of conducting public affairs. It found its first vocal expression in the summer of 2005 when monsoon floods were considered as badly handled by the administration in Mumbai. The local middle class then called for the replacement of the state apparatus by people trained in the corporate sector. This move was naturally supported by the role big firms had already played in reconstructing Gujarat after the 2002 earthquake.

There is no denying that some urban middle class people do not vote because they no longer trust parliamentary democracy. However, another major explanation for this new attitude lies in the dynamics of caste politics.

THE KEY ELEMENT OF CASTE

Indian sociologists have tended to de-link caste and class as much as they could, be it from a Marxist perspective or from a Weberian one. For the Marxists, of course, there is nothing compared to class, as a social category defined by the position of the people vis-à-vis the ownership of the means of production—one belonged either to the proprietary classes or to labour. B.R. Ambedkar exposed this flawed perception as early as the 1930s, showing that caste solidarity cuts across class sentiments simply because the 'caste system is not merely division of labour. *It is also a division of labourers*' (Ambedkar 1990 [1935]: 47, emphasis original).[5] The neo-Weberians, who acknowledge the importance of status in social relations, have constantly tried to maintain a distinction between class situation and status situation. André Beteille (1996: 513) argued along these lines:

a major contribution of analytical sociology has been to formulate and explore systematically the distinction between class and status. It is true that sociologists differ on how the distinction should be made, just as they differ on what they mean by status and by class. Nevertheless, they would agree upon the need to maintain as consistenly as possible some kind of distinction between the two.

For me, it is not possible, and certainly not desirable, to distinguish class and caste simply because both categories are closely connected, as André Béteille (2002: 74) himself has suggested recently when he wrote: 'It will be impossible to understand the morphology, leave alone the values, of the Indian middle class without taking account of the pre-existing differentiation of Indian society on the basis of language, religion and caste'. To look at caste and class separately would be an artificial exercise amounting to some wishful thinking that caste belongs to the past and that India has entered the era of class. This is what Jayaram assumes when he writes:

> The combination of caste and class status is no more a sociological axiom—the decline of the Jajmani system and the commercialisation of agriculture, the implementation of land reforms, the release from bondage of serfs, and the consequent changes in agrarian relations; and the rise of the land-owning 'upper-Shudra' caste groups, have all profoundly altered he economic bearing of the caste system (1996: 82).

Certainly, India has changed—though the land reforms have been stillborn in many states. Caste and class do not coincide any more, but they are still closely related anyway. Indeed, the 2000 National Sample Survey shows a remarkable correlation between caste and one's standard of living. According to this survey, more than 60 per cent of the urban upper caste Hindus had a per capita monthly consumption expenditure of Rs 775 or more, whereas less than 25 per cent of the urban Other Backward Classes (OBCs) and less than 18 per cent of the urban Scheduled Castes (SCs) were in such a position. Similarly, among the urban rich who spend more than Rs 1,500 of per capita consumption expenditure, 59.8 per cent are from the upper caste Hindus, 14.6 per cent from the OBCs and 3.8 per cent from the SCs (cited in Deshpande 2003: 112–13). Unsurprisingly, castes and occupations coincide to a large extent. According to a survey conducted thanks to the CSDS Data Unit, 24.5 per cent of the upper castes belong to the 'salariat' and 20.4 per cent to 'business', as against 9.5 and 10.1 per cent for the OBCs and 10.9 and 5.3 per cent for the SCs respectively (Kumar 2002: 4095).

One may object that standards of living and consumption patterns do not say everything—caste and class are also mindsets and even though the rich may come from the upper caste, they might have emancipated themselves from the hierarchical ethos of their original status group. Indeed, Béteille argues that

> Middle-class values are often contradicted by the values of caste and community, and the same individual is pulled in opposite directions. Individuals frequently act in ways that they condemn in others, justifying their own conduct by the press of circumstance (2002: 74).

I beg to differ again and rather consider that, far from being schizo-phrenic, middle class people combine rather easily both value systems to make one integrated new synthesis. A core element of this socio-political culture lies in the typical middle class value of individual *merit* and the correlative rejection of positive discrimination—the recurrent setting to fire of 'the corpse of merit' in anti-reservation protests is the most pictoral illustration of this correlation. Now, the defence of merit, which occupies the front row in the middle class repertoire, is well in tune with the hierarchical ethos of the upper caste Hindus. This is due to the fact that positive discrimination is largely based, in India, on the criterion of caste and, indeed, this major feature of the upper caste middle class worldview became prominent during the Mandal affair in the early 1990s. But this is also due to the elective affinities between the upper castes' ethos and the middle class value system. Comment-ing upon the book by Amitav Ghosh, *The Hungry Tide*, Sankaran Krishna shows that one of the characters, Kanai, 'an urbane, single and successful male entrepreneur from Delhi' can only oscillate 'between an ideational commitment to egalitarian values and an inability to practise it in reality', something the author implicitly attributes to caste consciousness or subconscious:

> so long as the subaltern's desire for a better life remains mimetic, aspirational and ultimately futile..., Kanai can be both indulgent and supportive. And yet, the minute it threatens the sedimented hierarchy of *an enduring social order*, he turns vicious, and a repressed inner-self surfaces with incredible hatred towards the subaltern'[6] (2006: 2328, emphasis mine).

It is very difficult to prove that this defence of hierarchy is rooted in caste feelings because no middle class man would confess that his behaviour is still dictated by the illegitimate social institution that is caste. But, here, political scientists could help sociologists understand what is going on. The starting point for such an analysis, once again, must be the Mandal affair. To my mind this affair made a bigger impact over the political culture of the urban middle class than the almost simultaneous decision to liberalize the Indian economy because of the changes in the polity that it entailed. New political parties emerged, which found their roots in two separate milieus, Dalits and

OBCs. The Bahujan Samaj Party, the Samajwadi Party and the Rashtriya Janata Dal are cases in point. The rise to power of these parties, which have governed Uttar Pradesh and Bihar over the last 15 years, permanently or intermittently, has transformed (north) Indian politics. It not only reflects the growing political awareness of the subalterns but also affects mainstream parties. For instance, the Congress and the BJP have given tickets to an ever larger number of OBC candidates. So much so that the declining presence of the upper castes among the MPs has taken them to their lowest points so far. This socio-political transformation results from the changing political attitude of the low caste voters. When they were included in clientelistic networks, they voted for their patrons—be they landlords, bosses or money lenders on whom they depended. But after the upper castes objected to the reservation policies, as they did in the streets in 1990 during the anti-Mandal demonstrations, they joined hands in a move towards horizontal solidarity and they now vote for their own caste fellows, be they candidates nominated by explicitly low caste parties or by mainstream parties.[7] This shift was bound to make a big difference to Indian politics given the sheer number of the lower castes: Dalits (17 per cent of the population) and OBCs (52 per cent) represented almost 70 per cent of Indian society. In 2004, upper caste MPs represented only one-third of all the MPs returned in the Hindi belt whereas the OBC MPs are almost one-fourth of the total (Jaffrelot 2007).

This plebianization of Indian politics has alienated the urban middle class from two points of view—first, the new social profile of the candidates is not to their liking because the nominees come more and more from the lower castes; second, they have started to wonder what difference their vote could make, given their small numbers. When I asked her why the middle class people of Delhi abstained from voting is such large numbers, Sheila Dixit, the Chief Minister of the state since 1998, replied:

Now there is a kind of cynicism about how is it going to make a difference if we go to vote or do not go to vote. They talk about politics most of them. But their attitude is 'I am not ready to try and make a difference', because they feel that they are not in numbers adequate enough to bring about a change.[8]

Things were different in the past when the addition of middle class votes could garner the plate of a candidate of their own milieu for whom plebeians had been requested to cast their vote according to a classic clientelistic pattern.

Caste politics is, therefore, largely responsible for the growing indifference of the middle class towards elections. In fact, instead of focusing on class as the more relevant variable, one should pay more attention to caste. Indeed, the difference between the electoral participation of the upper castes and the Dalits is even more significant than the difference between the electoral participation of the rich and the poor.

The idea that caste may be the most important variable when we try to understand the voting pattern of the middle class, is supported by the chronology of the change in turnout rates mentioned in Table 2.4. Indeed, the voters of the towns and cities of India where the upper caste middle class is concentrated started to vote less in 1991, precisely when low caste politics took off in the context of the Mandal affair.

Table 2.4   Turnout according to caste during the 1999 and the 2004 Lok Sabha elections in India (CSDS post poll survey weighted by actual turnout)

Caste groups	Voters		Non-voters	
	1999	2004	1999	2004
Dalits	60.6	63.3	39.4	36.7
Upper castes	58.0	57.7	42.0	42.3

Source: Adapted from data provided by the CSDS data unit.

Moreover, if we now turn to the Dalit middle class, we do not find the same apathy so far as voting is concerned and nor do we find the same rejection of parliamentary democracy. The notion of a Dalit middle class, though rather new, is not at all irrelevant, given the progress SCs have made in terms of education and socio-professional mobility thanks to the reservation policies in the university and the public sector. As pointed out earlier, the share of the Dalits in the salariat is bigger than that of the OBCs (and also of the Muslims), 10.9 per cent against 9.5 per cent (and 10.7 per cent) (Kumar, Heath and Heath 2002: 147). According to Gopal Guru, this Dalit elite has distanced itself from its original milieu:

The Dalit middle class keeps a safe distance from their caste people who normally reside in the slums of major cities. They have undergone a complete change in the value structures. Their past life has become so disgusting that they do not want to be reminded about it (2002: 147).

I do not share Guru's pessimism. Certainly, many Dalit *parvenus* lay themselves to the old cooption process that the Congress manipulated so well during the golden age of clientelistic democracy. And many of them probably do not visit the slums where their caste fellows continue to live. But it does not mean that they have severed their links with their original milieu. I do not agree with Guru's assessment that 'the Dalit middle class has nothing to do with the ideology of Ambedkar' (ibid.). Many Dalit civil servants and students have read some of his books and try to propagate his social as well as political views, as is evident from the social background of the members of the Backward and Minority Communities Employees Federation (BAMCEF), a union that has been the crucible of the BSP. These Dalit middle class people have lost no interest in electoral politics, on the contrary!

In order to explore the political culture of the Dalit middle class, I conducted dozens of interviews over the last 10 years. I shall reproduce below the main results of the one I conducted on 25 February 2005. It was a group interview with 18 Dalit students of Jawaharlal Nehru University (JNU), Delhi, coming from 10 different states.[9] The students definitely belonged to the middle class so far as their standard of living was concerned. Incidentally they were all fluent in English except one Hindi-speaking girl. I posed them a single twofold question: 'What is your assessment of Indian democracy and is it useful to vote?' Except one proponent of the naxalite ideology, they were all enthusiastic about the functioning of Indian democracy and positive about the act of voting. One of the interviewees said:

My own assessment is that the Indian democracy is working quite well, and is moving towards being more participative and giving power to the lower caste. And it is through this movement that the lower caste is asserting themselves. So I think it is within our reach through democracy only to upset that hegemony of the upper caste.

This respondent was not at all isolated. Most of the others were satisfied with Indian democracy insofar as it permitted the empowerment of the lower castes—they approved of a form of *democracy by caste*. One of them even declared:

> From the 1990s what we are seeing is that along with the Hindu nationalist forces, we are also seeing regional parties, different caste parties, and local parties; there is a kind of resurgence of protest against the Congress or against Hindu fundamentalist forces. There is a kind of resurgence of protest. That is again a part of the Indian democracy which from the last 20 years has been coming up. And of course caste politics and caste participation is compulsory in that.

These young Dalits of the intelligentsia very pertinently suspected that the upper castes were now giving a bad name to democracy because they were losing power in comparison to the lower castes. One of them made this very perceptive comment:

> There are moves now to subvert democracy. There has been a sense that in the early part since Indian independence, India was the only functional democracy in the third world, that its democratic values were great, etc.... But what happens when lower caste groups start coming into power, then the whole discourse starts being built up saying that democracy is fraud, the State is doing funny things, that people are grabbing, using the State to grab more than what they require through non-democratic means. Politics becomes something dirty suddenly. The whole point, even of this survey itself, is very interesting at what time it comes up. When democracy was in shambles in the beginning of the 1940s–1950s, Indian democracy was portrayed as the shining light of the world. And now when it is actually coming into its own, when people are participating, people are beginning to voice what they feel, then democracy becomes something on which we have surveys being conducted about if it is good to vote or not.

Another Dalit student makes a very similar analysis by paying more attention to the strategy of the upper caste middle class:

I feel the group of the upper caste and middle class who used to hold the political power, has moved to two spheres: NGOs and the media. It is through the media that the sense is created that politics is dirty. If you clearly analyse the media, where the upper caste is moving, especially the English media, the way Laloo Prasad Yadav is portrayed, Mayawati is portrayed, there is a sense amongst the middle class-upper caste, that Laloo Prasad Yadav is a criminal and corruption personified. And that Mayawati is another factor that should not come to politics. So the other option for them is military rule because democracy is not functioning. I am perfectly happy with the way Indian society and Indian democracy is functioning. And it is getting more and more democratised. NGOs also. You move to NGOs, and they say that politicians are bad and that it is not functioning etc., etc. So I will vote. Definitely I will vote.

In this perspective, voting is important. In fact all the respondents, except the follower of the Maoist strategy, said so. One of them expressed this view very well:

Social and economic democracy is not functioning in the Indian social structure, basically OBCs and SCs/STs communities. Still, if you consider OBCs and SCs/STs politics, they are asserting themselves in the parliament in a political way. Politics or the democratic way is the only way that they can assert themselves. Democracy is the only structure in which they can bargain and justify themselves. So voting is the only way to assert themselves.

Another interviewee made the same point in one sentence: 'you cannot make a change in this country without voting.'

CONCLUSION

The declining interest in elections among the urban upper caste middle class of India can primarily be explained by its growing rejection of the existing form of democracy and the rise of a new plebeian brand of politics. There, caste plays an important part—the urban middle class which abstains from voting is upper caste. The Dalit middle class people do vote and very much appreciate the empowering potential of democracy.[10]

The contrasting attitude of the upper castes and the lower castes regarding the act of voting partly explains one of the puzzling results of the CSDS 2005 'State of Democracy in South Asia' survey where we find that the percentage of those who considered that their vote had some effect increased, whereas the percentage of those who considered that it made no difference increased as well (see Table 2.5):

Table 2.5 Responses to the question: 'Do you think your vote has an effect on how things are run in this country?'

	1971	1996	2005
Has an effect	48.4	58.7	61.7
Makes no difference	16.2	21.4	26.1

Source: CSDS State of Democracy in South Asia Survey, 2005, New Delhi (roneo).

My hunch is that those who consider that their vote has an effect come more from the lower castes whereas those who think that it makes no difference come more from the upper castes. But is the upper caste middle class the real loser in India? Pawan Varma (2002: 90) argues that 'The middle class is no longer in the driver's seat in Indian politics'. At the same time, the urban upper caste middle class is benefiting more than any other group from economic liberalization. The 40 million people or so who earn US$ 1,000 a month form a group that increases by 10 per cent every year. The middle classes are powerful—so much so that they may think they do not need to vote to get what they want; they do not need to vote because they get the phone! One of the faculty members I interviewed elaborates very convincingly on this theme:

They think that they have accessibility, they are part of the governing system, and that they can influence and that they can get things done if the need be. So they are relatives or friends of a *neta* (political leader) or IAS (civil servant) or PCs (Police Constabularies). So they have their channels through which they can get their work done. So what is the need to go and vote for this leader or that leader?

Indeed, this is another major reason of the declining turnout of the upper caste middle class—it is so influential that it does not need to vote!

This point needs to be looked at in a wider perspective, beyond the focal point of this chapter that is the political culture of the upper caste middle class. If we take this larger view, we may argue that the way this social category abstained from voting substantiates a widespread view that it wants to secede 'from the rest of India'(Krishna 2006: 2327). Krishna, for instance, argues that 'one of the existential realities of being a middle class Indian is an inescapable desire to escape the rest of India' (ibid.). Given the fact that the upper caste middle class remains in command even though it does not vote as much as before, I would qualify this escapism. This class wants to escape from the growing influence of the plebeians—in order to continue to rule the country.

Notes

1. In 1920, 64.4 per cent of the delegates to the annual session of the Indian National Congress were lawyers, 7.4 per cent were journalists, 7.4 per cent were businessmen, 3.7 per cent were medical practitioners and 3.1 per cent were teachers (see Krishna 1966: 422).
2. In an interview to *India Today*, the middle class news magazine *par excellence*, Vajpayee declared in 1997 that 'where political parties are unable to form a government at the Centre, the President should carry on the administration with the help of advisers' (*India Today* 1997).
3. On the act of voting in India, see Jaffrelot (2007).
4. Yet, there is one element of the material process of voting which is relevant here, and that is the absence of 'none' or 'nil' on the Indian ballot papers (or on the screen of de EVMs)—the voters who are not willing to vote for any of the candidates (be they independents or supported by political parties) should be able to register a vote for none of them. The French system, for instance, makes this vote of protest, which may reflect the quest of some alternative, possible. It is known as a 'vote blanc' or a 'vote nul'. Interestingly, in France, the 'blancs et nuls' are increasing, along with the erosion of the mainstream parties and the rise of the extremes, both phenomena being symptoms of the growing rejection of the political parties.
5. For more details, see Jaffrelot (2005).
6. This article is primarily a fascinating review of the biography of the late nuclear scientist Raja Ramanna.
7. I have studied this process in a *longue durée* perspective in Jaffrelot (2003).

8. Interview with Sheila Dixit, New Delhi, 5 March 2005.
9. On the method of group interview, see Duchesne and Haegel (2004).
10. The idea that the support for democracy was widespread in the general public had already been substantiated by Peter Mayer in the 1970s (see Mayer 1972).

References

Ambedkar, B.R. 1990 (1935). *Annihilation of Caste*. New Delhi: Arnold Publishers.

Béteille, A. 1996. 'The Mismatch between Class and Status', *British Journal of Sociology*, 47(3): 513–25.

———. 2002. 'The Social Character of the Indian Middle Class', in I. Ahmad and H.I. Ahmad, I. and H. Reifeld (eds), *Middle Class Values in India and Western Europe*. New Delhi: Social Science Press.

Broomfield, J.H. 1968. *Elite Conflict in a Plural Society: 20th Century Bengal*. Berkeley and Los Angeles: California University Press.

CSDS. 2008. *State of Democracy in South Asia*. New Delhi: OUP.

Deshpande, S. 2003. *Contemporary India: A Sociological View*. New Delhi: Penguin.

Duchesne, S. and F. Haegel. 2004. *L'enquête et ses méthodes: L'entretien collectif*. Paris: Nathan/SEJER.

Graham, B.D. 1990. *Hindu Nationalism and Indian Politics*. Cambridge: Cambridge University Press.

Guru, Gopal. 2002. 'Dalit Middle Class Hangs in the Air', in I. Ahmad and H. Reifeld (eds), *Middle Class Values in India and Western Europe*. New Delhi: Social Science Press.

Hasan, Z. 2002. 'Changing Political Orientations of the Middle Classes in India', in I. Ahmad and H. Reifeld (eds), *Middle Class Values in India and Western Europe*. New Delhi: Social Science Press.

http://members.tripod.com/chandrababu/ consulted on 15 September 2006

http://www.statistics.gov.uk/cci/nugget_print.asp?ID=1008

India Today. 1991. 15 May.

———. 1997. 15 May.

Insee. 'Enquêtes participation électorale', *Octant*, n°102, juillet 2005, p. 5 (www.insee.fr).

Jaffrelot, C. 2000. 'Hindu Nationalism and Democracy', in F. Frankel, Z. Hasan, R. Bhargava and B. Arora (eds), *Transforming India: Social and Political Dynamics of Democracy*, Delhi: Oxford University Press, pp. 352–78.

———. 2003. *India's Silent Revolution: The Rise of the Lower Castes in North India*. Delhi: Permanent Black.

———. 2005. *Dr. Ambedkar and Untouchabiity: Analysing and Fighting Caste*. New Delhi: Permanent Black.

———. 2007. 'The Democratisation of Indian Democracy: The Rise to Power of the Plebeians', in S. Ganguly (ed.), *India, the World's Largest Democracy*. Baltimore and Washington: The John Hopkins University Press.

———. 2007. 'Voting in India: Electoral Symbols, the Party System and the Collective Citizen', in R. Bertrand, J-L. Briquet and P. Pels (eds), *Cultures of Voting: The Hidden History of the Secret Ballot*. London: Hurst, pp. 78–99.

Jayaram, N. 1996. 'Caste and Hinduism: Changing Protean Relationship', in M.N. Srinivas (ed.), *Caste in its Twentieth Century Avatar*. New Delhi: Viking.

Journal of Indian School of Political Economy. 2003. *Political Parties and Elections in Indian States, 1990–2003*, Special Issue, 15(1&2).

Krishna, G. 1966. 'The Development of the Indian National Congress as a Mass Organization, 1918–1923', *Journal of Asian Studies*, 25(3).

Krishna, S. 2006. 'The Bomb, Biography and the Indian Middle Class', *Economic and Political Weekly*, 41(23).

Kumar, S., A. Heath and O. Heath. 2002. 'Changing Patterns of Social Mobility: Some Trends over Time', *Economic and Political Weekly*, 37(40).

Mayer, P.B. 1972. 'Support for the Principles of Democracy by the Indian Electorate', *South Asia*, 2: 24–32.

Palshikar, S. 2002. 'Politics of India's Middle Classes', in I. Ahmad and H. Reifeld (eds), *Middle Class Values in India and Western Europe*. New Delhi: Social Science Press.

Seal, A. 1968. *The Emergence of Indian Nationalism: Competition and Collaboration in the Later 19th Century*. Cambridge: Cambridge University Press.

Sunday. 1994. 9 January.

U.S. Census Bureau. 2002. *Current Population Survey*. Available online at www.census. gov., accessed on 28 July 2004.

————. 2004. *Current Population Survey*. Available online at www.census.gov., accessed on 25 May.

Vajpayee, A.B. 1996. 'Challenges to Democracy in India', Desraj Chowdhary Annual Memorial Lecture, *The Organiser*, 24 November, p. 4.

Varma, P. 2002. 'Middle-class Values and the Creation of a Civil Society', in I. Ahmad and H. Reifeld (eds), *Middle Class Values in India and Western Europe*. New Delhi: Social Science Press.

Viraraghavan, V. C. 1956. 'Election Law and Procedure', in R .V. Krishna Ayyar (ed.), *All India Election Guide*. Madras: Oriental Publishers.

Weiner, M. 1989. 'Rajiv Gandhi: A Mid-term Assessment', in A. Varshney (ed.), *The Indian Paradox*. New Delhi: Sage, pp. 293–318.

Yadav, Y., S. Kumar and O. Heath. 1999. 'The BJP's New Social Block', *Frontline*, 19 November.

3

Rewriting the Code: Software Professionals and the Reconstitution of Indian Middle Class Identity

Carol Upadhya

The Indian software outsourcing industry has grown rapidly over the last decade or two, and has produced a fairly large population of 'information technology (IT) professionals' who can be said to constitute a new and socially significant segment of the 'new middle classes' in India.[1] Software professionals have a social and symbolic significance beyond their numbers (now approaching one million, according to official figures), for several reasons: they earn salaries that are much higher than other professional/technical/managerial employees with comparable educational qualifications, and so command high disposable incomes; their work is 'global' in the sense that they primarily work for customers located abroad and their work involves frequent travel to other countries; and as the key 'resource' for an industry that claims to have put India on the global economic map, they partake of the hype and the hope that has been created about the IT industry by the media, the state and the IT business class.[2] While software professionals and others employed in the IT industry are hardly representative of the much larger and broader 'Indian middle class' (howsoever this contested term may be defined), they are a crucial subject for study if one is attempting to understand contemporary social transformations in India under conditions of globalization. This is especially so because of the unique place that IT professionals hold in the social imagery of the middle classes as harbingers of the nation's future in the now promising era of liberalization.[3] As such, they may constitute the vanguard of a 'cultural revolution' within the middle class, or at least provide pointers to the ways in which the middle class is reconstituting itself in contemporary India.

In attempting to tease out of the narratives and interview responses of a large number of Indian software professionals some insight into their understanding of themselves, and especially of their 'middle classness' or other forms of identity, the researcher immediately runs into the perennial problem of reflexivity, for most of one's informants are asking of themselves and others the same questions that the researcher is posing: What does it mean to be Indian when the primary social field in which one operates is defined as 'global'? What is the cultural content of these categories (the 'global' and the 'Indian')? What does it mean to be 'middle class' when one's life and views are clearly so different from those of one's parents, most of who are also 'middle class'? How much 'tradition' can one reject while still retaining one's 'cultural values' and social identity and, conversely, how much can one embrace and still be a modern Indian and an employable 'global knowledge worker'? How do other 'traditional' forms of identity (caste, region, language) articulate with the new identity categories? More importantly, how does one produce and reproduce these identities in a social context that is far removed from the ones in which they arose? What are the effects of these multiple and conflicting forms of identity on the subjectivities of IT workers? Through what practices and discourses can one maintain a sense of self in such a rapidly changing world?

Of course, one's interlocutors rarely pose these questions so explicitly or in the same way, but these dilemmas are close to the surface of their narratives of self and are articulated through a range of discourses that are now circulating within the emerging public sphere of the new Indian middle class. And while these questions appear to address the old sociological problems of 'tradition' and 'modernity'—and similar dilemmas certainly have confronted the Indian middle class at every stage of its development from the colonial period onwards—my argument is that they have taken on a new meaning and form in the contemporary period due to the rise of a new consumerist culture in India, and the production and circulation of new cultural meanings and images within shifting transnational social fields.

As many theorists of globalization and postmodernity have pointed out, signs, commodities, images, ideas and cultural meanings now travel rapidly around the globe and have become widely available for public and private consumption, at least by those with the economic and cultural resources to access the media and other channels of circulation. The 'new middle class' of post-liberalization India has been constructed through such public discourses and images as a 'consuming class', due to which scholars studying the middle class have paid most attention to consumption and the media.[4] Yet, precisely because this class has been constructed as a consuming class, it is *discourses about* consumption, more than consumption itself, that have become constitutive of contemporary middle class identity. A central theme of this discourse is a subtle critique of the new consumer culture and cosmopolitan, transnational or 'global' lifestyle, which is articulated through an opposition between material comfort and social/spiritual well-being (itself a much older discourse in Indian public and political culture; cf. Chatterjee 1986).

The creation of a new middle class identity has also been closely tied to globalization, not only because of the wider availability and accessibility of new items of consumption (material and non-material), but also due to the emergence of a transnational discursive space occupied mainly by the highly visible Non-Resident Indian (NRI) community located in the US and other western countries. The middle class—especially the upper (managerial–professional) segment that has benefited most from globalisation—is:

> ... interpellated by globalisation in the same ... way that, a generation or two ago, it identified itself with development.... Having consolidated its social, economic and political standing on the basis of the developmental state, this group is now ready to kick it away as the ladder it no longer needs (Deshpande 2003: 150).

The growth of the IT industry has reinforced this interpellation of middle class identity by globalization. Software engineers—who primarily come from middle class urban backgrounds (Upadhya and Vasavi 2006) and whose work involves short or long stints of travel abroad and frequent interaction with foreign clients even while working in India—represent a new generation of transnational Indians as well as a new iteration of the middle class, with significant consequences for its culture.

While the media—film, television, advertising, and so on—are usually identified as the primary sites and conduits for the public circulation of images and ideas within the global cultural economy,[5] the public sphere of the middle class also consists of informal networks of communication and knowledge production that are more difficult to identify and trace, and yet appear to be crucial to the emergence of a pan-Indian middle class identity and to its reconstitution in the contemporary period. While it would be impossible to identify with certainty the sources of commonly expressed ideas about Indian-ness and markers of middle class identity (which, of course, have a long and complex history), narratives collected during interviews with software professionals and their families point to the wide currency of a rather homogeneous 'common sense' understanding of 'middle class-ness' and of 'Indian culture', and suggest that these may be derived from sources other than the publicly available discourses that are usually identified. In the following sections, examples of these narratives are given in order to illustrate the discursive processes through which the new middle class identity appears to be taking shape, and its cultural content. Many of these narratives revolve around the dilemmas of modernity and globalization—the problem of being Indian in a globalizing world—expressed through discourses about consumption, the family and Indian culture.

CONSUMPTION AND THE 'NEW MIDDLE CLASS'

The category of the 'middle class' is very slippery in the Indian (or any) context (Deshpande 2003), and in this paper I do not discuss directly the problems of definition and identification of this class. Instead, I am looking at the middle class basically as an ideological construct that has become a primary category of social identity for a significant

section of the Indian population, and at how the content and formation of that category is changing in the contemporary period.[6]

The post-Independence middle class had its roots in the Nehruvian
developmental regime, which, through the rapid expansion of the higher
education system, created a large contingent of professional, managerial and technical experts as well as a bureaucratic class to run the state
apparatus and public sector enterprises (Deshpande 2003: 144–45). It
is this section of salaried employees of public and private enterprises
and institutions, which is usually considered to constitute the bulk of
the middle class in India. These technical and professional workers
were imbued with the ideologies of nationalism and state-led development, but the demands of autarchic economic development meant
that they had to be content with somewhat austere material lifestyles,
which were justified by the ideal of 'high thinking, simple living'.

The advent of liberalization in India from the late 1980s precipi-
tated the present period of globalization, represented by the influx of
foreign branded consumer goods and new forms of media.[7] The opening up of the economy not only produced a growing public culture of
consumption within the middle classes, but also reconstructed the
middle class itself as a consuming class (Deshpande 2003: 134–39).[8]
The new middle class lifestyle that was being advertised through the
media was being produced primarily through the market, as specific
modes of living, fashion and types of consumer goods became defini-
tive of 'middle class-ness' (Mankekar 1999: Chapter 2). More importantly, consumption began to stand in for development, as visible
signs of wealth became the new symbols of national progress, replac-
ing the Nehruvian and Gandhian ideals of national economic progress
and austerity (Fernandes 2000: 614). The ascendance of what
Mazzarella calls the 'ideology of globalising consumerism', promoted
through media such as television and advertising, brought about significant shifts in the public culture of the urban middle classes and in
political discourses about consumption, representing a transition from
a 'developmentalist to consumerist vision of the nation' (Mazzarella
2003: 71). In a process of auto-referentiality, the consuming public was
being constituted in part through the consumption of its own image
via the media. The new commodity images and narratives that were
being retailed through television and advertising served to remove
the guilt traditionally attached to consumerism and change attitudes

towards spending money (Mazzarella 2003: 75). A spate of new Hindi films also celebrated this new culture, for instance through the 'spectacle of unlimited consumption' that is portrayed in *Hum Aapke Hain Koun...!* (Uberoi 2001: 334).

The explosion in consumption, especially of consumer and luxury goods, has been a very visible phenomenon in urban India over the last two decades, due to the rising incomes of some sections of the middle class, the growth of local business opportunities and the consequent emergence of new entrepreneurial groups, and the easier availability of such commodities. While reliable data on actual consumption patterns are hard to come by, what is more important for understanding the cultural transformation of the middle class is the way in which consumption has become central to its self-definition. Yet this linkage between middle class identity and consumption is not straightforward or transparent. Scholars such as Mazzarella have provided insightful analyses of the growth and contours of the new public culture of consumption in India by tracing the sites and conduits through which it has been produced and circulated, but the process of consumption and the reception of new images and discourses by consumers themselves has hardly been studied.[9] It can neither be simply assumed that the new consumer culture has had a homogenizing effect on the middle classes, nor that it has been uncritically absorbed without resistance or alteration. For instance, it is frequently noted that satellite television, rather than swamping the Indian airwaves with western fare, provided a space for an incredible flourishing of local and regional language channels, and for the Indianization of western programmes. Moreover, the 'middle class' is highly diverse in terms of cultural and social backgrounds, and one would expect to find enormous variation in attitudes towards, and practices of, consumption, across different sections, linked at least in part to 'traditional' identities of caste, region and community.[10] The question to be asked, then, is how middle class identity is being reshaped by public discourses about, and images of, the middle class consumer and desirable middle class lifestyles, and what are the other political, economic or cultural processes (such as travel and work) that are shaping this transformation? These questions are addressed through an analysis of the narratives and practices of people employed in the global software outsourcing industry.

Consuming the New Consumer Culture

The relatively high incomes of software engineers and other IT professionals place them easily within the upper segments of the middle class by any definition. They command large disposable incomes at a relatively young age, enabling them to engage in high levels of consumption. The economic standing of IT professionals sets them sharply apart from the 'old' middle class, to which most of their parents belonged.[11] Their parents, for the most part, had secure jobs but relatively low and slowly rising incomes, and many informants mentioned the difference in income as one of the most crucial differences between them and their parents. This inter-generational change in standard of living is a major theme of many informants' narratives. Typical is the following statement by an IIT Delhi graduate who is employed in the software development centre of a large American company in Bangalore; he is from a small town in Uttar Pradesh, his father is a lawyer and his mother runs a beauty parlour:

> My parents had to struggle for every small thing. For example, if they had to buy a couch they would have to plan for four years, whereas I can just go out and buy it. I remember that when they got a fridge it was planned for two years, and then they kept the same one for twenty-five years. So the biggest difference is due to income.

Similar comments were made by many others:

> Yes, I think I lead a better life than my parents. My father's last drawing salary was less than what I had as my first salary. All the comforts they struggled to get are available for us in one or two years. They could be electronic gadgets and other physical comforts.
>
> My dad could never afford a car. I am able to purchase a car at this young age.
>
> I never thought I would be shopping at huge malls, wearing a shirt of 2000 rupees and shoes of 3000 rupees.

Many informants spoke about the fact that their parents would rarely eat in a restaurant or buy branded clothing, and that they had to save their whole lives to buy a house, whereas they think nothing of eating in a five star hotel or buying expensive designer wear. The difference that was most frequently noted was the fact that they already own, or were planning to purchase, flats or plots of land, whereas their parents could afford to do so only close to retirement age.

Thus, many IT professionals define their new social and economic status in terms of their ability and willingness to consume more than their parents could, and on the surface it appears that many of them do conform to the 'new cultural standard associated with a hegemonic urban middle-class lifestyle' (Fernandes 2000: 619). Most of those interviewed possess all or most of the consumer goods that have become standard markers of 'middle class' status (a two wheeler or car, cell phone, elaborate music and home entertainment systems, and so on), wear branded or expensive clothing and shoes, and live in spacious, upmarket flats. They tend to spend more money than their non-IT friends and relatives, shop in the glitzy new malls and department stores that have come up in Bangalore rather than at the local market, and do not hesitate to eat out in expensive restaurants. This consumption style is a marker of difference between themselves and the previous generation, and between the old middle class and the new. Lavish expenditure is especially typical of 'techies' who have returned from abroad flush with cash, who tend to spend money in order to advertise their 'foreign-returned' status. (The same people are very frugal when they live abroad, in order to save money to bring back to India.) An informant in Germany said:

> When we go [to India], we start spending so much! We convert rupees into Euros and realise how petty the money is! Oh, 50 cents, that's all, *to kharidlo* [go ahead and buy it]! Standard of living certainly goes up. *Chota mota angadi types kuch nahi* [We don't shop in small shops]. Only Lifestyle, Weekender [large department stores] for us...

Despite this pattern of spending on consumer goods and their comfortable lifestyles, most IT professionals are not ostentatious. On the contrary, they tend to be conservative in taste. While they furnish their houses well with the latest gadgets and furniture, they do not exhibit the 'flashy' style of living or dress typical of the *nouveau riche* business class in cities such as Delhi and Mumbai. Similarly, while software professionals spend money on entertainment—movies, eating out at good restaurants and, especially, vacations—they do not do so in the highly visible way of the 'yuppy' crowd that frequents expensive discos, pubs and clubs of the city. They may dress reasonably well in expensive branded clothing (though often only in jeans and T-shirts), but most are not particularly fashionable or trendy: women software professionals are usually seen in the conventional *salwar kameez* with traditional hairstyles, and men in conventional office wear or casuals.

Differences in consumption patterns and preferences are discursively employed by IT professionals to distinguish themselves from other segments of the 'consuming classes'. For instance, they consciously attempt to differentiate themselves from the young and trendy call centre crowd, whose frivolous lifestyles and profligate consumption habits they tend to disparage.[12] In contrast, they see themselves as responsible consumers who plan for the future, save and invest money wisely, buy their own houses as soon as possible and take responsibility for the financial security of their families.[13]

Software professionals are, in fact, rather conservative in their expenditure patterns and financial planning and goals, and they tend to use their money to pursue 'traditional' middle class lifestyles (albeit on a grander scale than their parents could afford). This conservatism is suggested by the fact that the major expenditure incurred by most IT professionals interviewed in Bangalore was on a house, flat or plot of land.[14] The ability to achieve this conventional middle class goal early in life, which their fathers could do only after working for many years, is an important marker of generational difference and progress. But it is significant that the goals themselves have not changed substantially: own your own house, plan for economic security, and invest in whatever is required for the family's security and upward mobility, such as children's education. Thus, while the lifestyles of most software professionals differs from that of their parents in that they can afford larger and better furnished houses, cars and a variety of consumer goods, their orientation to consumption and planning of life remains much the same. This pattern reflects the social conservatism observed more generally among IT professionals, and the fact that in many ways the culture of the 'new' globalizing middle class is continuous with that of the 'old'. This is especially so with regard to what are seen as 'traditional middle class values' related to family and sociality.

MODERNITY AND NOSTALGIA

For IT professionals, the ability to support a better material life than their parents had is an important sign of upward mobility. However, the new consumerist culture contains both pleasures and dangers, and informants' attitudes about their sudden improvement in economic status are conflicting. Rather than simply absorbing the ideology of consumption as a symbol of India's (and their own) progress, their appreciation of their more comfortable lifestyle is in most cases leavened by a sense of loss and nostalgia for an earlier family- and community-based life that they believe has been destroyed by the demands of their work and the complexities of contemporary life. The most common complaint is, 'now I have enough money but no time to enjoy it'. While most informants believe that they have much better lives than their parents in terms of material comforts, the notion that progress and happiness are measured in material wealth sits uncomfortably with older middle class ideals of family, nation and sociality that they continue to hold.

In response to a survey question, many software engineers said that although their standard of living has improved, they do not think that their lives are better than those of their parents. In their view, their parents had the time and space to lead more fulfilling lives, keeping up relations with family and friends, pursuing outside interests and generally enjoying a more relaxed existence. Because IT professionals work long hours and move frequently, they say, they are often unable to fulfil family commitments, nurture significant social relationships, or pursue artistic or spiritual interests. Many of their narratives set up an opposition between the material gain and the social loss that result from their profession and lifestyle. The following interview extracts are representative:

> Earlier I couldn't spend money as I wanted. Now although I have more money I have no time to spend it.

I miss out on social life due to time constraints. My parents could give time to other people of the extended family that we cannot. Ours is a very nuclear family.

Income-wise, I lead a better life. However, my parents used to work till five in the evening and then take rest. They took care of health more. They used to spend more time with their parents. They used to express their concern for their parents. Now we have the time constraint.

An engineer with a large American MNC elaborated on this problem at length, with insightful comments on the changing nature of sociality:

My lifestyle has improved due to IT. In college I had just two trousers and two shirts. Now I don't know how many shirts I have, must be at least 20, but I haven't counted and don't care. I buy good quality clothes from Raymonds and I don't have to think about what I am spending. So definitely, working in software has added comfort to my life. Earlier there were a lot of financial problems in the family—my brothers and sisters were not able to study properly due to this, and I am very happy that I have been able to solve this problem by going to the US and earning. But it is a stressful and mechanical life; there is no social life, you don't even know your neighbours, there are no relatives around. In my hometown, there were always people around—neighbours and relatives. There was always someone to go and talk your heart out with—but here it's not like that. There is freedom—you can go out to pubs with friends, but you don't really enjoy it. Here everyone is 'professional'—all relationships are professional, no one has time for building social relations, they are busy earning, so no one really cares about anyone else.

Women IT professionals were especially critical of the social consequences of IT work, as in the following narrative:

Do I have a better life than my parents? Financially, may be yes. But I have lost the essence of life. I feel the previous generation used to be so happy. I still see my father feeling so happy when he purchases a new shirt! For me it is one more dress. We stop valuing things.

We have to strive hard to retain those small things of happiness. Nothing big makes you happy, it's always the small things. We college friends make it a point to go to our college and have ice-candy in front of the gate just to get back those small beautiful moments. I think we now have too many expectations from life. We see everything with money. *That is certainly not the Indian attitude.* The older generation used to value money, value life. Now it's only money. The IT industry has brought in the notion that all value is about money. It's the American attitude. IT is the gateway for American attitudes. Values are lost. Most people outside IT have a rich personal and social life. Here, all we value is coding! Coding is everything! We don't even attend our best friend's wedding when a delivery date is approaching. In other industries, they would ask, 'What, are you not going to your best friend's wedding?' Here we ask, 'What, are you going to your best friend's wedding leaving the delivery work?!'

Similarly, the main complaint of parents and spouses (mainly wives) of IT professionals is that their children/husbands have no time for them, and that they do not maintain kinship relations by attending family functions, visiting relatives, and so on.

As these comments suggest, many IT professionals believe that the price of their new-found wealth is the inability to maintain social and family relationships or even to have a meaningful existence outside of work.[15] This sense of loss is compounded by a more general discomfort with the new consumerist lifestyle that is promoted by advertising and the media. The 'old' middle class identity was based on a very different attitude towards consumption—self-denial of personal pleasures and materiality—out of devotion to the nation and family. Older employees in the IT industry spoke in negative terms about the change in culture that they see amongst their younger colleagues. The wife of a senior manager in a software services major had this to say about the IT phenomenon:

You must remember that IT in those days [when her husband joined the industry] was no big deal. It was just normal. It's only in the recent years that there has been such a big hype about this industry and people are enjoying the comforts. Even fresh graduates these days start at 17K. It's all about money today. But we were never after money right from the beginning. Money just happened to come. It was always job satisfaction that was important for him…I have a problem with the kind of fast money that young people make these days in this industry. There is just too much of it going around. During the early days, there was more emphasis on planning a family and carefully allotting money for household expenses and life. Now, young people have no control on the money they spend. They just go and spend. Before, people would think twice about eating out in five star hotels. Now nearly everyone at Bangalore can do so.

A group head in the same company made similar comments about the new consumer culture among software engineers:

There is a change in employees. Earlier one would be happy to work and devote time for home. They could manage with less money. But now you have more disposable income—that leads to a culture of its own…buying, buying. One is economically independent. That affects your perception at work and even at home. It breeds a whole set of problems, although one could say economic independence is there. There is a struggle between individualism of such a society and…priority for family life.[16]

These narratives suggest that more than consumption itself, it is *discourses about consumption*—both its positive and negative implications—that have become central to the self-definition of this segment of the new middle class. While the younger generation still values family and social relationships, and most informants reported that they spend most of their leisure time quietly with their families, they complained that there is never enough time for this because they often have to work late into the evening and on weekends as well. What are regarded as 'traditional' middle class values of family and sociality, exist in a state of tension with the new idealized middle class lifestyle that has been enabled by the IT industry.

Emerging residential patterns in cities such as Bangalore with large 'yuppy' and upwardly mobile middle class populations reflect and re-inforce the process of social fragmentation and disembedding, which was articulated by informants. Most software engineers and other young professionals prefer to buy flats in the large, upscale, self-contained apartment complexes that have sprung up around the city specifically to cater to this class. They find living in such enclaves convenient because services such as security, maintenance, recreation and domestic help are provided or readily available. Within these gated communities, an army of maids, cooks, drivers and nannies looks after family needs and domestic work, freeing professional couples from chores and child care so that they can concentrate on their careers. Working couples depend on hired help or their own parents for childcare, and what little entertainment and socializing they have time for is organized through commoditized and professional channels.[17] In addition, the standard layout of the flats in these complexes is producing a new model of middle class living that is very different from the pattern of small independent bungalows found in Bangalore's 'revenue layouts' favoured by the older generation of the middle and lower middle classes. These modern apartment complexes, and the lifestyles they promote, are helping to create a hegemonic and homogenized 'new middle class' cultural style, while fragmenting older kinship- or caste-based neighbourhoods.

CORE AND PERIPHERY

Although many software engineers expressed a sense of loss of family ties and other forms of sociality due to the demands of their work, most asserted (rather paradoxically) that they have not been *fundamentally* transformed by working in the IT industry or by their new lifestyles. Just as the emergent colonial middle class posed an opposition between the inner world of culture, tradition and values, and the outer and material world of modernity (Chatterjee 1986), Indian software engineers often draw a distinction between outward changes in material lifestyle and everyday attitudes and behaviour, and a stable inner core of cultural values and beliefs that they claim to have retained. When asked whether working in the IT industry has changed them, most answered in the affirmative, but cited what they regard as superficial changes in behaviour patterns (I have become more aggressive or assertive), attitudes (I am more confident and aware), or modes of living (cosmopolitan lifestyle). Such statements were usually followed by an assertion that their 'core values' or basic culture have not changed. The following quote from a software engineer recently returned from Europe is illustrative of this discourse:

[Has working in the IT industry changed you?] I don't party, booze, or smoke. I probably go to restaurants more frequently [after return-ing to India] and buy more branded clothes. Instead of purchasing clothes in Alankar Plaza, I now go to Commercial Street and buy Peter England shirts. If you call it change in lifestyle, then it has changed. But nothing more than that. I don't think my attitude or values have changed.

Outward changes in behaviour and appearance are contrasted with stability of values and self, a contrast that is consonant with the divi-sion between working and home life:

Your behaviour may change—for instance, you have to be very smart to succeed in corporate life. What you are at home is different from at office; I have to be aggressive at work, but this doesn't change my behaviour at home.

For some, 'core values' refer to family values such as 'giving respect to elders', while for others, they refer to religious traditions and rituals. One informant argued that most people 'do not forget their traditions' even if their lifestyle has changed, and he gave the example of his wife who was fasting that day, which was Mahashivratri:

She won't forget these things, and will call to find out from elders what is to be done. We place a lot of weight on traditions, and feel proud of them.

This discursive move echoes Fernandes' analysis of the representa-tion of certain commodities in advertising, which suggest that 'the core of Indian tradition' can be preserved even as 'the material context of that tradition is modernized and improved' (2000: 616). But unlike in the colonial context when the inner world of tradition and spirituality was shielded (largely through the medium of the patriarchal family) from corruption and westernization by the outer male-dominated world (Chatterjee 1986), in the contemporary era the private sphere of the family (and even of the self) is increasingly being penetrated by public discourses and external interests, such that the boundary between public and private life is becoming fuzzy. This is seen, for instance, in the increasing commodification of social relationships (child and elder care) and of domestic life (consumer goods, convenience foods, outsourcing of many mundane household functions) within the new middle class; the invasion of working time into the home and private time (late night conference calls, working from home on the laptop); and the requirement of the IT and ITES industries that workers revamp even their personalities and 'cultures' to fit into the new global workplace (Sathaye 2005; Upadhya 2005). As described in the previous section, this transformation has been sensed by many informants, who feel that the essence of their social selves has been destroyed by their new lifestyles and the pressures of work. Perhaps this feeling of loss of control over one's personal and social life, and even over one's self, explains why so many insisted that their 'core values' have not changed, that they retain the essence of their culture somewhere within them.

RECONSTITUTING AND CONSUMING INDIAN CULTURE ABROAD

While many informants drew a distinction between the changes in outward behaviour and appearance required by their work and new lifestyles, and an inner core of values and beliefs, identifying and retaining those 'core values' of Indian culture presents a problem. Software engineers living abroad most often articulated the feeling that they are cut off from their roots and their desire to preserve and reproduce their culture even while outside of India, and they emphasized their attachment to their country and family.[18] Their efforts to define those values and to retain their Indian-ness while living outside the country most often involve the reinvention and consumption of an objectified Indian culture—a process that has been noted among

NRIs in general. But among software engineers in Europe, this process of objectification also takes place through their work experiences, as they reconceptualize and relativize their Indian identities through juxtaposition with the 'Other'—mainly their European colleagues and customers.

For many Indians living abroad, 'Indian culture' consists of a collection of rituals, practices and holidays that they enact and observe, and which is displayed through material objects and practices such as dress, home décor, film viewing, language and food. Indian films have become a major vehicle for the learning and circulation of Indian culture, and Indian heroes such as film stars and cricket players have come to symbolize the nation. While Indian techies in Europe consume an objectified and highly commercialized Indian culture through these visible and public media, they still feel that they have 'lost their culture' and express nostalgia for what they imagine to be the rich social and cultural life of their relatives and forebears, which they are unable to reproduce or even remember because they are living outside of India. Several informants expressed a desire to 'learn' about their own culture, from which they clearly felt disconnected:

I am a Punjabi and don't know anything about our rituals. Here we don't celebrate things—not even Diwali—and don't know what to do for different rituals and functions. I would like to go there [to India] and learn about them.

According to a Maharashtrian couple:

You lose your culture because you are not in India.... Of course we are still vegetarians.... Our belief in God is stronger, as is our belief in family ties.... We can retain Indian culture here because we can easily watch Indian films, we can see Indian TV—Zee and Sony— although we don't get Marathi films.

But they find it difficult to keep up their culture and customs abroad:

Now Ganesh Chaturthi is coming, then there will be Dassara and Diwali, I really hate to be here on Diwali day—here it's just an ordinary working day, and we feel we miss so much. You can't get that atmosphere here, the festival feeling.

The experience of living abroad (even when it is temporary, as for most software engineers) has magnified the desire to retain Indian culture through the performance of rituals and festivals that they may not have observed in India.

> I used to find Diwali very embarrassing in India. [Why?] It was such a clichéd thing. But here, I make *besan ladoos* on Diwali. When I see people celebrating Christmas, I think, why should I not feel happy about my festivals? What makes it easier is you get all the Indian stuff here.

The problem of retaining and reproducing Indian culture for Indians abroad has been complicated by the transnationalization of the middle class in India. Although many Indian families interviewed in Europe expressed the desire to return to India for the sake of their children, at least one woman acknowledged that the choice is no longer so simple because Indian society (at least metropolitan middle class society) is changing.

> Now India is also westernized—I go to Bombay and see girls smoking in pubs. Therefore what is the difference? They speak English as if it is their native language. Sometimes I think bringing up your children abroad may help them speak their mother tongue and know about India. Maybe it's better here because we can keep our kids Indian.

The notion that children can be brought up as Indians more easily while living abroad than in India, captures in a nutshell the dilemma of the transnational Indian today. It also points to the hybrid and constructed nature of 'Indian culture'—a product that is desired and consumed (and often found to be elusive) as much by the new Indian middle class as by NRIs.

The narratives of Indian software engineers in Europe also point to a process of what Kirin Narayan terms 'emplacement' (as opposed to the *displacement* of diasporic subjects that is usually discussed), which refers to strategies of coming to belong somewhere—an imaginative process of 'orienting of self within multiple frameworks of meaning' (Narayan 2002: 423). While most of the software professionals we studied are not permanent emigrants but rather circulate between India and various sites in the global economy, this experience of mobility forces them to construct their life stories and sense of self out of the multiple, fragmentary, often conflicting discourses that are available to them, as well as from their direct experiences of working and living in 'other cultures'. In this process, the opposition between 'Indian culture' and 'European culture' (for example, Dutch and German) is a central organizing framework.

INDIAN CULTURE AND 'FAMILY VALUES'

In defining Indian culture and its core values, many software professionals emphasize 'family values'. There is nothing surprising about this—the family has become a key signifier of Indian tradition in transnational discourses about Indian culture. Nor is this something new—as Uberoi (2001: 339) points out, the joint family ideal has been promoted as an 'emblem of Indian culture and tradition' in films for the last 100 years. But the iconization of the family has taken on a new intensity and significance under globalization:

> ...as India globalizes and the 'imagined economy' can no longer convincingly iconicize the nation...the family remains...the sole institution which can signify the unity, the uniqueness, and the moral superiority of Indian culture in a time of change, uncertainty, and crisis. (Uberoi 2001: 340).

The location of Indian culture within the structures of family and kinship has also taken place in the context of the 'internationalization of the Indian middle class family' (Uberoi 1998), as many middle class Indians have relatives living abroad. Uberoi argues that the wave of 'NRI films', such as *Dilwale Dulhania Le Jayenge (DDLJ)* and *Pardes*, that became popular in the 1990s, use the figure of the NRI as a vehicle for constructing contemporary Indian identity, especially around norms and values of family, marriage and sexuality.[19] In these films, a particular model of the Indian family is iconicized as a marker of being Indian (Uberoi 1998, 2001, 2006). Indeed, the projection of a singular pan-Indian family system and 'family values' can be seen as an outcome of the process of formation of the 'secular' middle class in the post-liberalization period—a class whose lifestyles and cultural orientations are linked more to its class position than to ascriptive identities such as caste or religious community (Uberoi 2006: 20).

Although a new 'culture of kinship' has developed within the cosmopolitan all-India middle/professional class, it is not necessarily cosmopolitan in its marriage and kinship *practices* (2006: 22). Uberoi (2006: 25) points to the persistence of arranged marriages and the practice of dowry even in the face of the idealization of romantic love and 'love marriage'—a pattern that is found among our sample of software engineers as well. One might expect to find a shift away from traditional norms related to gender and marriage among employees of an industry where there are large numbers of women, where men and women work together closely for long hours, and where they are exposed to (and even inducted into) western and cosmopolitan cultures. Instead, our survey results suggest a pattern of social conservatism among software engineers with regard to family and marriage. Of those who were married, 62 per cent had arranged marriages, 28 per cent were self-arranged ('love marriages'), while a small proportion fell into the ambiguous category of being arranged through marriage bureaus, Internet chats, and the like. Of those who were not yet married, 59 per cent said that they would prefer to have their marriages arranged by their families, while only 25 per cent preferred love marriages.[20] Among those who prefer to search for partners on their own, marriage and dating websites have become popular, but even then, of the unmarried respondents, only 18 per cent were dating at the time of the interview (Upadhya and Vasavi 2006: 111–12). For many software professionals, the question is not a practical one as much as a social and emotional one—they believe that their parents are in the best position to find suitable partners for them, and an arranged marriage signifies adherence to 'family values'. The 'moral economy of the Indian family' as reflected in popular culture was voiced by many of the informants, who advocated the retention of 'traditional values' based on a sense of duty and the sacrifice of individual desire for the common good (Uberoi 2006: 33). Few, if any, would submit to an arranged marriage sight unseen—the final approval of the choice lies with the potential spouses, who may also meet several times before deciding to marry. Hence several respondents described their marriages as 'arranged love' or in similar terms, meaning that they were introduced to their spouses by relatives but made their own decision to marry. As Uberoi points out, the 'arranged love marriage' is a solution to the central contradiction between the cultural mandate to submit to parental authority and individual desire, or between 'tradition' and 'modernity' (2006: 36).[21]

The narratives of Indian software engineers living abroad reflect the discourses about Indian culture and family that have been circulating in the Indian middle class and NRI public spheres for at least a decade. But their reconstruction of Indian culture is also a dialogical and reflexive process that draws on their experiences of European culture, much along the lines of standard colonial discursive constructions of difference between East and West.[22] Predictably, a major theme of this discourse is the difference in values and practices of family, kinship and sexuality. Indian culture, with its emphasis on 'family values', is seen as superior to European culture, which is individualistic and materialistic. As one informant put it:

> The Dutch have no real family life. You don't have to get married, you can just live together legally, even have a child that way. They don't follow any strict religious family values. As a society they accept everything—they are very open and free. There is no specific Dutch food.

Many Indians make a conscious effort to avoid contamination by, and especially to shield their children from, the influences of European culture. Rajani, wife of a software engineer posted in Frankfurt, articulated this attitude:

> We cannot compare this culture with Indian culture. We cannot expect Indian values here. This is typical European culture. For children to grow up, it is not well and good.... We are from a middle class family, we don't accept this kind of culture. We feel homely in our country. People from posh society, hi-fi society who are used to going to clubs even in India may accept all this. But this is not for middle class people like us.... If you go out, you see that lovers will be hugging and kissing in the public. Our people hesitate to do all

this in public places. Public romance is very common here. Young ones also see it and think it is very normal. In Indian society, we cannot even imagine having it in public places. There are some things we can do openly, some things should be confidential and private. Here everything is open. They think there is nothing wrong in it. That we cannot digest. That is why we think we should not channelize our children in that direction and spoil our children. We should draw a circle of morality around the children.

For transnational subjects such as Indian software engineers, the family is all the more important because it is regarded as the primary site for the reproduction of the culture that they feel they are in danger of losing—it is the embodiment of Indian tradition as well as the means through which tradition can be retained and transmitted. The desire to inculcate Indian identity in their children is a primary reason why almost all the Indians we met in Europe plan or hope to return to India at some point. Many informants believe that their children can get a better education in India than abroad, but more importantly, they want their children to grow up in India so that they do not 'lose their culture'. One engineer in the Netherlands expressed the need to balance family and work in this way:

My daughter's growth is paramount to us. I can compromise my career, but we will be going back.... Her growing up in India is important, not that education is all that good in India...but culture is important...we can never feel at home here.

The other major reasons for wanting to return also have to do with family—to be near one's parents, friends and relatives, and to look after parents in their old age. An engineer in the Netherlands, referring to his unease at being so far away while his parents are growing older, said that his work gives him 'mental satisfaction', but

...you need to find a balance between unbridled ambition and a sense of managing things.... After all we are in a global workplace— time and distance are not supposed to matter any more. Of course we can send emails, make phone calls [to home], but something is missing. But we make a conscious choice to do this.

As noted above, many informants' narratives set up an opposition between the material benefits that their profession has brought and their ability to enjoy the rewards of a fulfilling personal and family life. For some, higher incomes have enabled them to contribute to the family budget and hence fulfil their filial duties towards parents, but many—especially those living for longer periods abroad—expressed regret at not being able to devote the kind of time and attention to their families (especially to parents) that would normally be expected of them (cf. Lamb 2002).[23]

Uberoi's analysis of the dilemmas posed in 'NRI films' pertain to what could now be labelled the first generation of NRIs and the early stages of transnationalization of the Indian middle class, when there was still ambivalence about migration. With the quickening pace of globalization and with large numbers of middle class Indians having lived or travelled in the West, one could argue that the process of transnationalization of the middle class has reached a more mature stage, and that there is now greater comfort, or at least strategies available to deal with the ambiguities and dislocations that this process has produced. Yet as the narratives quoted above suggest, family remains a central concern for circulatory IT workers at both the ideological and practical levels.

It is striking that the ideology of the family as an icon of Indian-ness continues to hold sway among transnational, upper middle class and cosmopolitan subjects, whose actual practices and family situations are far removed from the ideal. Software professionals may construct a sense of identity based on publicly available discourses about what it means to be Indian, but negotiating the complexities of their lives within and outside of their actual families often entails violating the ideals and norms that they espouse. They talk about 'family values' but at the same time acknowledge (with regret) that their own lifestyles often preclude living out those values. While the solidity and endurance of 'the Indian family' is contrasted with the individualism of western culture, the very nature of software professionals' lives and work produces the same pattern of individualization and fragmentation that they decry. Within the family as well, relationships tend to become instrumental, as for instance when elderly parents are invited to live with working couples primarily to look after their children (of course under the guise of the adult children wanting to take care of their parents).[24]

Apart from the validation of the family as the site of tradition and identity, other solutions to the problem of retaining Indian identity in the global world (which is equally pressing whether one is living abroad or in Bangalore) are being found. One such solution is the creation of a new Indian-global identity that accepts the hegemony of 'globalization' while invoking a new and assertive India as a major player on the world stage.

THE NEW NATIONALISM AND THE NEW GENERATION

Appadurai (1997) has suggested that globalization has produced new 'post-patriotic' identities that may be more significant than older national identities, especially among transnational subjects. However, what we are witnessing at present appears to be a reconstitution of patriotism within the discourse of globalization, at least among the social groups who have reaped the benefits of liberalization. While the earlier generation of NRIs had a somewhat negative, anti-nationalist image in popular imagination and the media, and had to struggle to prove their love for the country, the current generation espouses a new form of global nationalism, or nationalist globalism.

One indicator of this trend is that the ambition to settle outside of India that was common among IT workers and the Indian middle class in general until very recently, has subsided to a large extent. Very few of the software engineers interviewed expressed a desire to live permanently outside of India (although most appreciated the opportunity for travel and short stays in other countries that IT work provides). This shift is linked to the changing structure of the global economy, the opening up of opportunities in India after liberalization and also to the growth of the IT industry itself. While the earlier generation of NRIs had to migrate to the US in order to 'make good', and so struggled with the question of whether they (and most importantly, their children) are Indian or American, the new global professional (exemplified by software professionals) can choose to stay in India most of the time and to remain Indian, even while working and succeeding in the global economy. It is this combination that has now become available, especially in the IT sector, and is attracting many NRIs to return home.[25]

Moreover, largely due to the visibility of the Indian software industry, India has acquired a positive image among the new middle classes, who also take credit for much of India's transformation. Many of the software professionals we interviewed (especially those in Europe) voiced a nationalist pride about the IT industry and India's consequent prominent place in the global economy. Their identity as Indians in the wider world is largely pegged to their role in making this industry successful and to their reputation as Indian software engineers for technical expertise and professionalism. They see IT not just as a job or a new kind of business, but as an activity that will put India on the world map, turn it into a world economic power, and marshal respect for India and Indians. The country manager of one of the major IT companies spoke most eloquently along these lines:

> I had a vision: that the Indian IT industry must grow large enough to be taken notice of, and this is what has happened. This was in the mid-90s—a lot of young people wanted to become software engineers because they thought it was a ticket to the West, but my vision was to position India so that people would queue up to come to India. And this is what is happening now.

The wave of NRIs who have returned to India over the last several years, especially to Bangalore, is symptomatic of this trend. Returnees frame their decision in terms of a desire to be near their families and to have their children grow up in India, but they also speak of wanting to serve the nation by contributing to its economic development through their work or entrepreneurial ventures. A good example is Rajiv, who sold the successful telecom company that he had started in the US and returned to Bangalore with his family. Soon after their arrival, his relatives threw a welcome party for them. Rajiv's speech at the party:

> Thank you everyone. I'm overwhelmed. I don't know what to say.... Words fail me. But this I will say. I am happy to be back. To my country. To my family. To my people. This country gave me a lot of opportunities, and I am what I am because of that. Now I'm here to give back some of what I took. It's my turn to serve my country. I believe that if everyone who has left our shores and gone abroad were to come back and do their bit for our country, we would go

leaps and bounds ahead from where we are today. I am so glad to be back amongst all of you.... We felt this was the right time [to move back]. We wanted our children to grow with the values you and I have grown up with.

In a discursive move that neatly marries the global with the Indian nation, post-liberalization India—signified by the success of the IT industry—and the new globalized middle class are collapsed into one another. This logic is extended to the construction by young software engineers of inter-generational difference as an index of change. As one informant argued, India is changing because the younger generation is more 'aware' and more globalized:

Our generation is far different from our parents—more smart, global, we are more aware of things and less willing to take bullshit. When the customs officer stops and creates trouble, my father would not mind giving him some bribe. That is the way he has grown up. But I will not pay a bribe. This was the old socialist, corrupt system. Now we are globalized, we have Internet, Baywatch, McDonalds. In my family, I am the first person to have travelled abroad. The younger generation is very different. That is the good thing about India.

This theme was voiced by a number of informants, who asserted that working in the IT industry has given them a wider 'exposure' (to the outside world) and made them more aware, tolerant and confident.

While many software professionals see themselves as substantially different from their parents in that they are more open, cosmopolitan or 'global', this 'global' identity is, at the same time, reinforcing their Indian roots, producing a hybrid Indian identity that allows the 'global' to be articulated through the category of the nation (cf. Fernandes 2000; Mazzarella 2003).

CONCLUSION

The globalizing Indian middle class—increasingly divorced from its economic base in the public sector-driven economy, sceptical of

Nehruvian and Gandhian forms of nationalism, plugged into global economic and cultural circuits—is refashioning itself through the consumption and reproduction of ideologies and objectified elements of 'Indian culture' as well as the ideology of globalization. These include notions of 'tradition' and 'modernity', ideologies of the family, images of patriotism and discourses about the superiority of Indian culture, now filtered through celebratory discourses about IT and India's new place on the world stage.

For Indian IT professionals, and transnational Indians in general, the global nature of their work and workplaces sharpens the dilemma of Indian identity through the juxtaposition of Indian culture with other cultures. While working in the software outsourcing industry appears to have heightened their sense of Indian identity, it is a hybrid 'global Indian' identity that seeks to retain the essence of Indian culture while being tuned to functioning in the global economy. This identity hinges on a reconstruction of Indian culture that is a product of the process of 'consumerist globalization', which itself represents an intensification of a long-standing 'project of global difference-management' within global capitalism (Mazzarella 2003: 38). Thus, the identity of transnational Indian IT professionals is produced more through consumption of *ideologies* of the family and nation, and of the *idea* of Indian culture, than through consumption of new consumer goods and lifestyles. The transformations of identity and sociality observed in this class represent a rewriting of the code of culture, as older symbols and tropes of middle class-ness and Indian-ness, family and nation are appropriated and reconstituted to operate within a very different context.

While the media, advertising and film industries are important sites for the creation, articulation and circulation of ideas about cultural difference and Indian-ness, there are other sites that are less noticed, such as the software industry, which trains its workers in 'inter-cultural communication skills' and mandates a certain amount of personal restructuring in tune with the global workplace. A singular focus on the public and discursive construction of identity may also obscure the fact that processes of 'emplacement' and identity formation are inherently dialectical as well as reflexive, for as the 'new middle class' is being produced through the consumption of publicly available meanings and signs, it is also producing new narratives and understandings of itself that in turn feed into this process of cultural and class production. Commonality of experience, the creation of local social networks among Indians living abroad and the emergence of new social fields in urban India such as the 'IT community' should not be discounted as significant sites for the production of ideas and discourses about Indian-ness and middle class-ness.

Indian software engineers face similar dilemmas of how to remain Indian while living outside the country. Their experiences of working abroad have given rise to a common set of strategies—a clinging to 'core values' in the face of rapid social and cultural transformation; iconicization of the family as a symbol of Indian culture; and espousal of the new 'global nationalism'. The problem of Indian-ness is no longer the diaspora's alone, but confronts the new middle class even within India. For them, 'Indian culture' has become an object of nostalgic longing, reified into a set of traditions and values belonging to the past, but ever-elusive in a present that demands new dispositions and practices oriented to success in the globalizing economy.

Notes

1. This paper is based on a sociological study of the Indian IT/ITES (information technology and IT enabled services) workforce in India and abroad. One aim of the study was to explore the ways in which sociality, culture and identity among software engineers are being reshaped by their experience of working in a global industry. The research was carried out by A.R. Vasavi and myself, along with a research team, at the National Institute of Advanced Studies, Bangalore, and was funded by the Indo-Dutch Programme for Alternatives in Development (IDPAD), the Netherlands. Peter van der Veer was our research partner. The fieldwork was carried out over a period of more than two years, between November 2003 and March 2006, in Bangalore and in three countries in Europe. Research methods included formal and informal interviews with a large number of software engineers and BPO workers and their families, managers and others connected with the IT/ITES industries, as well as observations, informal interactions at their workplaces and outside. For more details on the study, see Upadhya and Vasavi (2006).

   This paper was first presented at the 'Conference on Consumerism and the Emerging Middle Class: Comparative Perspectives from India and China', held at New Delhi, 7–9 November, 2005. I thank Christophe Jaffrelot, Peter van der Veer and A.R. Vasavi for their comments on the earlier draft.

2. The software and services industry is often referred to generically as the 'IT industry', although technically 'IT' would include hardware as well as software.

Following common usage, I use the terms 'IT' and 'software' interchangeably in this chapter to refer to this industry and to 'IT' or 'software professionals'. Bangalore is well known as a major location of this industry.

The software and IT services industry in India is primarily oriented to providing services to customers abroad, although some companies also work on software products or provide consultancy services. Most of the Indian companies focus on software services outsourcing for customers in the US and Europe. There are also a number of multinational companies located in India (primarily software development centres that are wholly owned subsidiaries). In both kinds of companies, the work of software engineers usually involves short or long periods of work at the client site or head office located in the US, Europe or other countries.

3. I should clarify here that I use the term 'globalization' primarily in its ideological sense, to refer to a particular set of ideas about the economy and the future trajectory of capitalism that has become dominant around the world, including among prominent sections of the Indian elite and the middle classes. While 'globalization' may not be a very useful *analytical* category, in the Indian context the term does encapsulate a series of transformations in society, economy and culture that can be traced primarily to the opening of the economy under the liberalization programme—hence I use the term as shorthand to refer to these processes. Of course, 'globalization' does not imply cultural homogenization or even necessarily a tighter global economic integration, as much as the making of new connections between disparate places and people, both economic and discursive. In India, the software outsourcing industry is a primary site where these connections are being formed. The idea and social identity of the 'global' is a category that is deployed by political and business elites, as well as by software professionals, and so must be regarded as an object for analysis; it does not imply that there is a distinct 'global culture' that exists apart from its ideological deployment.

4. See Deshpande (2003), Fernandes (2000), Mankekar (1999) and Mazzarella (2003).

5. See Mazzarella (2003), Rajagopal (2001) and Uberoi (2006).

6. Any analysis of this type is inevitably partial and fragmented, and I neglect several crucial aspects of this process, for instance, the relationship between middle class and high caste (brahmin) identities. I thank Ramesh Bairy for pointing out to me the subterranean reproduction of caste within the discourse of middle class-ness, especially in the context of the IT industry in south India, but I do not address this question here.

7. A parallel and almost simultaneous process that is crucial to understanding the reconstitution of the middle classes from the 1980s, but that cannot be discussed here, was the communalization of politics and society, especially of the middle classes, and the growing caste divide (the 'Mandir' and 'Mandal' movements)—processes in which the media was also heavily complicit. See Mankekar (1999) and Rajagopal (2001).

8. Indeed, some have argued that the economic reforms initiated by Rajiv Gandhi were primarily oriented to increasing middle class consumption (Fernandes 2000: 613; Mankekar 1999: 75ff.).

9. But see Mankekar (1999) on the consumption of television in India, and Liechty (2003) and Kemper (2001) on other South Asian countries (Nepal and Sri Lanka, respectively).

10. Attitudes towards consumption and consumption itself have long been important markers of social status and cultural orientation in India, especially in relation to caste. Even among 'traditional business communities', for instance, there are striking differences among Gujaratis, Marwaris and Sindhis in their material culture and the ways in which they display wealth. While the Indian middle class is usually identified with salaried, white collar occupations, the 'consuming classes' are much broader and include traders and shopkeepers from older business communities, newly rich farmers and many other upwardly mobile groups. Thus, consumption style is as much a marker of community or caste as of class. Even within the newly rich classes there are various 'class fractions' that may have different responses to the 'ideology of globalizing consumerism'.

11. In the sample of software professionals interviewed for our formal survey, most informants' fathers (and many of their mothers) worked as managers or administrative or technical staff in public sector enterprises, banks or the government.

12. IT enabled services (ITES) include call centres and other back office operations (BPO or business process outsourcing), and the work is very different from that performed by IT professionals. However, business leaders and the state tend to categorize these two industries together under the 'IT' label, and this poses a threat to the self-identity of software engineers as highly trained global professionals. They do not want to be categorized with BPO workers, who they see as little more than clerical staff or telephone operators.

13. Even 26-year-old software engineers regard 20-year-old call centre workers as a different generation. They see them as the 'cable TV generation' that grew up being exposed to the new consumer culture available on satellite TV, and as too individualistic and fashion conscious. The BPO crowd is said to have imbibed new norms of sexuality and American culture, they earn easily and spend freely, and 'they do not know the value of the basic struggle for life', as one informant put it.

14. This trend of investing in real estate has been promoted during the last few years due to low interest rates and easy availability of house loans; but even then it is indicative of the persistence of 'traditional' middle class financial and social values.

15. This lack of a sense of social connection or community may account for the fact that a large number of IT professionals attend courses offering 'fast food' packaged spirituality, such as 'Art of Living'. Similarly, Fuller and Harriss (2005: 219) point out that both NRIs and middle class Indians in India attempt to fill the 'cultural vacuum' that they experience by turning to various 'god-men' and religious teachers. The teachings of spiritual leaders such as Dayanand appeal to the globalized middle class because they emphasize values and practices that enable devotees to function in the globalizing world.

16. This espousal of 'traditional' middle class values is not simply a reflection of generational differences (these two quotations are from people in their forties). As I have argued elsewhere, these values have been appropriated and promoted as a new business ethic by the IT elite. The IT industry has constructed an image for itself as being more transparent, open and socially conscious than 'traditional'

Indian business because of the fact that it is led by people from the 'middle class', and the two most prominent industry leaders—N.R. Narayana Murthy and Azim Premji—practise austerity to an extent unthinkable among most Indian industrialists (Upadhya 2004). This ethic of austerity has been absorbed by at least the older generation of IT employees. As one manager said, 'I have learnt values like simplicity, transparency, frankness and respect from these leaders'. But middle class 'family values' can hardly be lived out by software engineers who, due to the nature of their work, have little time or energy to fulfil what they regard as their obligations.

17. For IT professionals and other upwardly mobile professionals, time is their most precious and scarce resource, so they do not like to waste time on the mundane chores of everyday life. A variety of service providers have appeared in Bangalore to cater to this market—services that pay your electricity and phone bills, deliver movie tickets at home, cater food, provide domestic help, carry out plumbing and other such repair work, and even organise entertainment on the weekends. Needless to add, the social life of this group is sustained largely through the efficient medium of the Internet as they chat with friends, stay in touch with relatives, and search for friendship, dates and prospective marriage partners through the net.

18. As part of the IDPAD project, the research team carried out fieldwork in the Netherlands, Belgium and Germany during May to October 2004, for a total of four months. The purpose was to understand the work and other experiences of Indian software engineers employed in these countries. The software engineers interviewed in Europe included many who were on temporary assignments of a few months to a year or two, working at customer sites or at their head offices, as well as longer-term residents who were locally employed, some of whom were thinking of settling there permanently.

19. Uberoi (1998) shows that these films valorize specific norms of family and kinship (derived from the typical upper caste, middle class north Indian pattern), including the patrilineal, patrivirilocal joint family, the family as a patriarchal institution in which the father has the authority to arrange marriages of children, and the principle of marriage as an alliance between families. They also promote kinship-related values such as self-control of males, female virtue and obedience to parents.

20. However, we cannot assume that this pattern simply represents traditionalism: there are practical reasons for preferring families to arrange marriages, such as the difficulty of finding the right kind of spouse on their own, and little time available to socialize and meet potential partners.

21. Uberoi also argues that there has been a folding of Indian culture and family values into the new culture of consumption in films such as *Hum Apke Hain Koun*, which portray affluence as enabling a harmonious family life (Uberoi 2001: 334). In these films, '...wealth is no longer opposed to, but is metonymically linked...with Indian culture and tradition' (2001: 334). However, the experience and narratives of those interviewed does not reflect this equation—rather, there is a disjuncture between the new ideology of the Indian family as portrayed in popular culture and that which is articulated by at least one segment of the new middle class, the software professionals.

22. Another important source of cultural knowledge (especially about differences between Indian and western culture) for software engineers are the 'cultural sensitivity' programmes that most of them undergo before they are sent for 'onsite' assignments. The formation of the global Indian self while working abroad is also shaped by the conflict between the professional identity of the 'global knowledge worker'—a technical professional who is well adapted to the global workplace—and the stereotype of the *Indian* software engineer who is in demand because s/he is willing to work long hours for lower pay (Upadhya 2005).

23. Lamb's (2002) study of elderly Indian Americans points to a similar pattern among NRIs in the US, who often bring their aging parents to live with them because they want to look after them, but are unable to fulfil the ideal of 'inter-generational reciprocity' because they do not have the time to provide the kind of care and support that is expected. Instead of the reverse flow of care that is the norm once parents are old, giving continues to flow in the other direction, as elderly parents look after their grandchildren and perform other domestic tasks.

24. Within the transnationalized middle class, it is common for aged parents to circulate among their several married children living in India, the US and elsewhere, often in order to take over childcare duties from other sets of parents. These reconstituted 'joint families' do not represent adherence to 'tradition' or to the idealized joint family of Hindi films as much as a convenient solution to the domestic problems of the younger generation. These reconstituted three-generation households are often marked by an inversion of the inter-generational authority structure, for instance, when the younger generation challenge the beliefs and values of their parents in matters such as childrearing and food habits.

25. That the home they return to is not exactly what they had imagined, and that they also hope to recreate the comforts of their diasporic homes in India, is another matter.

References

Appadurai, Arjun. 1997. *Modernity at Large: Cultural Dimensions of Globalization.* Delhi: Oxford University Press.

Chatterjee, Partha. 1986. *Nationalist Thought and the Colonial World: A Derivative Discourse?* Totowa, N.J.: Zed Press.

Deshpande, Satish. 2003. *Contemporary India: A Sociological View.* New Delhi: Viking.

Fernandes, Leela. 2000. 'Nationalizing 'the Global': Media Images, Cultural Politics and the Middle Class in India', *Media, Culture and Society,* 22(5): 611–28.

Fuller, C.J. and John Harriss. 2005. 'Globalizing Hinduism: A 'Traditional' Guru and Modern Businessmen in Chennai', in Jackie Assayag and C.J. Fuller (eds), *Globalizing India: Perspectives from Below.* London: Anthem Press, pp. 211–36.

Kemper, Steven. 2001. *Buying and Believing: Sri Lankan Advertising and Consumers in a Transnational World.* Chicago: University of Chicago Press.

Lamb, Sarah. 2002. 'Intimacy in a Transnational Era: The Remaking of Aging Among Indian Americans'. *Diaspora,* 11(3): 299–330.

Liechty, Mark. 2003. *Suitably Modern: Making Middle-Class Culture in a New Consumer Society*. Princeton: Princeton University Press.

Mankekar, Purnima. 1999. *Screening Culture, Viewing Politics: Television, Womanhood and Nation in Modern India*. New Delhi: Oxford University Press.

Mazzarella, William. 2003. *Shoveling Smoke: Advertising and Globalization in Contemporary India*. Durham: Duke University Press.

Narayan, Kiran. 2002. 'Placing Lives Through Stories: Second-generation South Asian Americans', in Diane P. Mines and Sarah Lamb (eds), *Everyday Life in South Asia*. Bloomington: Indiana University Press, pp. 425–39.

Rajagopal, Arvind. 2001. *Politics after Television: Hindu Nationalism and the Reshaping of the Public in India*. Cambridge: Cambridge University Press.

Sathaye, Sonali. 2005. 'Combining Science with Sentiment: Psychologising Work (and Home) in Bangalore'. Paper presented to International Conference on New Global Workforces and Virtual Workplaces: Connections, Culture, and Control, National Institute of Advanced Studies, Bangalore, 12–13 August. Forthcoming in volume of conference papers.

Uberoi, Patricia. 1998. 'The Diaspora Comes Home: Disciplining Desire in *DDLJ*', *Contributions to Indian Sociology (N.S.)*, 32(2): 305–36.

———. 2001. 'Imagining the Family: An Ethnography of Viewing *Hum Apke Hain Koun...!*', in Rachel Dwyer and Christopher Pinney (eds), *Pleasure and the Nation: The History, Politics and Consumption of Public Culture in India*. New Delhi: Oxford University Press.

———. 2006. *Freedom and Destiny: Gender, Family, and Popular Culture in India*. Delhi: Oxford University Press.

Upadhya Carol. 2004. 'The Indian Middle Class in the New Economy: Corporate Culture and Strategy in the IT Industry', in Marika Vicziany (ed.), *Cultures and Technologies in Asia; The Paradigm Shifts*. Clayton, Australia: Monash Asia Institute, Monash University Press (CD-ROM).

———. 2005. 'Culture Incorporated: Control Over Work and Workers in the Indian Software Outsourcing Industry'. Paper presented at International Conference on New Global Workforces and Virtual Workplaces: Connections, Culture, and Control, National Institute of Advanced Studies, Bangalore, 12–13 August.

Upadhya, Carol and A.R. Vasavi. 2006. 'Work, Culture, and Sociality in the Indian IT Industry: A Sociological Study' (Final Report submitted to IDPAD). Bangalore: National Institute of Advanced Studies.

4

The Indian Corporate Hospitals: Touching Middle Class Lives*

Bertrand Lefebvre

'Now being in a hospital doesn't feel like being in a hospital.'
—Print Advertisement, Philips Medical Equipment Division,
September 2005

Introduction

Corporate hospitals are private, for profit hospitals (as opposed to charitable hospitals) offering general or specialized tertiary level care (for example, cardiac care). They differ from other nursing homes in their private corporate limited status. Some are now listed on the Mumbai Stock Exchange. Twenty years after the birth of the first corporate hospital in Chennai, the numbers are increasing in all states especially in the Indian metropolises. With the rise of life expectancy and the new expectations of a solvent middle class, the demand for hospital

* I would like to thank Christophe Jaffrelot, Allyson Pollock, Rajeshree Sisodia, Swati Sachdev and Paramita Banerjee for reviewing previous versions of this paper.

care is growing. The rise of degenerative diseases (for example, cancer and cardiovascular diseases) is transforming the hospital landscape. It has been estimated that this growing demand would require the creation of 80,000 new hospital beds each year (CII-McKinsey 2002). This compares with the public sector, which under financial constraints and management difficulties, struggles to provide an additional 8,000 new beds each year (CII-McKinsey 2002). Using incentives on tax exemptions and free land, public authorities have been trying since the early 1990s to attract private investors into the hospital sector. Indian investors (Apollo Hospitals, Fortis, Max Healthcare, Wockhardt, Artemis, and so on) as well as foreign hospital companies (like Parkway from Singapore) and foreign investment groups are investing in this fast-growing market.

This recent development is a complete u-turn from the founding objectives of the Indian healthcare system in 1947. Post-Independence, there were very few private hospitals apart from charitable institutions funded by big business families or missionaries. The optimistic goal of 'Health for All', which easily sums up 40 years of public healthcare policy in India, today sounds out of fashion. The emergence of the corporate hospital sector with a focus on profit-oriented goals has prompted denunciations of these new places of health reserved for the elite, characterized by an outrageous display of wealth and high-end medical technology in a country where public infrastructure and health status of the deprived section of population is so poor. The prices charged by the corporate hospitals are far higher than in the rest of the Indian hospital sector, for example, compare the cost of coronary angiography, a common medical procedure, that requires a full day hospitalization for checking the patient and his heart status (see Table 4.1).

Table 4.1 Coronary angiography prices in Delhi
(one day hospital stay)

Management	Hospital	General ward	Shared room	Single room
Corporate	Max Devki Devi	13,000	16,000	21,000
Corporate	Indraprastha Apollo	14,000	15,500	19,000
Trust	Sir Ganga Ram Hospital	13,000	13,500	19,000
Corporate	Fortis	10,000	11,000	12,000
Public	AIIMS	5,000		5,000

Source: Hindustan Times, 2006.

The cost in corporate hospitals is twice as high as that in AIIMS, the top-end public hospital in Delhi. For a single room, it is four times higher. The corporate hospital is designed not for the general population but the high and higher middle income population. Of course, for this price, patients have the guarantee of a high quality service and the best medical staff you can dream of.

In his essay *La société de consommation*, Jean Baudrillard looked at the first steps taken by the consumption society in France.

> Health today is less of a biological imperative linked to survival and more of a social imperative linked to status. It is less of a fundamental value and more of an 'assertion'. Consumption can be considered as a communication and exchange system, as a code of signs continually being emitted and received and reinvented, like language (Baudrillard 1996 [1970]: 218).

In this respect, healthcare service delivery does position the patient in a certain status group or a certain category of the population. With the rise of the Indian middle class, the choice of a certain type of healthcare is not only driven by the need of healing a disease but also by a certain sense of prestige and belonging to a particular social class. By producing discourses, images and ideas that aim at promoting their offer, corporate hospitals are positioning themselves at the edge of a consumerist vision of healthcare. This entry of consumerism in healthcare has been extremely well described in New Zealand and elsewhere (Kearns and Barnett 1997; Curtis 2003). Kearns and Barnett argue that the introduction of a market-based ideology in the healthcare system is transforming health into a commodity and healthcare into a product. 'The patients are refashioned as consumers and the healthcare system is becoming part of the consumer's world' (Kearns and Barnett 1997: 173). Corporate hospitals and their development in India has been studied by economists (Bhat 2006), who have described their model of development in the specific context of economic growth; some social scientists have looked at corporate hospitals more as an outcome of globalization (Baru 2000). Following the work of Kearns and Barnett (1997) in New Zealand, this chapter offers a rejuvenated perspective on the development of corporate hospitals in India. In an increasingly competitive environment, the Indian corporate hospitals have to build and promote a culture of healthcare consumption. In India, consumerism is expanding its base through the growing middle class and the higher income groups. The tricky side of healthcare is that it cannot be considered as a product per se. 'Rather it is a set of healing practices offered by medical doctors and other health care professionals—people who are afforded great respect in western society' (Kearns and Barnett 1997: 173). This argument can of course be extended to India. You cannot too explicitly promote a corporate hospital like a TV screen or a car as it would tend to give the patients a sense of distrust, an apprehension.

The main argument of this chapter is that today these hospitals are one of the most efficient vehicles that promote consumerism in healthcare. If we consider consumerism as an ideology, then the corporate hospital, as a place, is like the manifesto in the field of healthcare, which through place marketing is promoting newer perspectives of health and health service delivery. These places are creating confusion among the patients by mixing different symbols and signs from the consumption society.

THE CORPORATE HOSPITALS: BY THE MIDDLE CLASS, FOR THE MIDDLE CLASS?

Corporate hospitals are building images and narratives to attract people from the middle and upper classes. We can argue for a true retroactive process. The corporate hospitals, in building these images and discourses, are not only positioning themselves within the middle class, but also giving their patients a true sense of belonging to this emerging middle class. The corporate hospitals legitimate their development as well as fill the imagination of the middle class by using narratives to communicate about their roots, their management methods and their vision of Indian society. Through this, they make the middle class patients feel the echoes of their ideals of what India and the Indian healthcare should be.

Tales from the Corporate Hospitals

The emergence of the corporate hospitals in Indian healthcare is closely related to the emergence of the urban middle class in India. It has not been purely accidental that the middle class and the corporate hospitals both started to make their presence felt in the early 1980s. The liberalization policy launched by Rajiv Gandhi—even if it was a short step compared to the deeper changes that occurred after the 1991 financial crisis—opened a new era for the Indian middle class. Earlier the Gandhian ideals of frugality and simplicity were stressed, while today increased consumption and greater choice in commodities are more openly acknowledged values (Varma 1998). The corporate hospitals are prompted to explain their emergence by this sudden rise of new expectations among Indian patients, particularly the Indian middle class. The middle class had the money but the public hospitals were overcrowded and could not offer proper standards in terms of comfort and service. Middle class patients were looking for something better and they could afford it. Some middle class (probably the upper middle class) patients were even forced to go to the US or UK for treatment. The history of the corporate hospitals really took ground in the realm of the Indian middle class. A detailed examination of the history of the main actors of the corporate hospitals enables us to argue that this offer has been designed by middle class people to answer middle class needs. The founders of the corporate hospitals are refashioned by the media or through the marketing brochures produced by corporate hospitals as pioneers of the new consumption society and as heroes from and for the Indian middle class.

The first Indian corporate hospital was founded by Dr Prathap Reddy in Chennai in 1983. Son of a plantation owner from Chitoor district (Andhra Pradesh), Dr Prathap Reddy went to the US in the 1960s, like many other Indian doctors. Being homesick, he returned to India. He opened a cardiac clinic in Chennai. At that time, because of the custody taxes, importing top quality equipment was difficult and thus some hospitals were sending their patients abroad. In 1979, Dr Reddy was treating a young businessman who needed a coronary bypass surgery. Lacking the proper equipment he advised the businessman to fly to Houston in US. Unfortunately, this patient could not afford the travel and died. 'I pledged to myself then and there that I would make certain India would have world-class facilities before I died' (Reddy 2004). 'He was so devastated at the sight of a wailing young mother and her two small children that he decided to set up a hospital himself. Thus was born the Apollo Hospitals Group' (Financial Express 2004).

Many people at this moment doubted that starting and sustaining a profit-making hospital was possible. Dr Reddy had to fight the bureaucracy and the stringent regulation for land acquisition and import of medical equipment. Twenty years later, Apollo Hospitals is the largest Asian hospital chain.

The story of Dr Naresh Trehan, the mind behind the Escorts Heart Institute and Research Centre (EHIRC) in Delhi, is rather similar. Coming from a family of doctors who had to leave everything at Lahore to resettle in Delhi after the Partition, Dr Naresh Trehan went to the US in 1969 and by the mid-1980s was a famous Manhattan heart surgeon. His decision to come back to India was prompted by the Indians who kept coming to him in New York for heart care. They were all wondering why they could not get the same quality of care at home. Driven by 'a certain amount of arrogance—a kind of national pride' that he could do things better than most of his American counterparts, he took the decision to come back to India (Trehan 2003). With the support of the Nanda family, an industrialist family from north India, he set up the Escorts Heart Institute and Research Centre in Delhi in 1989.

Fortis was founded in 1996.

It was an idea whose time had come...making India truly come of age in healthcare. And it was the mission that fired the imagination of a visionary—the late Dr. Parvinder Singh. At the helm of one of India's leading pharmaceutical companies, Ranbaxy Laboratories, Dr Singh had already architectured its ambitious growth path for the 21st century.... His vision...creating a world-class integrated healthcare delivery system in India, entailing the finest medical skills combined with compassionate patient care (Fortis Brochure 2005).

His sons Malvinder and Shivinder Singh made sure that their father's dreams came true.

These three stories and others, tell us something about the relations that exist between the corporate hospitals and the middle class. The founding act in the case of Apollo Hospitals was the tragic death of a young businessman. The Indian patients, certainly rich enough to take a flight to New York for heart surgery, convinced Naresh Trehan to leave Manhattan. The truth behind the idea that the corporate hospitals have been created to cater to the needs of the Indian middle class makes more sense once these stories, which look more like legendary tales, have been read. Besides, national pride and the vision to bring to India, the best of facilities also seems an important consideration. As pointed out by Leela Fernandes (2000), the notion of 'abroad' is of primary importance to understand the Indian middle class. Before liberalization, accessing commodities from abroad was a sign of distinction. On the contrary, the limitation in accessing these goods was symptomatic of the limits of the Indian middle class prosperity. The moment Naresh Trehan, a Non-Resident Indian (NRI), one of the most skilful heart surgeons of New York, came back to India, the aspirations of consumption of the middle class could be realized in India, in the context of healthcare. The creation of Apollo Hospital by Dr Reddy, another NRI, was motivated by the desire to ensure that no young Indian businessman died because he could not afford or reach by-pass surgery (then not available in India and available in the US). The vision of Dr Parvinder Singh of bringing world class healthcare to India through Fortis, echoes the same wish of the middle class—to finally have the ability and the right to access the best of healthcare in India. Consumerism is about having choice.

Another interesting aspect lies in the social background of the founders of the corporate hospitals and the narration of the success stories of their groups. They are from the middle or the upper-middle class and are businessmen. Their stories perfectly fit the Schumpeterian entrepreneur's model. They took risks to make their way in the field of healthcare. The struggle of Prathap Reddy is also the struggle any Indian businessman who has to cope with regulation and public authorities, not to say corruption. The Singh family is one of the most respected business families of north India and Parvinder Singh has made Ranbaxy one of the top generic manufacturers in the world. These people are heroes of the business class and the middle class. They inspire confidence not only because they are like the middle class, but also because they work and manage their activity like a business enterprise and activity.

The Corporate Hospitals: A Business Like any Other

Corporate hospitals, in their brochures and communication through the media, mobilize and advertise their corporate identity thus establishing their business culture as a hallmark of quality that aims to build trust among middle class patients. Business in India is still a family affair as are corporate hospitals. In the story of Fortis, there is a true sense of filiations—the sons (Malvinder and Shivinder) doing their best to realise the vision of their late father, with the help of Shivinder's father-in-law, Harpal Singh. The top heads of the Apollo Hospitals are the three daughters of Prathap Reddy. With one of them studying in Harvard, the three have been groomed to take over control of Apollo Hospitals. The notion of family can also be extended to all the staff. Prathap Reddy is depicted as a kind of 'Heavenly Father' and his picture is usually placed at the gate, in the waiting rooms of every Apollo hospital and in every brochure of Apollo Hospitals. His speeches are full of the kind of wisdom one would expect from the Godfather of the corporate hospital. Leaving the day-to-day operations to his daughters, he has become the moral force behind the enterprise. Fortis reproduced this idea with the figure of late Parvinder Singh.

Being a business, the ideas of performance, achievement and success are not alien to corporate hospitals but an integral part of their set-up, and they want the middle class to know it. Healthcare is a peculiar business—the goal of profit is difficult to market and the emphasis is on medical excellence, management and corporate governance. The medical premier or the purchase of latest top medical electronic equipments give an idea of the excellence corporate hospitals can achieve. The important matter is to be the first—be it by the size, by the medical premier or by the number of awards and accreditations. The stiff competition between medical institutions now find some echoes in the media, with the yearly publication by *The Week* magazine of a ranking of the top Indian hospitals. Most of the corporate hospitals have an ISO licence like many other service businesses. This ISO licence of course means nothing about the quality of care a patient may get, but it means something about the quality of the management and the delivery of other services. ISO norm is familiar to the middle class and is a hallmark of the global level quality reached by these hospitals. Another important recognition for the corporate hospitals is to get the Joint Commission International (JCI) accreditation, which encompasses not only the quality of service but also that of medical procedures and practices. This accreditation, which is mandatory for any hospital in the US, has become the key to enter the medical tourism market.

The corporate hospitals are mobilizing medical tourism and their expansion abroad as the best arguments to celebrate, announce and prove their success as well as the quality of the service they offer. As one doctor of Fortis emphasizes, medical tourism is a good way to achieve and to promote medical excellence. Like other Indian Multi-national Corporations, corporate hospitals are mustering the recognition they receive from abroad to improve their image among the local population. After receiving the JCI accreditation for its hospital in Delhi, Apollo Hospitals was very proud to claim in its brochures that they are 'carrying the Indian Flame high'. This kind of statesmanship enables them to be in a position to tell and sometimes even dictate what is good for India.

A Vision for India and Its Healthcare System

The corporate hospitals reproduce social and political discourses to please the middle class, particularly when it comes to their social responsibility. Press interviews are an occasion to dismiss government action and the public authorities.

I am very disappointed that every government makes promises and does nothing. It is 30 years since I came back from the US and listened to all Budgets. Budgets just say increase Custom duty on this or reduce on that. Is that the health of a nation? In the West people enjoy good health, yet the priority of the governments is healthcare. Previously I used to represent, and request the government to declare health as infrastructure. But I don't blame the Government… when its officials want, they can get healthcare from anywhere in the world. The second thing is there is no powerful lobby for health (Reddy 2001).

The Health Summit, an event organized each year by the Confederation of Indian Industry, is often a moment where the crème de la crème of corporate hospitals gather and speak more freely about different aspects of their business and their forthcoming agenda. Being in this secure environment and having the attention from national media, one of their favourite sports is the bashing of public authorities. The usual complaint is about how the government is not helping them or worse even creating more problems for their activity. In their discourses, the relations with politicians seem really complex when it comes to finding a common framework to work. The lack of commitment of the politicians has to be blamed in on the failure of the Public Private Partnership (PPP). The change in governments necessitates that everything be started afresh. One of the most regular requests is to let the private sector be responsible for tertiary care and leave rural and primary care to the government. The only public institution that is not blamed during the Health Summits is the army, as it is less corrupt and filled with a sense of duty and commitment. As certain managers of the corporate hospitals claim, they share the same goals of efficiency for the good of the entire nation. It is an inspiring example for the corporate hospitals in terms of management and for entire India. We find former army officers among the top managers of corporate hospitals (for example, Brig. Joe Curian was the manager of Indraprastha Apollo hospital in Delhi).

Another key idea is that 'the business people are smart' (Prathap Reddy, CII Health Summit 2004) and thus are able to respond to the challenges of Indian society. Their success in business gives them a kind of legitimacy to assess and solve the problems of India. In the field of health, this discourse is coupled with a sense of national pride, a sense of duty towards society, as we have seen earlier. The talented NRI, forgoing his comfortable and secure life in the US to do something good for his homeland, is a modern hero and role model for the middle class. From Naresh Trehan to Prathap Reddy, this story has been told over and over again. The social responsibility of the business family is not really new in India. The big Indian industrial families, like the Tatas and the Bajajs, have often set up charitable hospitals for the good of the community. But corporate hospitals' charitable action more often than not echoes this typical middle class idea that civil society can take care of the national challenges and that nothing good has to be expected from the government and the babus of public administration. Apollo Hospitals sets aside some beds for free care and has established a financial trust to aid the needy. Recent advances in technology and telemedicine will supposedly help reach rural areas and remote populations. Escorts Heart Institute devotes 10 percent of its income to free care for the poor and subsidizes care for government employees, members of the military and retired persons. There is a heart check-up for 1,00,000 villagers per year thanks to Escorts vans. Fortis has a community outreach programme that relies on free health camps and health awareness programmes. As some insiders of the corporate hospitals, especially the medical staff explained, this is merely cosmetic. The surgery offered to poor patients, preferably children, is like a public relations operation that will hit the headlines and show how corporate hospitals are working for the health of all sections of the population in the nation. There has been regular controversy over the implementation of the free beds programme in Indraprastha Apollo hospital (The Hindu 2004) and other hospitals (Public Account Commission 2005).

Using promotion material, press interviews and primary sources, we have been trying to analyze the production of discourses that are aimed to attract middle class patients to the corporate hospitals. We tried to show how indeed a retroaction is occurring between the middle class and the corporate hospitals in the creation of these discourses. Thus, in our opinion, it is really within the hospital itself that the discourses produced by the corporate hospitals are the most powerful and influential. It is in the hospital that the patient from the middle class can experience what the brochure and interviews in the media are selling and narrating.

THE CORPORATE HOSPITALS IN THE NEW LANDSCAPES OF CONSUMPTION

The Five Star Hospitals

There is a mythical construction that makes the hospital more than a simple building—rather it has a symbolic dimension. The functionalist approach that has led hospital architecture for decades has now been replaced by more imaginative architecture. With the rise of consumerism, in New Zealand (Kearns and Barnett 1997), in UK (Gesler et al. 2004) and as we will see in India too, healthcare providers are keen on integrating symbols of the consumer world into the hospital to attract more patients. If the therapeutic impact of environment and architecture has been increasingly recognized, the experts in design and architecture are not free from the values and ideologies of their time (Gesler et al. 2004). Gruffudd (2001) studied two health centres built in London in the 1930s and showed how they were both built as an

Figure 4.1   Max Devki Devi Hospital, Delhi

answer to the declining standard of public health in the downtown area. Guided by a modernist architecture, based on hygienic and naturalist principles, they were seen by the professionals and the population as a symbol of the capability of the society to improve low health standards. The Indian corporate hospital is full of signs and symbols that create a specific sense of place. Everything is done to create a true sense of distinction from the worn-out public hospitals and small private nursing homes. The premises, with their display of prosperity, wealth and modernity, enable patients to assert their difference and identity, and gives them the feeling that they are part of the elite. The corporate hospitals try to market themselves as a specific place in the Indian healthcare system. If the Max Devki Devi hospital's slogan is 'The heart institute with a difference', it has to be put into practice (see Figure 4.1).

In India, one of the best points of comparison to describe and analyze the corporate hospitals remains the five star hotels. So relevant is it that even the expression 'five star hospitals' is often used by the managers and the media in-charge people to describe their corporate hospitals. The corporate hospitals are not only imitating the five star hotels in their design but also in the experience the patient will have in the hospital. Let us enter the Indraprastha Apollo Hospital in Delhi. First, you come through the main entrance, with its well mannered porters using the same ceremony like in any five star hotel. After crossing a large atrium, there is a second gate to access the in-patients building, with a well-designed information desk made of marble. According to his/her means, a patient can choose from different types of bedrooms ranging from the shared bedroom to the first class bedroom. This last category offers a wonderful view of the surroundings. It is also very well equipped with a TV, a personal bathroom, a sofa for the guests and an attached bedroom for the relatives. All the corporate hospitals in Delhi are now equipped with a presidential suite.

The quality of the service is of course said to be excellent. From the food to the medical and nursing staff's attitude towards patients, everything is done to give satisfaction to the patient. In case you are not satisfied, you can always fill a form to complain and rate the different aspects of your stay. Entering a corporate hospital is like entering the 'King Patient' era. The corporate hospitals and the five star hotels share a common target population. The business people receive very special attention. Some health packages are specifically designed for them (for example, the Apollo Executive Cheq). In the Fortis Hospital of Mohali (Chandigarh), you can find a business centre, where Internet connection, computers, desks and phones are accessible to businessmen. In the Indraprastha Apollo Hospital, you find a Premium Lounge for VIPs. Just like the famous French chefs in any five star hotel, the 'NRI' surgeons or doctors, graduated from the best American or British medical colleges, are a must in the Indian corporate hospitals. This NRI mark echoes back to the position that the NRI occupies in the middle class imagination—particularly when it comes to the ideals of consumption, and economic and social success. There is a tight concurrence among corporate hospitals to have the best medical team as part of their infrastructure. The corporate hospitals also want to make patients aware of this. Near the gate of the Fortis Hospital in Mohali, a large board depicting the entire cardiac team of the hospital welcomes the patient. In the communication brochure, the testimony of the patients is taken, based on their experiences regarding the quality of services and the quality of the surgeons or doctors. In a realm where people are sometimes putting their life in the hands of the corporate hospitals, it is of primary importance to build a strong reputation for the hospital. The reputation of a surgeon and his team can help attract more patients and enhance the quality of the hospital. The recent departure of Dr Naresh Trehan from EHIRC to the Indraprastha Apollo Hospital increased the number of patients in the cardiology department of the latter.

Another interesting point of comparison is to look at the Information Technology (IT) sector. The hospital sector and the IT sector both rely to a large extent on electronic equipment and informatics for their activities. The purchase of medical equipment now accounts for 30–40 per cent of the initial investment in a tertiary care hospital in India. The medical electronic equipment is often considered by the managers of private hospitals as the best way to increase their market share (Sukanya 1996). The corporate hospitals also make intensive use of information technologies. Patient management is very IT intensive, with medical records now being stored on data servers. From x-rays to the last prescription of medicines, everything can be accessed by the medical staff. As one doctor from Apollo said:

It helps to give a better diagnostic. You don't need to discuss ten minutes with the patients regarding their previous visits. It saves a lot of time. And the patient feels more comfortable. Sometimes it can be stressful or disturbing for a patient, to recall past moments when he suffered.

According to another doctor it creates also an 'IT office' atmosphere that is praised by the patients, particularly children. This IT atmosphere is reinforced by the interior design, which uses typical postmodern architectural materials like wood or white metal. The Fortis Hospital in Mohali, displays the pictures of the employee and the doctor of the month in its halls. The management culture from the IT sector or the BPO sector has been applied to the hospitals and this is too evident today. All these symbols put together, create an image of efficiency and cleanliness that seems far different from what you can usually experience in a public hospital. It associates, through these symbols, the corporate hospitals with the IT sector, one of the most successful sectors of the Indian economy.

One last interesting point of comparison is the shopping centre. The rise of the middle class and consumerism is giving birth to new places of consumption such as malls and shopping complexes in the suburbs of the Indian metropolises. We can read the rise of the corporate hospitals as its counterpart in the field of healthcare. As the malls are offering a large choice of items and shops, corporate hospitals are always proud to remind its patients of the profusion of various medical electronic equipments, various medical services and, as we have seen earlier, non-medical services available under the same roof. The Indraprastha Apollo Hospital offers more than 50 medical or surgical services to its patients. In this hospital, you can find a monumental atrium between the in-patients and the out-patients buildings, with different services, which are not always related to health—a travel agency, pharmacy, some health insurance desks, a Premium Lounge for the VIPs and a fast-food restaurant (Nathu's). At the Max Heart and Vascular Institute in Delhi, you can find a Café Coffee Day, a Book Cafe and a Subway, all franchises which are very common in the Indian malls. As the director of sales and marketing of Max Healthcare puts it: 'Through these facilities we are trying to provide an unhospital like ambience to our visitors. It helps them to unwind and take away the blues' (Express Newsline 2006). These hospitals also put a lot of effort to control smells and to ensure that no 'medical' smell prevails to remind the patient that he is actually in a hospital.

The five star hotel, the IT office and the mall have been interesting sources of comparison. The corporate hospital can be analyzed as a mix of all these different places. The corporate hospitals are particularly keen on using the codes of postmodernist architecture, which can be associated in the imagination of the patient to other places of consumption such as shopping centres, five star hotels or high-tech places such as IT research centres or offices. Everything seems to be done to project the corporate hospital as anything but a hospital. The corporate hospital as a building creates an environment where the patients and their relatives are surrounded by consumerist signs. This is reinforced by the location strategy of the corporate hospitals.

In the Landscapes of Consumption

It is common in health geography to study the location choice of a new hospital and even sometimes to help along in the decision making process. Is the hospital close to the targeted population? Does this population have an easy access to this hospital? This material dimension has been well explored for decades now. But the symbolic and mythical part of the location can teach us a great deal about the nexus that exists between healthcare and consumerism.

The choice of location is of primary importance for the corporate hospitals, as in any retail business. In the context of a competitive market like in Delhi, the choice of location appears to be a matter of even greater concern. Every piece of land leads to intense rivalry between the different groups (for example, between Max and Fortis). It has led some groups to sign some surprising deals with so-called Charitable Trusts, where the corporate group is considered as the manager of the hospital but not the owner of the building itself. The Delhi Development Authority does not allow charitable trusts to sell their land. The Devki Devi Foundation has signed a management contract with Max Healthcare, while Fortis took over the management of the Jessa Ram Hospital. This way, corporate hospitals have access to land at a cheaper price.

In the case of Delhi, most of the corporate hospitals are located in south Delhi and its extensions, namely, Noida, Gurgaon and Faridabad. This area is welcoming the new middle class that has emerged in Delhi over the last 15 years. The choice of these localities places these hospitals in the new areas created by India's consumer society, with their multiplex movie theatres, malls and gated communities. They are very well integrated with the landscapes of consumption and indeed play a pioneering role in most of the cases. The Indian media has devoted a lot of coverage to the recent mushrooming of shopping centres in Delhi and around, but this trend—which has occurred in the last two years—seems very recent compared to the development of corporate hospitals. At a micro-level, we can see shopping centres taking ground near the corporate hospitals like the Indraprastha Apollo in Sarita Vihar or the Max hospitals in Saket (see Figure 4.2).

In Europe, the creation of a new hospital, either private or public, is often used to restore and glamorize deprived areas. The role of the hospital in the gentrification process has been very well described by geographers (such as A. Vaguet and J-M Toussaint, University of Rouen) studying the insertion of a new private hospital in the industrial town of Le Havre (France). In UK the creation of new hospitals

Figure 4.2   The huge Metropolitan Shopping Complex will
open in a couple of months near the Max Hospital campus
(Max Devki Devi and Max Super Speciality Hospitals)

under the Private Finance Initiative—instead of funding the renovation of previous public hospitals—makes a clear statement about the
new orientation taken by British hospital policy (Gesler et al. 2004).
The commodification of the urban landscapes is also at work in the
creation of the new urban landscapes in Delhi. The corporate hospitals are markers of these new landscapes of consumption. The proximity of shopping centres, restaurants and cinema complexes reinforces
what we have described earlier about the saturation of consumerist
signs inside and around the corporate hospitals.

We have discussed new landscapes of consumption but another trend
related to consumerism is transforming the urban landscapes of south
Delhi. The commercial activities are gradually gaining ground in
residential areas of south Delhi. The fashion boutiques, the jewellers,
the restaurants and, increasingly, services or retail businesses are spreading out from the markets. Their presence is increasingly visible through
banners or advertisements. The corporate hospitals are of course part
of this process. There is no question of settling a 250-bed hospital in

the middle of a 'posh' residential area but the corporate hospitals groups have a specific strategy to enter such areas. It is part of the 'Hub and Spokes' model imported from the US. Sometimes based on a franchise system, this model allows corporate hospitals to create a network of primary and secondary care structures that enter in frontal concurrence with the next door specialist (dental care, paediatrics, and so on) or general practitioner. The hospital groups can create their patient base much earlier from the primary care level and offer packages to families as well as quality healthcare closeby. Another advantage lies in improving the tertiary facility's turnover by sending the patient to a secondary structure for the post-operative period. If these care units often develop their own symbols with different colours or logos, their brand (The Apollo Clinic, Max Medcentre) echoes the main hospitals. Capitalizing on the brand name, they offer the best of care to the neighbouring patients. As one manager of an Apollo Clinic explained to us, this type of infrastructure aims to save the patient from the trouble of hospitalization:

> A family is in chaos if the wife has to stay in the hospital. Who is going to cook or to take care of the children? And if the husband has to stay in the hospital for a night, the wife will be worried because there is only one nurse for 15 patients.

Like any 'five star hospital', secondary structures need to be clearly identified in the more densely built-up areas than the tertiary hospital. (see Figure 4.3). They clearly differentiate themselves from the rest of the healthcare system by reproducing some of the architectural or design clichés that can be observed from other franchisee business (for example, Barista and McDonald's). In the case of an Apollo Clinic, the company sends architects to supervise the transformation of the site. The franchise has to follow the specifications of Apollo Clinic for not only the medical equipment but also for the furniture and the interior design. The way medical staff welcomes and treats the patient comes under scrutiny. The contrast with the usual next door chemist or doctor is really appealing with the use of stained windows and their brand name put in good place. Their strategy in terms of design, to create a more appealing place, is now even spreading to other private actors of healthcare, like nursing homes and diagnostic centres. In the

Figure 4.3   The Escorts-Kalyani Heart Centre in
Gurgaon and an Apollo Clinic in south Delhi

case of an Apollo Clinic, the local investor has to propose different
sites for its future clinics. The site will be selected in agreement with
Apollo Clinic Company. Often located close to a very intense market
area (for example, Greater Kailash M-Block Market in south Delhi and
MG road in Gurgaon) frequented by the middle class, their insertion
into these landscapes of consumption reinforces the idea that health
and healthcare are like any other product or service.

Conclusion

The mythical dimension attached to the corporate hospitals is interesting as it echoes some of the values attached to consumerism and the
Indian middle class. The promotion of the personal history of the
founders, the location strategy or the marketing strategy can offer
interesting elements to understand how healthcare is gradually being
commodified in India. The corporate hospital may represent a part of
Indian society, a place to assert its identity. In 'Of Other Spaces', Foucault characterises heterotopia as the following:

First there are the utopias. Utopias are sites with no real place.... There are also, probably in every culture, in every civilization, real places...which are something like counter-sites, a kind of effectively enacted utopia.... Because these places are absolutely different from all the sites that they reflect and speak about, I shall call them, by way of contrast to utopias, heterotopias (Foucault 1967).

This concept of heterotopia has been extremely useful for us to explore medical tourism (Bochaton and Lefebvre 2006) and the experience it can give to the patient. The corporate hospital can be read as an enacted utopia for the Indian middle class, as a monument dedicated to consumerism in the realm of healthcare. The concept of heterotopia certainly needs to be further explored in the near future.

The hospital as a building or by its location is also a powerful entry point in helping to understand an ideology and discourses. This dimension is very important because the hospital helps to bring reality and facts to the discourses. This is a true retroactive process as Kearns, Barnett and Newman describe in the case of New Zealand:

We argue for a recursive link between these material and ideological landscapes of health care: the increasing representations of private hospitals in New Zealand (e.g via buildings and advertising) lead to the legitimation of their presence within 'health care talk' by policy makers, politicians and the public at large. In this respect, places such as hospitals, exist not only as empirical entities, but also as social productions, reflecting changing underlying relationships of power.

The discourses make the corporate hospitals key actors, even if they hardly tap 7 percent of the total spending in private healthcare (CII-McKinsey 2002). The corporate hospital's lobbying (through the Confederation of Indian Industry and the Indian Healthcare Federation) is incredibly powerful and enables them to obtain more and more incentives from local and central governments to open new structures—new structures that are reinforcing their presence in healthcare dialogues and discussions. In the same manner, the patients are confused seeing this mix of health, ostentation and business. Some scientists have pointed out how environment can structure values and beliefs. But with the rise of consumerism, the patients also have new expectations in terms of hospital design. In this retroactive process, Indian public hospitals seem excluded because of their lack of funding. It seems as if health is no longer a quality or right but simply a commodity which you have to pay for to get the best.

The final outcome of such a nexus between healthcare and consumerism can be seen in the 'medicity' or 'health city' projects that are mushrooming in the suburbs of Delhi, Hyderabad and Kolkata. Gathering together hospitals, medical colleges, medical research facilities and in certain cases hotels and residential plots, these projects are good examples of the disneyization—hybrid consumption, performative labour or merchandising that Bryman (2004) found to have originated from the Disney theme park—of the hospital sector in India. The main objective is to nurture more profits for hospitals through increased synergies and theming. These projects also appear to be the answer to the challenge of medical tourism. There will no longer be any five star hotels or five star hospitals, but just a health theme park where you can have knee replacement treatment after having a yoga lesson. Here comes the time when 'being in a hospital doesn't feel like being in a hospital'.

References

Baru, R. 2000 'Privatisation and Corporatisation', *Seminar*, 489. Available online at http://www.india-seminar.com/2000/489/489 baru.htm, accessed on 4 May 2006.

Baudrillard, J. 1996. *La société de consommation*. Paris: Gallimard, Folio, Essai.

Bhat, R. 2006. 'Financial Health of Private Sector Hospitals', Indian Institute of Management of Ahmedabad, Working Paper, 2006-01-01.

Bochaton, A.and B. Lefebvre. 2006. 'Medical Tourism in India and Thailand: An Heterotopia in the Time of Globalisation', paper presented at the international conference on 'Of Asian Origin': Rethinking Tourism in Contemporary Asia, National University of Singapore, 7–9 September.

Bryman, A. 2004. *The Disneyisation of society*. London: Sage.

CII-McKinsey. 2002. *Healthcare in India: The Road Ahead*. New Delhi: CII-McKinsey.

Curtis, S. 2003. *Health Inequalities: Geographical Perspectives*. London: Sage.

Express Newsline. 2006. 'Blue Chip Diners', *Express Newsline*, 29 July.

Fernandes, Leela. 2000. 'Nationalizing the Global: Media Images, Cultural Politics and the Middle Class in India, *Media, Culture & Society*, 22(5): 611–28.

Financial Express. 2004. *Financial Express*, 4 April.

Foucault, M. 1967. 'Of Other Spaces', *Architecture/Mouvement/Continuité*, 5: 46–49. Available online at http://foucault.info/documents/heteroTopia/foucault.heteroTopia.en.html, accessed on 4 May 2006.

Gesler, W., M. Bell, S. Curtis, P. Hubbard and S. Francis. 2004. 'Therapy by Design: Evaluating the UK Hospital building Programme, *Health & Place*, 10(2): 117–28.

Gruffudd, P. 2001. 'Science and the Stuff of Life: Modernist Health Centers in 1930s London', *Journal of Historical Geography*, 27(3): 395–416.

Kearns, R.A. and J.R. Barnett. 1997. 'Consumerist Ideology and the Symbolic Landscapes of Private Medicine, *Health and Place*, 3(3): 171–80.

Kearns, R.A., J.R. Barnett and D. Newman. 2003. 'Placing Private Health Care: Reading Ascot Hospital in the Landscape of Contemporary Auckland, *Social Science & Medicine*, 56(11): 2303–15.

Public Account Commission. 2005. *Allotment Land to Private Hospitals and Dispensaries by Delhi Development Authority*. New Delhi: Lok Sabha.

Reddy, Prathap. 2001. *The Hindu Business Line*, 11 February.

————. 2004. *Wall Street Journal*, 26 April.

Sukanya, S. 1996. Investments in Medical Equipment: Study of Private Hospitals in Madras, *Radical Journal of Health*, 2(1): 9–25.

Trehan, Naresh. 2003. *The New York Times International*, 18 May.

The Hindu. 'Apollo Hospital ticked off', *The Hindu*, 28 July.

Varma, P.K. 1998. *The Great Indian Middle Class*. New Delhi: Penguin Books.

5

Chinese Middle Class:
Reality or Illusion?*

Xiaohong Zhou

The discussion on the Chinese middle class has recently become a major concern of Chinese sociologists as well as the general public. Ever since the early 1990s, works on the middle class—in spite of all the existing ideological constraints—have been released successively due to the increasing interest in the matter by publishers and the mass media. The fundamental cause underlying the occurrence of such a phenomenon can be attributed to recent changes in China's social stratum conditions which, for the past 30 years or so, have more or less remained unaffected. The most striking change noticed is the emergence of another class or stratum, or, at least, a new group of people with medium incomes, than the two traditional classes—the working and farming classes.

* This paper is one of the results of the Project on Comparative Research of the Western Social Construction, supported by Chinese National Foundation for Social Science (No. 05 & ZD037).

IS THERE A MIDDLE CLASS AT ALL IN CHINA?

This question was raised with the release of our book *A Survey of Chinese Middle Class* in 2005. Our investigation, based on telephonic interviews of 3038 households, indicated that the middle class or middle stratum accounted for 11.9 per cent of the population in Beijing, Shanghai, Guangzhou, Nanjing and Wuhan, the five major cities in China. Three main indices, namely, financial conditions, occupation and educational background, were adopted in our study for a comprehensive survey of the interviewees' situation.

The publication of our investigation created much stir in sociological circles and other sectors of society as well. Shortly after it was published, *China Youth Daily*, an influential newspaper in China with a circulation of millions of copies a day, devoted a whole page for the report on our study. The investigation as well as its follow-up discussions were given full coverage at home and abroad. Almost as many as 75,400 web pages were available using the Internet search engine Google for *A Survey of Chinese Middle Class*, and no less than 39,700 using Baidu (a leading Chinese search engine). Apart from objective reports on our study, there were also comments presented on these web pages. One-third of the comment writers felt that our estimation of the percentage of middle-income households in the city population at 'merely 11.9 per cent' was much lower than their expectations, whereas the other two-thirds challenged not only our estimate of the total middle class population but also the criteria for our judgments. According to them, if 11.9 per cent of the Chinese population was classified as the middle-income group, the total would reach an amazing 150,000,000! Moreover, it was doubtful whether a person with over 5,000 yuan monthly income, a white-collar occupation and formal college education was qualified for the middle class.[1]

As a matter of fact, challenges of this kind never really detached themselves from studies on the middle class. When Lu Xueyi declared in *A Study on Modern China's Different Social Strata* (2001) that the estimated number of middle class households in China was 80 million, it gave rise to widespread heated discussions. Then, in 2004, another stormy discussion on the same topic ensued when the National Bureau of Statistics issued the standard for China's middle annual income as ranging from 60,000 to 500,000 yuan per household. In September 2005, Lu Xueyi again caused much agitation when he further proclaimed, during 'The Second China-Europe Senior Forum on Government Management', that, based on an annual growth of one percentage point, the middle class in China was expected to make up for 40 per cent of the total work force in 20 years (Lu Xueyi 2005).

Actually, the debate on whether there is a middle class or a middle stratum at all in China goes far beyond cyber talk. Some scholars, a few of whom are experts on social stratification, also deny the existence of the middle class in present China. As far as they are concerned, 'there is more a middle-income group than the middle class' (Wang Yi 2003). Some others even claim that 'the so-called middle class in China is no more than a myth invented by media reporters and scholars' (Cai Zhenfeng 2004).

The Chinese middle class has long endured much hardship for its survival in the same way as studies on this particular class. The former subject is well handled in my book *China's Middle Class: What They Can Do and What They Should Do* (Zhou Xiaohong 2002), whereas the latter will be dealt with in the current study with a focus on one question—How come, after 25 years of social reforms and opening-up, most people are still rather sceptical about the presence of the middle class or the middle stratum in China?

One reason accounting for this skepticism lies in our misinterpretation of the English term 'middle class. This is also true for other East Asian countries like Taiwan and Korea (Xiao Xinhuang 1994). In Hongkong and Singapore, where English is generally used by the public, the term 'middle class' is used to refer to a particular group of people, almost free of any misunderstanding; the term 'the new middle class' is usually used interchangeably with 'the professionals'. In both Taiwan and Korea, however, the translation of the English term 'middle class in their local languages implies 'the possession of middle property'; consequently, it is no longer appropriate to follow Mills' (1951) practice of identifying professionals and white-collar workers with 'the new middle class. In mainland China, the conventional translation for the term 'middle class' is *zhongchan jieji*, which means 'the middle property class' and, obviously, this translation adds to people's overemphasis on the amount of assets owned, at the cost of total ignorance of occupational characteristics of the modern middle class or the new middle class.

Even in the United States, as a matter of fact, the income, absolute or relative, of the middle class is far less than our expectations—'The great bulk of the.new middle class are of the lower middle-income brackets', Mills puts it bluntly. Again, when it comes to the transition of the old middle class to the new middle class, he asserts that 'negatively, the transformation of the middle class is a shift from property to no-property; positively, occupation' (Mills 1951: 64–65).

The second reason why people challenge the existence of the middle class in China can be attributed to their confusing 'middle class' with 'middle class society.' A close inspection of articles refuting the existence of China's middle class shows that most authors have cited, as a supporting argument, the five standards of middle class society proposed by Niu Wenyuan, leader of a research team for sustainable development strategy studies at the Chinese Academy of Social Sciences (CASS). These include: (i) a rate of urbanization of over 70 per cent; (ii) a white-collar work force of the same, if not larger, size as the blue-collar one; (iii) an Engel coefficient lower than 0.3 on an average; (iv) maintenance of the Gini coefficient between 0.25 and 0.30; and (v) an average term of over 12 years of education for an individual.

Anyone who has some knowledge of the middle class would know that these standards are not intended for the judgment of the presence or absence of the middle class in a society; rather, they are the criteria for a middle class society, that is, a society composed mainly of middle class people. Still, it is open to discussion whether these standards are indeed valid for the evaluation of middle class society. A case in point would be the United States—the Gini coefficient for the nation is as high as 0.4, but no one would deny the fact that the US is a typical 'middle class society'.

Apart from the two reasons listed earlier, another fact that may give rise to sceptical attitudes has something to do with an overestimation of the middle class and its social properties. In an Internet article entitled 'The Concept of "Middle Class" Misinterpreted: High Income Does Not Mean High Quality', the author argued that:

As far as an individual is concerned, the middle class does not mean comfort and luxury, but responsibility and devotion.... The very reason why the middle class is a social group with extraordinary sense of social responsibility lies in the fact that the middle class people have full supply of the necessities of life… (Wen Wen, 2005).

After reading this article, one would have a better understanding of who has misinterpreted the middle class, especially when you compare it to the following phrases from the book *White Collar: The American Middle Classes* by Mills, 'the decline of the free entrepreneur and the rise of the dependant employee on the American scene has paralleled the decline of the independent individual and the rise of the little man in the American mind' (Mills 1951: XII).

WHO ARE THE MIDDLE CLASS PEOPLE IN CHINA?

The Chinese middle class, in the modern sense, came into being between the late 19th century and early 20th century, and the concept was gradually enriched in the first half of the 20th century. It was the metropolis of Shanghai that became a hotbed of its emergence. However, before 1949, the growth process of the middle class in China was marked with difficulties and hardships, both due to the invasion by Japanese imperialists and the problems of the old China (Lian Lian 2005).

The Chinese middle class was deprived of its breeding ground after the revolution in 1949. Although the middle class did not undergo the same rough treatment as was meted out to the landlord and bureaucratic-capitalist classes, the great majority of the class who used to be members of the national bourgeoisie and the petty bourgeoisie became almost extinct after a series of political movements (ranging, for example, from the Three Antis and the Five Antis to the Anti-Rightists and the Cultural Revolution) and economic reforms (for example, industrial and commercial reforms). Not until the adoption of the open policy initiated by Deng Xiaoping in the year 1978, did the middle class find its new way to come into Chinese society. In other words, the prosperity of the modern Chinese middle class or middle stratum owes most to the social reforms and the opening-up or social transformation of China since 1980. As early as 2001, it was estimated that the proportion of middle class people or households, that is, those with 10,000–1,00,000 yuan per capita annual income or 30,000–100,000 yuan's worth of family assets, was about 20–25 per cent of the whole population (Xiao Wentao 2001). At the same time, it was also calculated, according to a sample survey in urban and rural China, that the middle-career people constituted 15.9 per cent of the whole population, the middle-income people 24.6 per cent, the middle-consumption people 35 per cent, the self-approved-middle-class people 46.8 per cent and the percentage of people who fell into all these categories only 4.1 per cent (Li Chunling 2003). However, our own study shows that middle class people—those who can meet the three composite indices on career, education and income—comprise 11.8 per cent of all the citizens in Beijing, Shanghai, Nanjing, Guangzhou and Wuhan (Zhou Xiaohong 2005a: 45). No matter how high the percentage or proportion is, the middle class or middle stratum in modern China should include following basic components:

1. The owners of newly-born private and township enterprises, a group of people spawned by China's free market agenda over the past 25 years. According to statistics, by the end of 2002, the number of self-owned enterprises in mainland China reached 2,435,000, with total employees involved being as many as 34,093,000. Among them, the number of investors who could be classified as members of the middle class or the middle stratum was 6,228,000 (National Statistics Bureau 2003: 148).

2. Other kinds of self-employed people like petty proprietors and small trades people, who emerged almost at the same time as private and township enterprises owners. By the end of 2002, the total number of this group of people was 23,775,000, and the employees involved were 47,429,000 (National Statistics Bureau 2003: 149). Of course, a small part of this group had such small businesses that they could hardly be labelled as the middle class.

3. Some officials and intellectuals who serve, directly or indirectly, the Party and the government, as well as the leaders of state-owned enterprises. This group was derived from the middle layer of the planned economy–society or, as Li Qian put it, the quasi middle class. Whereas some leaders of state enterprises may have experienced big changes in their economic and social status, Party and government officials and intellectuals, owing to both their

own cultural and personal qualities as well as the privileges their work units enjoy, have reserved their superiority, although no longer in an overbearing manner.

4. Chinese people who work in white-collar and senior managerial occupations in joint ventures. Statistics suggest that by the end of 2002, mainland Chinese workers employed by foreign-investment enterprises numbered 3,675,600, those employed by Hong Kong, Macao and Taiwan funded enterprises were 3,529,500, and the total was 7,205,100 (National Statistics Bureau 2003: 138).

5. A great number of managers of enterprises and social organizations. With increasing social demand, there has been a rise in MBAs, MPAs and Masters of Laws. This group, while steadily increasing in number, is in every way qualified to be part of the Chinese middle class.

6. High-income people working in the new hi-tech professions such as returned overseas students, architects, lawyers, accountants, real estate appraisers, salespeople, film and TV programme producers, stock investors as well as other types of professionals.

Some problems are worth our attention when it comes to the estimation of the size of the middle class population. First, the middle class in China did not spring up until 1978. In western countries, the middle class has undergone a fairly long development process, and many families of the class can be traced back to their early ancestors. On the contrary, the middle class in China was almost eradicated by the revolution, after 1949, so that what exists now in modern China is in a sense the first generation of the middle class. But, we should also notice that some of the post-1978 middle class people owed much to the social and economic resources they possessed in the planning economy. In his study, Lu Xueyi confirmed that the maintenance of superiority by officials and intellectuals in the middle class greatly depended on how they adjusted their own social positions and made use of acquired social connection resources, power resources and knowledge resources in the market economy (Lu Xueyi 2001: 255). The study carried out in Shanxi by David Goodman indicated that China's middle class, be it private entrepreneurs or managers of state enterprises, maintained a good rapport with national and Party organizations, which is a prerequisite for acquiring economic resources (Goodman 1999).

Second, in the western world, there was a gap of over one century between the emergence of the old middle class and of the new one. The former was mainly a result of industrialization, whereas the latter was formed during the transition from industrial to post-industrial society. But, in China, the two kinds of middle class were forged almost simultaneously after 1978. The reason for this is that the old middle class in China, like owners of private and township enterprises and petty proprietors, was, strictly speaking, not a result of industrialization itself—in China, industrialization boomed even before 1978, when the modern state system and a hierarchy of power were established—but of market transformations in the wake of reforms and opening-up. Reforms and opening-up allowed China greater visibility in the world arena. Based on industrialization, she soon formed the new economic system, which incorporated post-industrial elements like tertiary industry and technology-intensive industry. This finally led to the emergence of the new middle class including professionals and managers. The short interval between the emergence of the old middle class and the new one can be better illustrated through a comparison between the abnormal situation where 'intellectual labour is less well paid than manual labour' in the 1980s and the return to a 'rational relation between mental labour and manual labour' in the 1990s. The current phenomenon of the harmonious co-existence and co-development of the two types of middle class or, the conspicuous heterogeneity of the development of the middle class in mainland China, makes it possible for the middle stratum to be vividly described as 'multiple collars'.

THE SOCIAL BACKGROUND FOR THE EMERGENCE OF CHINA'S MIDDLE CLASS

In the western world, the transition from an industrialized to a post-industrial society provided a social background for the emergence of the middle class; in China, industrialization itself did not impose as much influence on social class transformation. As discussed earlier, industrialization only began to have an effect on the formation of the middle class after the reforms and opening-up in 1978 and the consequent massive social transformation.

This conclusion is better justified when considering the remarkable achievements China's industrialization made during the 30 years between 1949–78, with a yearly growth rate of about 7 per cent, not counting the hazardous Big Leap Forward period. However, apart from all the political devices that were meant to contain the emergence of the middle class, some economic factors also made its emergence a mere dream. The political means employed concerned two seemingly contradictory respects. One was to plant a symbolic 'exploiting class', as an opponents of existing working and peasantry classes, for as long as 30 years. The other was to apply the equalitarian de-stratification strategy[2] among 'the masses'. There were multiple means for the realization of de-stratification, ranging from the equalitarian salary system to the allotment system for daily consumption, the housing distribution system and the abandoning of the piecework system as well as the premium system.

The economic factors were multiple in the same way. To begin with, under the influence of the Russian economic mode, Chinese industrialization gave priority to the development of heavy industry, sacrificing light industry and the service industry, which were closely related to the daily life of common people, but seriously lagged behind people's demand for enhancing the quality of life. Also, owing to the principle of 'regarding agriculture as the key link in national economy' and the quasi-militarized administrative system in the people's commune, the movement of farmers was greatly restricted. Especially after the monopolization of the purchase and marketing of grain in 1953, agricultural and related products were in great shortage, the various coupons prevalent in the Mao Zedong era being a sure proof of that. Finally, military confrontations with the United States and afterwards with India and Russia made defence expenses a considerable proportion of the national income. All these factors contributed to the fact that the income of the average Chinese had hardly any substantial increase from 1952 through 1980.[3]

All these changes came only after 1978. The Third Plenary Session of the Eleventh Central Committee of the Communist Party of China set off large-scale reforms and the opening-up movement in China.

The movement started with the contract responsibility system of linking remuneration to output in agriculture, and later spread to many urban economic fields. In the following 20 years or so, China's economic development made achievements of world interest. The yearly increasing rate of GDP remained 8 per cent after 1978, and it even achieved a rate of 11–13 per cent during the three years between 1992 and 1994. The strategic objective of quadrupling GDP during the 20 years between 1980 and 2000, set by Deng Xiaoping at the Twelfth National Congress of the Communist Party of China, was also met five years ahead of time.

If the fast development of China's economy during the last 20 years of the 20th century laid the basic foundation for the betterment of life in China, it was the social transformation after 1978 that lent much to the emergence and growth of China's middle class. Here, the social transformation includes the following three primary aspects: first, to carry the industrialization from 1949 through 1978 further so as to assist the social transition from an agriculture-oriented one to an industry- and service-oriented one. Second, and more importantly, to transit from a mandatory planning economy to a modern market economy. Last, to transit from a political system featured by extreme centralism to that of a socialist democratic political system. Soon we would find that it is the social transformation, together with all the changes it has brought to social life, that has rendered possible the emergence and growth of China's middle class.

The first change that can be attributed to social transformation is the dissociation of people's everyday life from the political life of the state and the appearance of 'public fields', a term coined by Jurgen Habermas, in certain spheres, as a consequence of the relaxed and well-regulated political environment and the readjustment of national and social relationships. This change is one of the necessary conditions for the emergence and growth of China's middle class. After China adopted the reform and opening-up policy, the first meaningful change noticed was the removal of labels on landlords and rich farmers by the Central Committee of the Communist Party of China after 1979, for one thing, and the modification of the basic line so as to make economic construction, rather than class struggle, the central task, for another. This change, accompanied by some other changes, especially the subdivision of careers, finally led to the stratification of Chinese society following, in place of the former 'symbolic' class standard, a career standard. While this serves as a prerequisite for the emergence of the middle class, the further weakening of the interference of the state in social life, economic as well as political (China has taken its first step towards village autonomy in rural places), the formation of a civil society and the expansion of all relevant public fields, will definitely contribute a lot to the maturity of the Chinese middle class.

The second change lies in how the sustained, steady growth in the national economy, the adjustment of economic construction, the expansion of the tertiary industry, the rise of marketing levels and the quickening of the pace of urbanization have all fulfilled the conditions for the emergence and growth of China's middle class. The achievements made by the Chinese economy during the past 20-odd years, which is widely acknowledged by the whole world, continues the world's confidence in China's promising future. As for the creation of the Chinese middle class, the growth of the economy may lay the foundation, whereas the rise of national income and its increasing rate may be a more direct reason. The fact is that national income made up 57 per cent of GDP in 1980, 71 per cent in 1993 and, hopefully, as much as 81 per cent in the year 2010, which means more and more of state wealth is now in the hands of common people. Moreover, a draft of the Constitutional Amendment, submitted by the National People's Congress (NPC) Standing Committee to the NPC session in 2004, made formal alterations to Article Thirteen from 'The State protects citizens' lawful income, deposit, housing and the ownership of other lawful property' to 'Citizens' lawful private property brooks no violation'. Although it was only about one year ago that the clause recognizing 'protection of private property' was included in the Constitution, the successful practice of encouraging the individual economy by the Chinese government already hinted that citizen's legal private property would be protected.

The third change is that the diversification of culture and the shift from elitist education to mass education have prepared the ground, both culturally and psychologically, for the emergence and growth of the middle class, especially the new one. In the Mao Zedong era, culture, literature and art worked exclusively for politics and as a means of propagandizing official ideology. Thus, the exclusiveness and the orthodoxy of the worker-peasant-soldier culture, literature and art left it impossible for the middle class (even if there were such a class in terms of economic income) to possess its own cultural property. The diversification of culture and people's tolerance of multi-culture only came up following the reforms and opening-up in 1978. Moreover, as Mills (1951: 266) put it, 'mass education has also been one of the major social mechanisms of the rise of the new middle-class occupations, for these occupations require those skills that have been provided by the education system'. The development in China's higher education is perfectly obvious. For instance, Chinese People's University's enrolment rate was above 15 per cent in 2003, which is good evidence of the transition from elitist education to mass education. However, the development of higher education and the rise in people's educational levels do not suffice for the emergence of a middle class. It was again confirmed by William's study that while the number of years spent in education by the average Chinese kept rising from 1930 through 1978 (except for the 1960s when the Cultural Revolution led to a decline in educational levels), their occupational ranks and incomes deteriorated (William 1984). The situation was altered only after 1980 when education started to yield increasingly profitable returns for people, with a rate of increase as high as 6–7 per cent in 2000 (that is, one extra year of education brings about a rise of 6–7 per cent in one's income), which was almost equal to that of developed nations. This also provides favourable conditions for the emergence of the middle class, the new one in hi-tech fields in particular.

GROWING PAINS, OR THE BOTTLENECK IN DEVELOPMENT

We have discussed how over 20 years of reforms and opening-up has resulted in tremendous transformation and change in almost all aspects of Chinese society, including social construction, and how this fact has caused the emergence and growth of China's middle class. Just because the Chinese middle class has exerted much influence on China's modernization process and because of its own growth rate, the rise of such a class in China has aroused a worldwide concern. As we have discussed, a whole set of policies carried out by the Chinese government after the reforms and opening-up were all favourable for the emergence and maturity of the middle class or, using a term from the state discourse system, the middle stratum. After the first 10 years of implementation of the open-door policy, most people, including farmers, benefited from it. A group of people emerged who had above average incomes, encouraged by Deng Xiaoping's slogan, mentioned earlier, 'allowing some people to become well-to-do ahead of others'. In the last 10-odd years, the number of the middle class people has multiplied so enormously that some overseas media are alarmed at their own judgment that 'China has stepped into a middle class era.'

While we cannot deny that China's middle class has taken its shape and is now rapidly growing, this does not mean that China has stepped into a middle class era. In western developed countries, that is, the so-called post-industrial or middle class societies, middle class people account for 80 per cent of the population (hence referred to as 'the masses') and the social structure is 'olive' styled. In present day China, however, the middle class constitutes less than 20 per cent of the whole population. Even after over 20 years of reforms and opening-up, the former 'pyramid' styled social structure has only been replaced by an 'onion' structure, one with a slightly expanded middle part and an even bigger base. Moreover, no matter whether it is for the rapid development of the economy, the distribution of wealth, the transformation of social structure or the realm of ideology, the maturity of China's middle class is doomed to rigorous test.

The first difficulty for the maturity of the Chinese middle class lies in the distribution of wealth brought about by the rapidly growing economy. We have discussed the legitimacy of incomes by China's middle class, especially those new middle class people who live on their own intellectual output. But, at the same time, it is also evident that the upper 'capital class' and a fraction of the middle class in Chinese society are either derived from the former power centre or, at least, have something to do with it. Part of their wealth is acquired through unfair competition or utilization of the loopholes in the state system and policies. More importantly, this group of people, while small in number and proportion, own a great part of the social wealth. Statistics suggest that the financial capital for China today is over 1,000 billion yuan, but the majority of it is under the control of a tiny minority. In 2003, the per capita GDP for Beijing, counted on the permanent population, reached US$ 3,074; it was US$ 6,000 for Shanghai and US$ 4,000 even for the whole triangular zone, which has, in every way, reached the level of the moderately developed countries (Li Yang 2004; Oriental Morning Post 2005). But at the same time, the increase in the gap between the poor and the rich is also apparent—the seriousness of the problem is fully demonstrated by the Gini coefficient of 0.457. Obviously, if the efforts in constraining the over-concentration of wealth in the hands of a tiny minority fails, the result would not only be a more striking poor–rich disparity but also conflicts among different social strata. Such a situation will not be beneficial for the growth and maturity of China's middle class; on the other hand, it is quite possible that the middle class will be made the 'scapegoat' for the existence of social inequality. Therefore, the government should, through perfection of the legal and tax systems and the establishment of an appropriate social security system, protect the economic interests of the lower-income groups and, at the same time, facilitate a rational and effective flow of the national wealth to the middle class or middle stratum. Also, to ensure that the middle class does not seek 'special privileges' for the improvement of its own economic status, which is sure to invite criticism and boycott from the lower middle classes and lower social classes, the government should not neglect legal constraints on the middle class.

The second difficulty for the expansion of China's middle class is related to the unsolved problem of demand and pressure that the large rural population has on industrialization. Ever since the reforms and opening-up policy, we have observed a nationwide, large influx of rural labourers into cities and developed areas, where industrialization has begun to take its effect. According to the fifth national demographic census, the number of rural labourers in cities is 88 million. With China being admitted into the WTO, most villages, especially those in backward rural areas, will confront more severe challenges. Consequently, the numbers of farmers who will have no other choice but to move into cities for a living will continue to shoot up. Nevertheless, the cities' absorption of the rural labour force is rather limited because the pace of industrialization lags behind the flowing rate of farmer labourers, the business of state-owned enterprises is generally depressed and township enterprises which used to display prosperity are now losing their momentum (most villages in China's rural areas have not been affected by industrialization yet). Apparently, even if the millions of Chinese farmers can successfully find their places in cities, owing to the labour force requirements of industrialization, it is quite likely that they can only place their hopes on their next generation, that is, 'the second generation immigrants', to enter into the ranks of the middle class. Therefore, it remains a remote dream for China to have the same 'olive' structure as some western societies.

The final difficulty for the growth of the Chinese middle class stems from ideological pressure. As we all know, the present Chinese regime is a socialist one which is characterized by the leadership of the working class and the alliance of workers and farmers. But, with more and more state enterprises caught in extreme difficulties, the leading position of the working class meets great challenges and, as we have seen, it is these challenges that have delayed the legal recognition of the legitimacy of China's middle class. Most officials and official documents prefer to address this class as the middle-income class or the middle stratum. Obviously, it is disadvantageous for the future development of the middle-property class or stratum if it cannot be properly acknowledged in theory. In fact, on second thoughts, it is not so contradictory to acknowledge the socialist regime of present China and, simultaneously, the existence of the middle-property class or the middle stratum as we would think. On the one hand, our analyses have made clear that the middle class is far from being the mainstream of society in China, a developing country still in its process of industrialization. Even in the following decades, the growth rate of the working class (the so-called blue-collar workers), in its traditional sense, is sure to surpass that of the middle-property class or stratum, especially when considering that more and more rural labourers will enter into the group of industrial workers. Consequently, the expansion of the middle class will not shake the fundamental regime of China. On the other hand, Deng Xiaoping's proposal of viewing intellectuals as a part of the working class has both a theoretical basis and practical necessity. In western society, it is just commonsense to view mental workers as 'white-collar workers', in that their vocational feature and their middle income do not change the nature of their work. As a consequence, I would argue that the expansion of the middle class in China could just as well be perceived as the wax and wane of the two groups, the white-collar group and the blue-collar group, of the same working class. One visible change in the 21st century will be that, along with the continuous flowing of farmer labourers into cities as demanded by industrialization, the majority of the working class, through further improvement of their economic and social status, will become members of the now minor middle-property class or stratum.

Notes

1. We have every reason to believe that those who challenged our results in this way have read neither the book by us nor the whole-page coverage by *China Youth Daily*. It was specified in our study that the survey was done among urban citizens living in the five major cities in China and, hence, our findings were not applicable to the rural population, which makes up for over 60 per cent of Chinese population, or to citizens of other cities lower in the economic and development level.
2. According to William's (1984) study, China was the most equal society among all the socialist countries during the period from 1960 through 1970, when the higher income was only 2.2 to 2.3 times that of the lower one, with the Gini coefficient being a mere 0.20 to 0.21.
3. Statistics provided by *China Agricultural Yearbook* (1980) and *China Statistical Yearbook* (1981) suggested that the average per capita annual income for Chinese civil servants was 446 yuan in 1952 and 529 yuan in 1980, the total increasing rate being 18.6 per cent, and that the average per capita annual income for peasants was 38.8 yuan after collectivization in 1953 and 54.4 yuan in 1975, with a total increasing rate of 40.2 per cent.

References

Cai, Zhenfeng. 2004. 'China's Middle Class Has Not Taken Form Yet', *Global Times* (Beijing), 28 January.

Editing Committee of China Agricultural Yearbook. 1980. *China Agricultural Yearbook*. Beijing: Agricultural Press.

Goodman, David. 1999. 'The New Middle Class', in Merle Goldman and Roderick MacFarquhar (eds), *The Paradox of China's Post-Mao Reforms*. London: Harvard University Press.

Li, Chunling. 2003. 'The Composition and Proportion of the Present Chinese Middle Class', *Chinese Journal of Population Science*, 6: 29–36.

Li, Yang. 2004. 'Beijing's Per Capita GDP has Surpassed US$ 3000', *Beijing Business Today* (Beijing), 17 September.

Lian, Lian. 2005. 'The Middle Class in Shanghai prior to 1949', in Zhou Xiaohong (ed.), *A Survey of Chinese Middle Classes*. Beijing: Social Sciences Academic Press.

Lu, Xueyi. 2005. 'The Chinese Middle Classes will Account for 40 per cent of Whole Population of Employment within 20 Years', *Daily Economic News* (Beijing), 15 September.

———. (ed.). 2001. *A Study on Modern China's Different Social Strata*. Beijing: Social Sciences Academic Press.

Mills, C. Wright. 1951. *White Collar: The American Middle Classes*. New York: Oxford University Press.

National Bureau of Statistics. 1981. *China Statistical Yearbook*. Beijing: Chinese Statistics Press.

———. 2003. *China Statistical Yearbook (2003)*. Beijing: Chinese Statistics Press.

Oriental Morning Post. 2005. 'The average output per capita of Shanghai goes far ahead, leading the whole economy of Long Delta', *Oriental Morning Post* (Shanghai), 5 April.

Wang, Yi. 2003. 'How Many Middle-class People Are There in China?' Available online at http://news.eastday.com./epublish/paper148/20030626/calss01480001.

Wen, Wen (ed.). 2005. 'The Concept of 'Middle Class' Misinterpreted: High Income Does Not Mean High Quality'. Available at http:// finance.news.tom.com/ 1001/ 1002/200596-280249.html.

William, L. Parrish. 1984. 'Destratification in China', in Waston, J. (ed.), *Class and Social Stratification in Post-Revolution China*. New York: Cambridge University Press.

Xiao, Wentao. 2001. 'The Present and Future Situation of China's Middle Stratum', *Sociological Research*, 3: 93–98.

Xiao, Xinhuang (ed.). 1994. *Taiwan's Middle Class in Change*. Taipei: Juliu Book Company.

Zhou, Xiaohong. 2002. 'The Middle Class: What They Can Do and What They Should Do', *Jiangsu Social Sciences*, 6: 37–46.

———. (ed.). 2005a. *Survey of the Chinese Middle Classes*. Beijing: Social Sciences Academic Press.

———. 2005b. *A Report of Middle Classes in the World*. Beijing: Social Sciences Academic Press.

6

Power of Knowledge: The Imaginary Formation of the Chinese Middle Stratum in an Era of Growth and Stability

JEAN-LOUIS ROCCA

'In the present stage how to structure and expand the middle stratum in our society?'

—Zhou Xiaohong 2005

The emergence of a Chinese middle class has become a hot topic. Political leaders, researchers, journalists and potential members of this stratum discuss and write extensively about the consequences of this phenomenon. The objective of this paper is not to produce a new contribution to an already active field of research but to understand how researchers and intellectuals construct a 'class', which they are supposed to define. It is the preliminary step in a long-term research project focusing on the analysis of lifestyles, conflicts and the concept of class in contemporary China.

In academic literature, classes and strata are generally perceived as both objective and subjective realities. The middle class, for example, is to be analyzed not only in terms of income, levels of education, and so on, but also in terms of lifestyle. According to Max Weber, Pierre Bourdieu and Norbert Elias, the concept of 'social class' is mainly a imaginary phenomenon, linking objective conditions and subjective perceptions. Some groups of people define it as an *ethos* that constitutes a guideline for behaviours and actions. Individuals who desire to belong to this group have to respect this framework by respecting signs of 'distinction' (Bourdieu 1979; Elias 1983). However, 'objective criteria' and 'subjective perceptions' are not 'given realities' but a matter of knowledge. Every attempt at understanding a social phenomenon is based on a certain set of methodological principles and moral perceptions which play the role of a filter between scholars and reality. In other words, in trying to define a phenomenon—the emergence of the middle class—researchers, journalists and middle class members themselves contribute to the establishment of characteristics of this stratum. In a parallel movement, the establishment of these characteristics not only enables insiders to determine their position in society but also lends clarity to outsiders about their own class membership. Every identification process supposes a reference of class. This phenomenon is particularly true concerning the middle class since this stratum is very difficult to define in terms of occupation, income, ways of life, and so on. In all 'modern' societies, including China, feelings of membership of lower or upper strata usually refer to this middle class. As a consequence, frontiers between classes are not clearly established because ambiguities enable people to define themselves as members or future members of the middle class even though they do not possess the objective characteristics of this stratum.

In brief, the 'middle class' problem cannot be analyzed in terms of an objective phenomenon to be described and to be understood but as the formation process of an imaginary stratum in a context of political struggles. What I mean is not that reforms have not produced a new stratum, but that definition of this stratum is at the core of the imaginary reshaping of what a 'modern' society is. Under such a perspective, the imaginary is not the 'spectacular', or 'the reflection of the "fictive"'— 'It is the unceasing and essentially undetermined (social historical and psychical) creation of figures/forms/images, on the basis of which alone there can be a question of "something". What we call "reality" and "rationality" are its works' (Castoriadis 1987:3).[1] According to

Michel Foucault, the knowledge of reality is not external to the reality; it contributes at once to the perception and to a certain extent to the formation of it. As such, to understand the 'middle class' phenomenon, my starting point will not be a 'definition'. I use the same method Boltanski used when he analyzed a significant part of the French middle class—*les cadres*. He considered 'common stereotypes' both as 'tools of knowledge' and 'tools of legitimacy' (Boltanski 1982: 23).

The imaginary nature of the middle class is even more obvious than other 'classes' for two reasons. The first lies in the fact that the 'producers' of the concept of middle class—researchers, intellectuals and media workers—themselves belong to this group and to a certain extent are the main symbols of the middle stratum. In other words, they contribute to the setting up of their own identities and status. Besides, not only do the blurred limits of this group lead to endless controversy but also often result in unsatisfactory conclusions; the middle class is very often defined in negative terms as the 'remaining' one, once the lower strata and the higher strata are defined. As such, the middle class is usually an aggregation of 'sub-groups' which have very few things in common in terms of prestige, income, level of education, and so on. What is at stake is to determine the criteria, which could transcend these differences, or to determine a 'reference group', which could be the 'core' of the aggregation.

Under such a perspective, my main hypothesis is that the middle class is becoming a hot topic because it plays a determinant role in the reshaping of power relations introduced by economic growth. The players of the stage aim at defining a group, which could be both a factor of social dynamism and a factor of stability. It is true for the ruling class but also for the middle class members themselves, who identify their fate with the future of 'modern' China. Therefore, the goal of the discussion is clearly normative—how can we build up a middle class society with Chinese characteristics?

First, the emergence of a middle class is considered to be the consequence of successful reforms. Different related groups have taken advantage of the new economic context in gaining higher incomes. This increase in standards of living would have led, almost automatically, to a radical change in the ways of consumption and in the perceptions of social life. This phenomenon is viewed as an aspect of the 'transition' to modern society (Li Peilin et al. 2004).

Second, the Chinese middle class is perceived politically as a 'stabilizing' element. Situated between the elite and the lower strata (the 'have been'), it is expected to play a 'go-between' role. In this way, political tensions between the rich and the poor could be, if not eliminated, at least, largely alleviated.

MOBILITY AND DYNAMISM

A great majority of researchers and journalists consider that the emergence of a middle stratum is the consequence of a reform policy. Everybody seems to consider that before 1978 Chinese society was a one-class society (with slight differences between groups) in which the class origin was more important than any other characteristic. Yet, it is not groundless to consider that during the Maoist years, the 'working class' played the role of the middle class, occupying a place between the cadres and the peasants. In the same way, it is interesting to remark that the 'new middle class' is composed, for a part, of people coming from the 'old middle class' rank and who convert their 'capital' (notably in terms of education and relations) to a new position. Finally, the distinction between class (*jieji*) and stratum (*jieceng*) has not been dealt with at length. Researchers seem to be reluctant to use the word 'class' but the problem is easily solved in remarking that in English, class and stratum now have very close meanings.

The first matter of discussion is the number of people we can gather under the term—'middle stratum'. Figures are all based on surveys but they use different criteria and are thus very different. Li Chunling (2003)[2]—one of the few sceptics of the Chinese middle class 'blossoming phenomenon'—points that the middle class constitutes only i4.1 per cent of the total population, that is, around 40 million people. Lu Xieyi (2002) estimates the real figure at 80 million people for the beginning of 21st century. According to the Chinese Academy of Social Sciences, it represented 15 per cent of the total population in 1999, 19 per cent in 2003 (48.5 per cent of the urban population) and will reach 40 per cent in 2020.[3] Xiao Wentao (2001) considers that 20–25 per cent of the families earn from 10,000 to 1,00,000 yuan a year and they own property worth 30,000–1,00,000 yuan. BNP Paribas defines members of the middle stratum as educated professionals and white collar professionals earning between 25,000 and 30,000 yuan per head per year. They represent 13.3 per cent of the total population.[4]

Nearly everybody seems to be optimistic about the growth of this social group. According to the National Bureau of Statistics, which conducted a survey of 3,00,000 people, the middle stratum represents 5 per cent of the total population but the figure is expected to reach 45 per cent in 2020.[5] A newspaper states that from 2001 onwards, 200 million people will enter the middle class within 5 years.[6] In 2002, the Canadian Ambassador to China announced that the Chinese middle class will comprise 500 million people in 2010.[7]

Actually, the essential question concerns the income thresholds of the stratum. The upper threshold is a subject of controversy—it has ranged from 10,000 to 10,00,000 yuan (Xiao Wentao 2001), from 25,000 to 30,000 yuan[8] and 60,000 to 5,00,000 yuan per household per year,[9] that is, more than 5,000 yuan per month.[10] The lower threshold is important because it helps to define socially and economically as well as politically who the winners and the losers of the reforms are. The more important the winners' group, the more stable is society. But the delimitation of the border between the middle and the upper class is also of significance. As an intermediary group between losers and winners, the middle stratum has to be distinguished from the 'new rich' or the elite. However, it is apparently more difficult to draw a line between losers and winners than to make a difference between the rich and the 'middle' class. The emergence of a middle stratum and of the new rich and the elite are often confused. Lifestyle and job characteristics seem to be very difficult to differentiate (Luigi Tomba 2004). The picture of the middle stratum given by Xin Baoping in *Touzi kexue* (Investment Science) uses some criteria which are obviously characteristic of the behaviour of a very small elite. Besides high income (2,00,000 yuan per year), the typical middle class members spend three years abroad, use foreign words in conversation, have a house in the country and display an American lifestyle, though 'in his heart he prefers Europe'! (Zhang Wei 2005).

The amount of income is generally not considered as the main criterion. Two other criteria are at stake. The first is profession. For example, in Zhou Xiaohong's book a certain number of groups are determined: (*i*) bosses of private and countryside enterprises (*siying qiyejia, xiangzhen qiyejia*) and middle class investors (6.22 million in 2002), (*ii*) small bosses, small traders and bosses of individual enterprises (*getihu*), their numbers reaching 47.42 million, (*iii*) people who have close relations with the Party and government organs, that is, officials and intellectuals, as well as leaders of state-owned enterprises (SOEs), (*iv*) white collar professionals in foreign firms such as high tech workers and managers (7.2 million), (*v*) managers of social organizations and enterprises, people with an MBA, MPA or law degree and (*vi*) people with high technical qualifications, working in the new economy— lawyers, architects, accounting clerks, real estate and stock exchange agents, movie technicians, all of them having studied abroad (Zhou Xiaohong 2005). As we can see, profession and education level is perceived as highly connected. Actually, some people insist on the fact that middle class success is mainly based on education (ibid.). For Lu Xieyi, middle class members have a 'knowledge capital', they work with their brain and have expectations concerning job 'qualities'. They earn money from wages and have execution power in labour organizations (Lu Xieyi 2002). For Zhu, the definition is simple—middle stratum members use their brain and work as white collar professionals (Zhu Guang 1998).

The second criteria is based on a distinction between the objective and subjective definitions of class. Some people only refer to the objective side, for example, Zhang Jianming (1998) who considers only three elements—income, education level and job. But for a majority of researchers, the middle class is characterized as a specific group in terms of behaviour and lifestyle. Using Bourdieu's analysis, Zhou's book emphasizes the importance of 'distinction' in middle stratum behaviour. Middle stratum members would have a tendency to work more than other groups, to strive continuously to climb the social and professional ladders. They have more social relations; they read more than the lower strata members (Zhou Xiaohong 2005: 125; Zhang Wei 2005; Li Peilin, Li Qiang, Sun Liping 2004). They have resources (*ziyuan*) and capacities (*nengli*). More important, Zhou's book gives an ideal picture of the middle stratum. The success of its members would only be based on their effort, on accumulation of education capital and not on 'relations' or corruption. As such, the emergence and the growth of the middle stratum appears as fully legitimate.

The success of the middle stratum and its change of its social position is able to constitute an example for common people, not only because the means they used are rational and then cannot create a feeling of injustice but also because everybody can see that this success is based on education (Zhou Xiaohong 2005).

Middle stratum is then a model for lower classes which note that it is possible to earn high incomes without cheating, with moral values and legal rules. This statement opposes the common view that usually considers success to be the simple result of relations and corruption.

Finally, the lifestyle of the middle stratum appears as an important factor of economic growth. They consume a lot and mainly sophisticated products: house, cars, and so on. The amount of money they spend on elementary products is weak. They contribute to the flourishing of a leisure industry (Deborah Davis 2000; Zhou Xiaohong 2005). More important, they spend in a rational way—they plan for buying, they save money before spending, and so on. In other terms, not only do they personify the appearance of hedonism in China but also introduce a reasonable approach of consumerism. As such, their attitude to consumption is considered as 'modern' and should play a role as model for other classes (Kang Xiaoguang 2002; Li Peilin, Li Qiang, Sun Liping 2004).

How to Limit Conflicts

The emergence of a middle stratum is not only perceived as a determinant economic factor, but also considered as an absolutely necessary political ingredient. Middle stratum members are supposed to have a citizenship conscience (*gongmin yishi*) and a moral conscience (*daode yishi*). They take care of society (*guanhuai*). They are interested in political participation, they are more involved in social organisations and associations than other people. They constitute a basis for the development of a citizenship culture (*gongminxing wenhua*), that is, the emergence of a rational, right-oriented citizen (*lixing gongmin*), involved in social and political movements. Some surveys reveal that they have more trust on direct political participation (like elections) rather than on traditional participation (like contacts with leaders and government departments). These statements are indirect criticisms of both a (supposed) lack of interest of lower classes in politics and the (supposed) exclusively money-oriented behaviours of the new rich (Zhou Xiaohong 2005; Zhang Wei 2005). Besides, the middle stratum can play a go-between role. Its members 'cannot be dominated by another group and they cannot freely dominate other groups'(Zhang Wei 2005). In other words, they possess quite an important degree of autonomy, an autonomy that we can see in their lifestyle and as well in work attitudes. On this point, Chinese researchers largely refer to classics (for example, David Riesman, C. Wright Mills and William White) dealing with the American middle class.

The 'go-between' role of the middle class takes place in a context of growing inequalities. Nearly every article provides figures (mainly Gini rate) and examples of discrepancies between the poorest and the richest Chinese. This became a very hot topic in all circles of society. The struggle against peasants' low income, migrants' hyper exploitation, increase in unemployment and extreme flexibility is now considered the government's primary task. The emergence of a middle class appears as part of the answer to the unavoidable and unpredictable consequences of reform. The growing influence of its lifestyle and social behaviour gives it the ability to counterbalance excesses. It could limit the excess (in terms of income and reasons of success) of the new rich by participating in social movements and by intervening in political life but without challenging the regime as such. It could also limit excessive criticisms coming from low classes by proving to them that it is possible to change life without taking the road to criminality. For many researchers the problem is that the middle class is not developed enough to play this role. They are all in favour of political initiatives aimed at developing education, employment, social organizations, and so on, to give the 'go-between' people more space.

Unfortunately, the examples of involvement in social movements are very few. As discussed later, Zhang talks of home-owners' protest movements in a very general manner. He seems to consider that these movements, which oppose infringements to the rights of 'ordinary people', are a good example of political modernization (Zhang Wei 2005).[11] According to him, these people do not defend an ideology but their interests and rights; they try to get the support of the media and of government leaders. They behave rationally. In that case, protest movements evolve from 'reaction' to autonomy, from ideological claims to 'modern political concepts' (that is, interest-based), from unique-type of protest to several-types of protest, from mass participation to interest group participation (Zhang Wei 2005).

However, this analysis is at odds with the social origin of middle stratum members as revealed by the researchers themselves. Most of these people succeeded because of their connections in the political field. Goodman has shown that in Jiangxi most of 'the new middle class' are largely connected with power holders (Li Lulu 1998; David Goodman 1999; Li Jian and Niu Xiaohuan 2003). Li Chunling (2004) explains that political cadres and intellectuals who have improved their position are those who had the ability to transform political resources to economic resources. Therefore, there is a contradiction between the economic dynamism of the middle stratum members that enables them to climb the social ladder and the political conser-vatism which follows from the fact that their success is largely due to good political connections. Besides, we also have to take into account that having once entered the ranks of the middle class, there is no reason that they leave the door open for other people. For Zhou, 'they hope to make continual progress in a stable social order' (Zhou Xiaohong 2005). In other words, they do not want to see their pro-minent position challenged by people who refuse the new rules of the game.

To get out of this contradiction, researchers try to distinguish van-guard groups from the mainstream of the middle stratum. If many members of the middle class are not particularly keen to 'fight for rights', maybe some of them could be more open to political change. The first distinction made is between the old middle stratum (*lao zhongjian jieceng*) and the new middle stratum (*xin zhongjian jieceng*). The former is the result of industrialization and is considered as quite conservative and routine-minded. The latter, a by-product of post-industrializa-tion, is defined as more open-minded and politically active. A parallel distinction is proposed in Zhou's book between the rearguard middle stratum (*zhongjian jieceng houwei*), characterized by a high degree of connection with the political apparatus (for example, SOEs leaders), and the vanguard middle stratum (*zhongjian jieceng qianwei*), com-posed of professionals who show more independence. Finally, it is also possible to distinguish between people 'within the system' and people 'outside the system', the latter having entered the middle stratum thanks to the 'market'. In the different cases, what is viewed at stake is the ability of the groups to accumulate wealth, legitimacy and power outside the political apparatus. These distinctions give some insights into conflicts within the middle stratum but do not lead to a real analysis of the relations between power holders and the middle stratum members. The true question is to determine the conditions by which the middle stratum or a part of it would 'break off' the present political consensus with the regime. Actually, very few examples of this sort are given. When it is a question of 'political participation' (*zhengzhi canyu*), the analysis is vague. Zhang Wei (2005) deals with conflicts concerning real estate—a topic that is perceived as typical of the interest-oriented movement, which could contribute to the 'modernization' of political participation. But when he distinguishes between different attitudes among home-owners in conflict with 'power', the link with political challenge is not very clear. The people who buy houses for investment purposes prefer to deal discreetly. The victims of expropriation are quite passive. The only active group—the leaders of protest movements—is composed of those young people who want to get a 'piece of land under their feet' (*luojiao zhidi*).[12]

An Ideal Society

What is clearly emphasized by researchers is an ideal society of small owners, an olive-shaped society (*ganlan shehui*),[13] in which the poorest and the richest people would constitute marginal groups. To a certain extent, the entire society would identify itself to this central stratum. As such, an ideal society needs an ideal class for reference. Thanks to the middle class, the 'poor' could notice that it is possible for everyone to improve their living conditions by taking advantage of market opportunities and the elite could see that to be modern and dynamic does not mean to use illegal or immoral tricks. These statements depend on the obvious phenomenon of identification (*rentong*) to this new group. All surveys reveal that most people think they belong to the middle stratum or, at least, that they would like to belong to it (Zhou Xiaohong 2005 ; Zhang Wei 2005; Li Chunling 2003).

Considering this ideal society, two problems arise. The first lies in the fact that the middle stratum should be at the same time a stabilizing factor and an active element of political change. It is supposed to be rational, to provide the 'middle of the road' political option, but it is also defined as the only protagonist able to force the regime to introduce political reforms. How could a stratum, which is a result of the reform policy handled by the regime, and also the main winner of the new game, be able to question this regime?

The second problem arises from the nature of the protesting movement. The hope of change seems to lie in the ability of the middle stratum to launch interest-based movements and to base demands on the new legal rights provided by the government apparatus. Yet, whether or not this kind of movement threatens the regime or reinforces the regime is an essential question which is rarely handled by researchers. The notion of 'group interest' is now at the core of policies, including social policies. We talk, for example, of 'vulnerable groups' (*ruoshi qunti*) as groups whose interests are infringed (Jean-Louis Rocca 2003, 2006). The home-owners protesting movement is another interesting example. According to Zhang, the most active people in protest movements are those whose aim is to get a place to stay. In principle, such people are not particularly keen on taking risks. A class that owns is a class that fears change. The middle stratum members desire essentially to preserve their own (egotist) interests and not to defend the 'rights' of the society. As long as these interests are not called into question by a turn in government policies or by the effect of an economic crisis, there is no doubt that they will not challenge the political system. In the case of China, as elsewhere, the traditional opposition between 'state' (or 'political system') and market have no sense. It is impossible to imagine a stratum whose autonomy is based on the 'market' since the 'market' has become a core element of the strategy of the Chinese leaders (Mengin and Rocca 2005).

Besides, the laws are not adopted to endanger political order but, on the contrary, to protect political order. To take advantage of rights does not mean questioning power but participating in its legitimation and institutionalization. In other terms, the evolution towards an 'olive society' perfectly fits the plan of more open political leaders who provide a peaceful and gradual process to modern society.

Notes

1. 'Everything that is presented to us in the social-historical world is inextricably tied to the symbolic. Not that it is limited to this. Real acts, whether individual or collective ones—work, consumption, war, love, child-bearing—the innumerable material products without which no society could live even an instant, are not (not always, not directly) symbols. All of these, however, would be impossible outside of a symbolic network' (Castoriadis 1987: 117).
2. See also an interview of Li Chunling in *Renmin Ribao*, 27 October 2004.
3. *Xinhuanet*, 26 March 2004.
4. *Xinhuanet*, 26 March 2004.
5. *China Daily*, 20 January 2005.
6. *Xinxi shibao*, 21 July 2001.
7. See http://www.forestnet.com, accessed on April 2002.
8. *Xinhuanet*, 26 March 2004.
9. *China Daily*, 20 January 2005.
10. *Zhongguo qingnian bao*, 2 September 2005.
11. The fact is that 45.2 per cent of urban dwellers have bought flats.
12. For a western view on the home-owners' struggle, see Reed (2003).
13. *Renmin Ribao*, 27 October 2004.

References

Boltanski, Luc. 1982. *Les cadres. La formation d'un groupe social*. Paris: Les éditions de minuit.
Bourdieu, Pierre. 1979. *La Distinction*. Paris: Editions de Minuit.
Castoriadis, Cornelius. 1987. *The Imaginary Institution of Society*. Cambridge, UK: Cambridge University Press.
China Daily. 2005. 20 January.
Davis, Deborah (ed.), 2000. *Consumer Revolution in Urban China*. Berkeley, California: University of California Press.
Elias, Norbert. 1983. *The Court Society*. Oxford: Blackwell.
Goodman, David. 1999. 'The New Middle Class', in Merle Goldman and Roderick Mac Farquhar (eds), *The Paradox of China's Post-Mao Reforms*. London: Harvard University Press.
Kang Xiaoguang. 2002. 'weilai 3–5 nian zhongguo dalu zhengzhi wendingxing fenxi', *zhanlue yu guanli*, 3-2002, pp. 30–36.
Li Chunling. 2003. 'Zhongguo dangdai zhongchan jieji de goucheng ji bili' (Proportion and Structure of Contemporary Middle Class), *Zhongguo renkou kexue*, 6-2003, pp. 25–32.
————. 2004. *Renmin Ribao*, 27 October.
Li Jian and Niu Xiaohuan. 2003. 'The New Middle Class(es) in Peking: A Case Study', *China Perspectives*, 45(January): 4–20

Li Lulu. 1998. *Zhuanxing shehuizhong de siying qiye zhu -shehui laiyuan ji qiye fazhan yanjiu* (Private Enterprises Owners in a Transitional Society: Study on Enterprises Development and Social Origins). Beijing: Zhongguo renmin daxue chubanshe.

Li Peilin, Li Qiang, Sun Liping (eds). 2004. *Zhongguo shehui fenceng* (Social Stratification in China Today). Beijing: Shehui kexue wenxian chubanshe.

Lu Xieyi. 2002. *Dangdai zhongguo shehui jieceng yanjiu baogao* (Research Report on Contemporary Chinese Middle Class), pp. 250–60. Beijing: Shehui kexue wenxian chubanshe.

Luigi Tomba. 2004. 'Creating an Urban Middle Class: Social Engineering in Beijing', *The China Journal*, 51(January): 1–26.

Mengin, Françoise and Jean-Louis Rocca. 2005. 'State and Market: A Reciprocal Formation', paper presented to IIAS/CASS/CERI/CSH/IIC Workshop Series, Number 1, Leiden, Netherlands.

Reed, Benjamin. 2003. 'Democratizing the Neighbourhood: New Private Housing and Home-Owner Self-Organization', *The China Quarterly*, 49(January): 31–59.

Renmin Ribao. 2004. 27 October.

Rocca, Jean-Louis. 2003. 'The Rise of the Social and the Chinese State', *China Information*, XVII(1): 1–27.

—————. 2006. *La condition de la Chine. La mise au travail capitaliste à l'âge des réformes.* Paris: Karthala.

Xiao Wentao. 2001. *Zhongguo zhongjian jieceng de xianzhuang yu weilai fazhan* (Present situation and future development of the Chinese Middle Stratum), *Shehuixue yanjiu*, 3-2001, pp. 93–98.

Xinhuanet. 2004. 26 March.

Xinxi Shibao. 2001. 'Weilai wunian woguo zhongchan jieji renkou da liang yi' (In five years the number of middle class members will increase of 200 million), Xinxi Shibao, 21 July.

Zhang Jianming. 1998. 'Zhongguo chengshi zhongjian jiecengde xinzhuang jiqi weilai fazhan' (The Future Development and Present Situation of the Chinese Middle Stratum in Urban China), *Renmin daxue xuebao*, 5-1998, pp. 27–34.

Zhang Wei. 2005. *Congtu yu bianshu: zhongguo shehui zhongjian jieceng zhengzhi fenxi.* Beijing: Shehui kexue wenxian chubanshe.

Zhongguo gingnian bao. 2005. 2 September.

Zhou Xiaohong (ed.). 2005. *Zhongguo zhongchan jieceng diaocha* (Survey on the Chinese Middle Stratum). Beijing: Shehui kexue wenxian chubanshe.

Zhu Guang. 1998. *Dangdai zhongguo shehui gezhong jieceng fenxi.* Tianjin: Tianjin renmin chubanshe.

7

A Requiem for Songpan, or Once More about China's Civilizing Mission

PÁL NYÍRI

ACT I

Songpan, Ngawa Tibetan and Qiang Autonomous Prefecture, Sichuan Province, China, September 2003[1]

I find Songpan much the way the 1996 *Lonely Planet* described it: 'This bustling, friendly town merits a visit of its own' (p. 849). 'A fair number of its old wooden buildings are still intact, as are the ancient gates.... Farmers and Tibetan cattle herders clop down the cobblestone streets on horseback....' The book is especially impressed with the horse treks offered in the town to surrounding 'valleys and forests so pristine and peaceful that you may not believe you're still in China'. The 2000 edition of the upmarket German guidebook, the *Dumont Kunstreiseführer*, also suggests 'a longer stay' in Songpan for its 'colorful market and picturesque streets with old wooden houses' (p. 335). Primarily for the horse rides, Songpan is a popular destination for western backpackers.

Songpan's unusually well preserved North Gate (Figure 7.1) and the remaining parts of the wall were built in 1380, when a Ming general pulled in to 'pacify' the Qiang (Songpan 1967[1924]:83). Songpan still has a spectacular mix of 'ethnicity,' which should work as an asset in tourism development. Elsewhere in Ngawa, a village renamed and promoted as the 'First Village of Western Qiang' has been designated an Ethnic Arts Village by the National Cultural Relics Bureau (Xu Xinjian 2001: 204–05). Yet surprisingly, Songpan is missing from Xu Xinjian's (2001) review of tourism development in Ngawa. Scholar-officials Wei Xiaoan and Zhang Guangrui, high priests of Chinese tourism, shrug when asked about it. A growing number of individual Chinese tourists do come to Songpan for horse riding during the three 'golden weeks'—weeklong holiday periods introduced in 1999—but mainstream domestic tourism pulls right through the town. The few groups that stay here overnight on their way to or from Jiuzhaigou—a National AAAA Level Scenic Spot listed in UNESCO's World Natural Heritage and one of China's most popular tourist attractions—lodge at new hotels built just outside the town, not at the simpler ones in the historic core. Of the 17 guidebooks covering Sichuan, available in the closest provincial capitals, Chengdu and Lanzhou, only two mention

Figure 7.1   The North Gate of Songpan in 2003

Songpan as a destination. One of these, a backpackers' guide, notes that the town, 'though not large, is quaint (*gupu*) and picturesque (*jingzhi*). Bilingual Chinese-English shop signs in the streets reveal an unusual atmosphere of internationalization' (ZITO 2003: 73).

The deputy head of the county's Tourism Bureau admits that the popularity of Songpan with foreigners is not the result of policy but due to the activities of two trekking companies. Guo Shang, the general manager of the older company, Shunjiang Horse Treks, now an influential businessman, says he started his business in 1987 when Israeli and Swiss students came from Beijing and wanted to go horse riding. Now, the two companies employ almost 100 guides with their horses.

The official at the tourism bureau admits to being surprised by the appearance of foreign tourists, but, he says, they gradually got used to it. In Guo Shang's words, the bureau's attitude to foreign tourism has been 'Nothing. They don't support it but don't oppose it either.' Gradually, the town, which used to depend entirely on agriculture, developed a dependency on foreign tourism. Tourism revenue in the county increased ten fold between 1996 and 2002, when it exceeded ¥ 250 million (around $ 28 million), and it has become the largest sector in the economy. The phenomenal growth has been mainly due to tourism in Jiuzhaigou and its twin site, Huanglong, as well as the hotels of Chuanzhusi, the twin site's satellite town—they served over 4,40,000 guests in 2002. Nonetheless, the revenue from Songpan Town, with over 1,80,000 hotel guests, is about the same as that from ticket sales in Huanglong, where according to the county government's statistics, over 8,70,000 visitors spent ¥ 89 million in 2002. Around 70,000 hotel guests in the county were foreigners, who stayed chiefly in Songpan town. This suggests that the status of Songpan as an international tourist destination, while unstated and low-key, has nonetheless made a significant contribution to tourism's overall economic effect on the town, an effect that is comparable to that of one of the most visited nature reserves in China. Tourism has left its mark on the town, but in a way that is very different from a 'scenic spot' developed for mass tourism. The Internet café that advertises ADSL and displays the English sign 'English, Korean, Vietnamese, Arabic' comes as a surprise to the traveller arriving in the small centre of Songpan after the 10-hour trip from Chengdu. Agents from two companies approach foreign visitors, distributing business cards printed in English and offering horse treks.

They have learned English from their clients. The trekking companies' signs display English-language recommendations by the *Lonely Planet* instead of titles granted by Chinese tourist authorities; indeed, their destinations, Erdao Hot Springs and Zhaga Waterfalls, are nowhere to be found in Chinese travel brochures, not even the ones published by the Songpan Tourism Bureau. Emma's Kitchen, 'the best Pizza in Songpan', is wallpapered with postcards sent by foreign backpackers (Figure 7.2) and offers an English-language book swap. Emma's brother, the former manager of the other trekking company, Happy Trails, has moved to England after marrying a British backpacker. Yulan Pancake House, recommended by *Lonely Planet*, features banana pancakes and milkshakes as well as the more enigmatic 'Israeli fried noodles'. Both have addresses of backpackers' hostels in Chengdu. Unlike restaurants at Jiuzhaigou, they are local family enterprises.

Having been left officially 'undeveloped', but having in fact quietly grown as a tourist industry oriented towards western backpackers outside the pale of tourism authorities and corporations, the town has, to me and my German companion, an intimate, harmonious feel that scenic spots and officially designated 'old towns', not to mention new

Figure 7.2 Postcards on the wall at the old Emma's Kitchen

developments like Chuanzhusi, lack. The zone inside the old city gates is a living part of the town; it functions as a pedestrian street where locals stroll leisurely. At night, part of the effect comes from the yellow streetlights, rarely seen in Chinese cities that prefer neon. Here, there are no neon signs at all inside the gate, although the tower on the gate itself is illuminated with colourful lights. Unlike other city gates that have been developed into scenic spots such as the one in Nanjing, this one has no fence or ticket; locals sit and smoke on the wide terrace of the tower. Although the businesses in the main street of the old town, selling Tibetan clothes, curios and yak meat to tourists, employ an increasing share of the locals and many find jobs in Chuanzhusi and Jiuzhaigou, agriculture is still an important part of the economy. So far, modernity has arrived here, at least in part, not by the diktat of tourism developers replicating 'success models' elsewhere or the imagery of national media shows. It has taken a gentler shape that, like the milkshake made of yak milk because no cow's milk is available, feels at once more local and more global than scenic spot fare. What is missing, by contrast, is a strong sense of the national.

ACT II

Songpan, Ngawa Tibetan and Qiang Autonomous Prefecture, Sichuan Province, China, April 2005[2]

This time, I arrive in Songpan from Chuanzhusi, where the Jiuzhaigou-Huanglong Airport was built just after my first visit. Some of the work is still being finished even as an expansion is already being prepared because the waiting hall is too small to accommodate the passengers. After the airport's opening, the number of visitors to Jiuzhaigou nearly doubled, from 1.1 million in 2003 to 1.9 million in 2004 (Dombroski forthcoming). In the same year, Huanglong received 800 thousand visitors (Kang 2005). The growth was helped by the fact that the second Sichuan International Tourism Festival was held at the Jiuzhai Paradise resort and in Songpan. For the event, the Songpan county government ordered businesses and residents to remove tile fronts from buildings and paint façades with 'Tibetan patterns', that is, geometrical patterns in shades of ochre along where the lintel of a wooden building would be and around the windows—as well as to replace the iron shutters of shops with colourful 'Tibetan-style' iron doors, all at their own cost (see Figure 7.3). Hui Muslim businesses appear to have been given the option of painting their buildings with green crescent motifs, although the yellow paint and the doors remained 'Tibetan'.

Figure 7.3   'Tibetan-style' shop doors and the new Emma's Café, repainted in hybrid 'Hui-Tibetan style'

The project's masterminds in the Tourism Bureau had apparently changed their minds since my first visit, when they wanted to 'rebuild' late imperial Ming- and Qing-era houses, and—perhaps impressed with a similar transformation of Zhongdian, a new tourist region in northwestern Yunnan recently renamed 'Shangri-la' (Hillman 2003)— decided instead on what they refer to as Songpan's 'restoration in Tibetan style'. They were apparently untroubled by the fact that the very purpose of Songpan and its fortifications from the Tang on was to be a military outpost *against* Tibetan and other 'barbarian' incursions (Songpan 1967 [1924]: 5, 31).

Songpan's change is not limited to repainted houses and replaced doors. Inside the gate, I can hardly recognize the old town. Cars can now enter, and the old, warm yellow streetlights have been replaced. The city wall, most of it long gone, has been rebuilt, and the surviving parts mended and repainted a matching grey. All of the houses that used to lean on the ramparts, and many of those around them, have been torn down and their inhabitants moved out of the old town and given plots to build houses. According to Emma, who has moved her café farther away from the gate, the money they received for their houses from the government covered most, but not all, of the costs.

Figure 7.4   Demolition of houses in front of the town wall east of the North Gate in 2003 and the rebuilt wall in 2005

Many of the houses along the main street have also been torn down and rebuilt (see Figure 7.4). There is a new square in front of the county government (it too has received the 'Tibetan' makeover), with the concrete finery that marks ceremonial spaces in China, and what looks like a review podium, made of the same concrete, outside the newly built East Gate (see Figure 7.5). Next to the 'reconstructed' covered bridge hangs a poster showing the next phase of development—a new quayside (see Figure 7.6).

Figure 7.5   New ceremonial spaces in front of the county government and East Gate

In front of the North Gate, another new square has been built, at the centre of which is there is a statue of the Tang Dynasty princess Wencheng and her Tibetan king-bridegroom, with a tablet that says 'Han Zang he qin' (Han and Tibetan: harmony and amity) (see Figure 7.7).

This is where the tourists take their photos. They are much more numerous than in 2003, in groups and largely middle-aged. The Chinese backpackers of two years earlier are nowhere to be seen. Westerners still sit in Emma's Café, but she complains of a steep drop in business. Foreigners who come to Songpan now, she says, are Singaporean and Malaysian groups rather than backpackers. The Yulan Pancake House has been rented out to migrants from Mianyang in the

Figure 7.6   Poster depicting planned quayside development

Figure 7.7   The North Gate in 2005 with the
statue of Han-Tibetan amity

Chengdu plain, who—though they still have the old 'Israeli Fried Noodles' menu—cannot prepare the food on it and do not speak English (or, for that matter, Mandarin).

This reflects two changes at once. The first is that westerners no longer put a stamp on the town. The atmosphere of 'homespun globalization' is gone and tourist business is now determined by the needs of domestic and, to a lesser extent, overseas Chinese group tourists. Rather than pursuing the 'authentic' and 'unspoiled', these tourists seek what they view as the modern comforts of lodging, transportation and shows. After all, as I have argued elsewhere (Nyíri 2006), instead of being the continuation of a post-Enlightenment quest for the sublime as in the West, contemporary Chinese tourism grew out of a tradition of pre-modern literati travel—visiting places that had been enshrined by past cultural heroes and properly recognizing their canonical meanings—that was picked up by the state as it decided to turn citizens into consumers in the 1990s. The second change is what locals point as large-scale migration from elsewhere in Sichuan (mostly from the Chengdu plain) as well as from Hunan and Zhejiang Provinces. In fact, the increase in the numbers of locals in the street is even more striking than the growth of tourists. Some migrants are workers, but others now rent most of the shops in the old town. All are attracted by the new tourism boom. Contrary to the perceptions of locals' resentment of migrant business people in tourist places like Lhasa (see TIN 2002) and Lijiang (see Peters 2001), Songpan natives I spoke with, do not, for now, appear to see the outsiders as rivals. On the contrary, they welcome them as a boost to the economy and the government 'strongly welcomes' them too, issuing temporary residence permits liberally. Moreover, some of the locals take it for granted that they lack the skills or looks for certain jobs in the service sector. As a taxi driver explains, it is normal that front desk staff at Jiuzhai Paradise are from the plains, because 'if they were from here they would have bad skin'.

Similar to the Songpan residents interviewed by Kang (2005), all the locals I spoke with evaluated change as 'good' or 'very good'. Even Emma, who was quite critical of the government and its plans for demolition and forcible relocation in 2003, and who is concerned about her own business, says that seeing her town so clean and neat for the first time makes locals feel very happy. 'I understand that you might not like the makeover', she repeats, 'but for the locals, it is very good'.

Indeed, the government promotes tourism as one of the core elements of the 'Great Northwestern Development' strategy (Wei 2002), designed to reduce the wealth gap between the country's prosperous coastal and poorer inland provinces. The 2001 State Council resolution, 'On further accelerating the development of the tourism sector' (*Guanyu jin yi bu jiakuai lüyouye fazhan de tongzhi*), calls for the establishment of 'Experimental zones for poverty alleviation through tourism' (*lüyou fupin shiyanqu*) as well as the construction of new airports and roads in the west. The Committee on Nationalities and Religions of the People's Political Consultative Conference also issued a 'Proposal to accelerate the development of the tourism sector in nationality areas' (*Guanyu jiakuai fazhan minzu diqu lüyou chanye de jianyi*) in August 2001.

But Emma and the others we spoke with do not talk about increased prosperity, the most frequently mentioned positive effect of Songpan's relaunch is that the 'quality (*suzhi*) of the people' has improved. To my question as to how this could happen so suddenly, Emma answers: 'Because their environment improved! If you live in dirt then you don't care! But when everything is clean, and you throw away some rubbish, people will stare.' Echoing Hillman's findings in the southwest Chinese county recently named Shangri-La (2003: 185), she says that she was happy and impressed to see the musical and dance performances by various 'minorities' from the area during the International Tourist Festival, and cites the fact that in the evenings now, people gather in the new square in front of the government and listen to music or dance. Thus, the changes have 'improved their bodily and spiritual health'. I ask again how people could discover their inner virtues so suddenly, but Emma maintains that a change in the environment can bring out such qualities.

Discussion: The Civilizing of Songpan

Chinese authors have interpreted the spatial transformation of touristified villages and towns as a result of the intrusion of the global market whose inexorable force locals are unable, and often unwilling, to resist (see Duan and Yang 2001). Clearly, commercial developers or local governments bound touristic spaces and erect ritualized markers such as gates and walls because they believe that these correspond to tourists' expectations and will improve their experience by directing them to the 'nice' parts of the place, and thus attract more visitors.

But, although the exigencies of the market are often cited in China as a catch-all rationale, they provide only part of the explanation. True, the social and spatial engineering Songpan has been subjected to was intended to generate an income, and it would be easy to cynically dismiss the government's civilizing rhetoric as eyewash to cover plainly economic motives. Underestimating the disconnect between ideology and everyday life has been a mistake not uncommon to researchers of state socialism. Yet the effects of Songpan's civilizing—as opposed to just market-induced change—have been real, precisely *because* they have been linked to the inducements of the market. The town's spaces have been nationalized and its inhabitants civilized in order to make it suitable for tourism. Specifically, Songpan has been fitted into the standardized category of 'old town' (*gucheng*), a touristic genre represented by hundreds of sites across today's China (see Anagnost 1997: 167–70), from Zhouzhuang near Shanghai to Lijiang in Yunnan (which Tourism Bureau officials said in 2003 they wanted to emulate). The old town has now been clearly bounded by the wall, and the border between mundane and touristic spaces ritualized through gates and pedestals. It has several wide ceremonial spaces, its little Tiananmen—which every student learns in third form to see as 'majestic and grand' (Woronov 2004: 303)— and standard monuments, identifying it explicitly and implicitly with the Chinese nation and used for the 'healthy' activities of photo-taking and dancing, and its tourist streets with Zhouzhuang-like lanterns and fake flower beds just like the Wangfujing pedestrian street in Peking (see Figure 7.8).

Soviet officials liked to describe the culture they promoted as 'national (ethnic) in form, socialist in content'. Wei Xiaoan (2000: 139) describes the 'tourism culture' he promotes as having 'ethnic form [but] modernised content'. With the intention of emphasizing 'ethnic form' for the development of tourism, the public spaces of Songpan, which, thanks to its poverty, had escaped the great spatial standardization of early Communist times, have belatedly acquired 'socialist content'. The logic of these developments is not antagonistic but synergistic. From

Figure 7.8   The main street in 2003 and 2005

the government's standpoint, the relationship between tourism and civilization is evidenced by the simultaneous appearance of slogans about Party members' education and the environment in the made-over town. That the project actually works is reflected not only by tourists taking photos at the monument, but also in the endorsement of the changes and purchase of the state discourse of 'quality' (much more than emphasizing economic benefits) by Emma, who owes her rise as self-educated businesswoman to the cosmopolitan backpacker discourse of 'freedom'.

A number of authors have recently attempted to theorize the Chinese government's concern with population 'quality', tying it to the state's drive to create modern consumer-citizens (Anagnost 1997, Friedman 2004, Murphy 2004, Woronov 2004, Yan 2003). Appropriately directed consumption simultaneously stimulates the economy and provides a new process of identification with the nation-state, reinforced by the recognition of one's 'quality' (Pun 2003). John M. Flower (2004: 651) has described the campaigns to build 'material and spiritual civilizations' (*wuzhi wenming, jingshen wenming*) as 'a Chinese inflection of the global development discourse'. There is, however, more at stake here. The late 'socialist' Chinese state's civilizing discourse is formulating a very distinct idea of the 'good life', one that Peking University academic Sun Xiaoli (2004) describes as a 'modern, healthy, and civilized lifestyle'. According to Sun, the modern (and, clearly, productive) personality, which possesses qualities like openness, orientation towards the future, respect for science and friendliness, as well as an environmental consciousness and a respect for time and planning, is achieved through both eugenics as well as a 'scientific view of consumption' rather than 'Mammon worship and hedonism' (Sun Xiaoli 2004). Sun's colleague, leisure researcher Chen Luzhi (2004, cover flap), writes: 'Through "leisure", it is not only possible to promote the multifaceted development of human beings; moreover, it is possible to perfect, to elevate human beings; to improve the quality of labourers from the inside; to promote harmony between man and nature, man and man, man and society.' Another leisure researcher, Ma Huidi, writes that 'the state's governance and control (of society; *zhili yu tiaokong*) requires not only economic, administrative, scientific, technological and legal means; even more, it requires the workings of cultural guidance' (*wenhua yindao*) (Ma 2004: 170). As Pun Ngai (2003: 475) suggests, this 'cultural turn' represents 'a new mode of governmentality', and it tallies with the Hu-Wen leadership's promotion of 'harmonious society' (*hexie shehui*), 'community building' (*shequ jianshe*) and 'cultural construction' (*wenhua jianshe*). Indeed, in 2006, Hu Jintao announced a new list of 'eight honourables and eight shamefuls'.

Tourism, which is undergoing a proverbial growth in China and is now firmly established as an element of urban consumer lifestyle (see Nyíri 2006), is an arena with the potential to both civilize the 'tourees' (Oakes 1998) and respond to officials' calls for the 'propagation of correct notions of leisure' in order to 'lead the masses to plan their leisure and cultural lives in a scientific, healthy, and reasonable manner' (Ma 2004: 218–19). Indeed, officials often repeat that tourism 'synthesizes the material and the spiritual civilization' (see Lin 1998: 52, Xiong and Zhao 1998: 5). The ideal of the consumer-citizen is almost explicit in the State Council's 1993 'Opinion on actively developing the domestic tourism industry' (*Guanyu jiji fazhan guonei lüyouye de yijian*), which declares that 'the emergence and development of a domestic tourism industry has satisfied the popular masses' demand for material culture, which grows day by day, and strengthened the popular masses' patriotic cohesion.' With a different inflection, the 2001 'Notice on further accelerating the development of the tourism industry' calls for 'closely connect[ing] the development of tourism with the construction of socialist spiritual civilization; cultivat[ing] superior national culture through tourist activities; strengthen[ing] patriotic education.' In a 2004 paper, a trio of Hubei University law students capture the unusual combination of a belated mass-bettering socialist tourism with the ideology of modernization through consumption—an idiosyncrasy perhaps typical of contemporary China. They claim that 'tourism improves the quality of labour' by letting people 'enjoy natural landscapes and immerse themselves in historic culture and modern civilization'; that it 'strengthens national cohesion'; but that it is hindered by the 'backward sense of consumption' that makes people abstain from taking tourism loans. 'Therefore it is necessary to further guide residents to change their sense of consumption and [thereby] fundamentally improve people's quality of life' (Zhu, Zhu and Wu 2004: 72).

The Chinese state—as many others over the course of history—thus sees the *correctly framed* consumption of places as an instrument for strengthening national consciousness; indeed, many scenic spots are also designated as Patriotic Education Sites, to which schoolchildren are taken.[3] Songpan's transformation into a scenic spot has necessarily entailed the conversion of spontaneously evolving local ways of consuming space into national spaces of civilization. Just as Zhang Gu, Deputy Director of the provincial Tourism Bureau declared:

The construction of scenic spots and scenic areas must both fully reflect modern material civilisation and fully display the positive and advancing spiritual civilisation of the Chinese race (*Zhonghua minzu*). Indeed, this is what distinguishes the socialist tourism industry with Chinese characteristics from the western capitalist tourism industry (Zhang 2000: 121).

Notes

1. Act I is abridged from Nyíri (2006).
2. Act II fieldwork was funded by a Macquarie University grant, which the author gratefully acknowledges.

3. Analyzing the representation of monuments in Chinese history textbooks, Nicola Spakowski (1997: 291) comes to a similar conclusion. She points out the timeless and 'totalizing view of built structures as monuments symbolizing the greatness of the nation', whether by representing the historical unity of the nation, its 'resilience' (*shengmingli*), its 'civilizational evolution (ideally represented by feats surpassing the contemporary West), or the heroism of individual sacrifice. More specifically, Woronov notes that schoolchildren learn 'the appropriate attitude towards these places, and display awe at the magnificence and power Tiananmen and other national spaces represent' (Woronov 2004: 303). School visits to national historic sites are occasions of not edification but also of rehearsing exemplary discipline and solemnity (Woronov 2004: 306). 'Children are supposed to see and then appreciate China's history and aesthetics in specific ways... the attempt always exists on the part of all pedagogues (parents, teachers, state textbook writers) to make the experience 'right' by appreciating the site' (Woronov 2004: 307).

References

Anagnost, Ann. 1997. *National Past-Times*. Durham, N.C. and London: Duke University Press.

Chen Luzhi. 2004. *Min xian lun* (On leisure). Peking: Zhongguo Jingji Chubanshe.

Dombroski, Kelly. Forthcoming. 'The Whole Nine Villages: Local Level Development through Mass Tourism in Tibetan China', in J. Connell and B. Rugendyke (eds), *Tourism at the Grass Roots: Villagers and Visitors in the Asia Pacific*. London and New York: Routledge.

Duan Ying and Yang Hui. 2001. 'Quanli bianyuan de Manchunman—Lüyou zuowei xiandaixing yu minzu yishi de gean yanjiu' (Manchunman at the periphery of power: tourism as a case study in modernity and ethnic consciousness), in Tan Chee-Beng, Sydney C. H. Cheung and Yang Hui (eds), *Tourism, Anthropology and China*. Kunming: Yunnan Daxue Chubanshe, pp. 94–115.

Flower, John M. 2004. 'A Road is Made: Roads, Temples, and Historical Memory in Ya'an County, Sichuan', *Journal of Asian Studies*, 63(3): 649–85.

Friedman, Sara L. 2004. 'Embodying Civility: Civilizing Processes and Symbolic Citizenship in Southeastern China', *Journal of Asian Studies*, 63(3): 687–718.

Hillman, Ben. 2003. 'Paradise Under Construction: Minorities, Myths and Modernity in Northwest Yunnan', *Asian Ethnicity*, 4(2): 176–88.

Kang, Xiaofei. 2005. 'Tourism, Two Temples and Three Religions: A Three-Way Contest on the Sino-Tibetan Border', paper presented at the 2005 Annual Meeting of the Association of Asian Studies, Chicago, 31 March.

Kausch, Anke. 2000. *Dumont Kunstreiseführer*. Ostfildern, Kemnat: DuMont Reiseverlag.

Lin Yanzhao. 1998. 'Lüyou chengshi jingshen wenming jianshe de tedian ji cuoshi' (Distinguishing characteristics and measures of the construction of spiritual civilization in tourist cities), *Lüyou yanjiu yu shijian*, no. 4: 52–55.

Lonely Planet. 1996. *Lonely Planet*. Footscray, Victoria: Lonely Planet Publications.

Ma Huidi. 2004. *Xiuxian: Renlei meili de jingshen jiayuan (Leisure: The Making of a Beautiful Home for the Human Spirit)*. Peking: Zhongguo Jingji Chubanshe.

Murphy, Rachel. 2004 'Turning Peasants into Modern Chinese Citizens: "Population Quality" Discourse, Demographic Transition and Primary Education', *The China Quarterly*, 177: 1–20.

Nyíri, Pál. 2006. *Scenic Spots: Chinese Tourism, Cultural Authority, and the State*. Seattle: University of Washington Press.

Oakes, Tim. 1998. *Tourism and Modernity in China*. London and New York: Routledge.

Peters, Heather. 2001 'Making Tourism Work for Heritage Preservation: Lijiang—A Case Study', in Tan Chee-Beng, Sydney C. H. Cheung and Yang Hui (eds), *Tourism, Anthropology and China*. Bangkok: White Lotus Press, pp. 313–32.

Pun Ngai. 2003. 'Subsumption or Consumption? The Phantom of Consumer Revolution in "Globalizing" China', *Cultural Anthropology*, 18(4): 469–92.

Songpan xianzhi. 1967 (1924). Taipei: Taiwan Xuesheng Chubanshe.

Spakowski, Nicola. 1997. *Helden, Monumente, Traditionen. Nationale Identität und historisches Bewusstsein in der VR China*. Münster: LIT.

Sun Xiaoli. 2004. 'Xiuxian yu xin de shenghuo fangshi' (Leisure and the new lifestyle), talk at the seminar '2004—Zhongguo: Xiuxian yu shehui jinbu' (2004—China: Leisure and social progress), Peking, 2–6 June.

Tibet Information Network (TIN) 2002. '"Rebuilding" and "Renovation" in Lhasa'. Special report, http://www.tibetinfo.net/news-updates/2002/1009.htm, accessed on 4 March 2004.

Wei Xiaoan. 2000. 'Zhongguo lüyouqu (dian) de xianzhuang yu fazhan qushi' (China's tourist zones [sites]: current situation and development trends), in Zhang Guangrui, Wei Xiaoan, and Liu Dejian (eds), *2000–2002 nian Zhongguo lüyou fazhan: fenxi yu yuce* (China's tourism development, 2000–2002: analysis and forecast). Peking: Shehui Kexue Wenxian Chubanshe, pp. 126–43.

———. 2002. 'Xibu lüyou fazhan zhanlüe' (A strategy for tourism development in the West [of China]), opening speech at the Western Tourism Development Strategy Seminar, Guiyang, 23 April. Electronic file courtesy of author.

Woronov, T.E. 2004 'In the Eye of the Chicken: Hierarchy and Marginality among Beijing's Migrant Schoolchildren', *Ethnography*, 5(3): 289–313.

Xiong Xuezhong and Zhao Ling. 1998. 'Yunnan lüyou wenhua jianshe de zhanlüe gouxiang' (A strategic plan for the construction of tourism culture in Yunnan), *Chuangzao*, no. 5, pp. 33–35.

Xu Xinjian. 2001. 'Developing China: Influence of "Ethnic Tourism" and "Ethnic Tourees"' in Tan Chee-Beng, Sydney C. H. Cheung and Yang Hui (eds), *Tourism, Anthropology and China*. Bangkok: White Lotus Press, pp. 193–214.

Yan Hairong. 2003. 'Neoliberal Governmentality and Neohumanism: Organizing Suzhi/Value Flow through Labor Recruitment Networks', *Cultural Anthropology*, 18(4): 493–523.

Zhang Gu. 2000. 'Gengxin wu da guannian, jiakuai fazhan Sichuan lüyou chanye' (Refresh five big concepts, accelerate the development of Sichuan's tourism industry), *Lilun yu gaige*, no. 5, pp. 120–22.

Zhu Guangxi, Zhu Lixia, and Wu Guangyun. 2004. 'The Value Analysis of Tour Golden Week Policy', *Yunnan Geographic Environment Research* (in Chinese), 16(3): 70–72.

ZITO. 2003 *Zhongguo Zizhuyou (A Tour Guide for Chinese Backpackers)*. Xi'an: Shaanxi Shifan Daxue Chubanshe.

8

History and Heritage Woven in the New Urban Fabric: The Changing Landscapes of Delhi's 'First City'. Or, Who Can Tell the Histories of Lado Sarai?*

ANAND V. TANEJA

GOLF

Delhi, October 2005. Hole 17 of the Qutub Golf Course, built by the Delhi Development Authority (DDA) on what used to be the agricultural land of the village of Lado Sarai (see Figure 8.1). I am photographing a large 14th century wall mosque next to where players tee

---

* This paper is based on preliminary work on a much wider project on the contemporary practices and politics around medieval ruins in Delhi. Much of it is based on interviews conducted in Lado Sarai village in September and October 2005. I would particularly like to thank Shehryar and Minhazz, who gave me my first contacts in the village. In Lado Sarai, I would like to thank Devinder who, along with being a hardheaded man of the world, is a great and generous friend, and has a deep understanding of history and of the burdens of the researcher. Through him I met many people, but

Figure 8.1   Hole 17 of the Qutub Golf Course, built by the Delhi
Development Authority on what used to be the agricultural
land of the village of Lado Sarai[1]

off—though this was recorded in the Archaeological Survey of India's
(ASI) 'Zafar Hasan List' back in 1920, it does not appear in the Indian
National Trust for Art and Cultural Heritage's (INTACH) magisterial
two volume guide to Delhi's built heritage, published in 1999[2] (Hasan
1997[1920]: 119; Nanda et al.1999: 197–200). It is a large structure, 63
feet wide and 76 feet long, as Zafar Hasan tells us. It is in reasonably
good repair. How does a structure like this disappear from the records,
when it is so manifestly present?

One of the two golfers playing the hole turns to me and asks me
what I am doing. I tell him that I am a historian and a researcher, and
am photographing this structure because it is not in the records. 'Just
don't put us into any history books', he says. I ask him if he knows
anything about the structure.

here I would like to single out Karan Pal Singh and Manphool Pradhan, who in their
laconic wisdom and generosity embody a world too rapidly disappearing. And finally,
I would like to thank Awadhendra Sharan and Ravi Sundaram at CSDS for suggesting
future directions for my continuing research.

Friend, I've been playing golf here for ten years, but I don't know anything about this. It is much cleaner now than it used to be. But so far no one has come and occupied it, or made a nuisance and disturbed our game.

Then he walks off to finish his game. I am left looking at the context-less ruins, isolated from meaning by the undulating, manicured greens.

To know the history of a ruin, a piece of land, is to acknowledge the claims upon it. It is not something that you necessarily want to do. Consider the case of the Qila Rai Pithora.

In 1981, much of the agricultural and non-residential land of the village of Lado Sarai was notified and taken over by the DDA. Lands of the adjacent villages of Hauz Rani and Saidulajab had already become the large 'modern' housing colony of Saket. Much of Lado Sarai's land came under the 'Green Belt', and agricultural land very soon turned into wooded tracts. In 1991, V.K. Jain, then Land Acquisition Collector of the Delhi Government for south Delhi, and a keen golfer, started a golf driving range on this land, after the success of a similar driving range started in the Siri Fort Sports Complex. By January 2000, it was opened to the public as a 9-hole golf course, widely advertised as Delhi's first 'public' golf course. Presumably due to the proximity and visibility of the Qutub Minar, the iconic monument adopted as symbolic of Delhi's history, the course was named the Qutub Golf Course.

By December 2000, the DDA was already planning to expand it into an 18-hole golf course, and had initiated proceedings to acquire more of the notified land. Here, they seemingly ran into trouble with the central government, led by the Hindu nationalist Bharatiya Janata Party. For the lands of Lado Sarai village, and hence of the land acquired by the DDA, were traditionally bounded by the vast fortified walls identified as Qila Rai Pithora, or the fort of Prithviraj, the last 'Hindu' ruler of medieval Delhi's 'first city'.[3]

History and Heritage

Extensive quotes from the statement made by the then Urban Development Minister Shri Jagmohan to the Parliament on 21 December 2000:

An honourable member of this august house had raised the issue regarding development of Prithviraj Chauhan's Qila Rai Pithora in south Delhi and the occupation of the land earmarked for it by the DDA Golf Course.

I wish to make it clear that the government attach great importance to the project and development of the Qila Rai Pithora complex which was conceived by it in November 1999.

The project has two basic objectives in view. First, to preserve, protect and strengthen our architectural and cultural legacy. Secondly to weave history and heritage in the new urban fabric that is being presently spun in Delhi...and acquaint the youth with the great acts of valour of our leaders.

It is unfortunate that some senior functionaries of the DDA, without informing me, have caused occupation of huge lands, which had been earmarked for the park, for building and expanding the golf course which it has no powers to do....

Jagmohan ordered an inquiry, and outlined plans for the cultural centre, which included a mounted statue of Prithviraj (see Figure 8.2),

Figure 8.2   The statue of Prithviraj Chauhan atop the cultural centre Inaugurated in 2002 (The ruined wall of Qila Rai Pithora is in the foreground)

18 feet high, to be placed on top of the cultural centre. This was obviously meant to be seen by the traffic passing on Press Enclave Road.

Let us consider Jagmohan's phrase,'History and heritage woven in the new urban fabric'. Press Enclave Road is the major route for people travelling to PVR Saket, Delhi's first multiplex, symbolic of the new urban fabric, and the shift in the government's imagination of its own public. In 1997, PVR Saket, a formerly run-down and low profit disreputable hall, was 'gentrified' (a term which has great resonance in Delhi cinema history as well as in urban studies) and almost overnight became a space for elite consumption and flânerie, attracting a public from all over Delhi and its satellite cities. One of the major reasons for PVR to become possible was the Delhi government's deregulation of cinema ticket prices, indicating a shift from governmental thinking of cinema as working class entertainment—which allowed PVR to sell tickets at much higher prices, and market itself as a 'global' elite cinema experience.[4] The Prithviraj Memorial is less than half a kilometre from PVR Saket, and is adjacent to A-Block, Saket. On an acrylic panel under the statue, Jagmohan recounts a story very similar to the story told of the transformation of the cinema hall. 'This was a wilderness', he says, 'the walls were overgrown and people from the nearby slums used to come and defecate on it, I cleared the walls and made a beautiful garden all around, and now 5000 people a day come here for their morning and evening walks.'

The Prithviraj Memorial is one of many initiatives to assert the Hindu past of a historic cityscape dominated by the traces of an Islamicate past. The policies of Shri Jagmohan were only the most public of these initiatives. In Delhi, these included the creation of the Indraprastha Park, invoking the mythical founders of Delhi, the Pandavas; an attempt to grant the Purana Qila, also associated with the Pandavas, World Heritage status;[5] and an attempt to make the Yamuna riverfront near the Nigambodh Ghat a site for 'pilgrimage tourism'. Many of these plans required the removal of settled communities. Unideal citizens were removed so that landscapes could be remodelled for tourists. But which tourists? Since many of these new spaces are unticketed, foreign exchange earning does not seem to be the immediate logic. Instead these spaces are built for the Indian citizen as a tourist, relearning the history of the (Hindu) nation through looking at the reconstituted landscape.

Figure 8.3   Jagmohan and L.K. Advani at the
unveiling of the statue, 7 June 2002

Source: The Hindu.

In June 2002, the then Home Minister and Deputy Prime Minister
L.K. Advani inaugurated the Qila Rai Pithora Cultural Complex (see
Figure 8.3).

'If Pakistan does not put an end to cross-border terrorism and
India reacts in accordance with popular sentiments, it would be con-
sidered appropriate', Mr Advani said after unveiling the statue of the
Rajput warrior, Prithviraj Chauhan (*The Hindu* 2002).

Advani went on to invoke US support for India's actions against terrorism, and to say that world opinion had shifted in India's favour in
the War on Terror, 'from Agra to Almaty'. The walls of Qila Rai Pithora
were burdened with the narrative of not just a national history, that of
the last Hindu king being defeated by the Muslim invader for lack of
national unity, but also a global history, where Prithviraj Chauhan was
the first martyr of the War on Terror, being fought continuously for 800
years since, against Islamic terrorists from Pakistan and Afghanistan.

The past, as landscaped by Shri Jagmohan, is not a foreign country.

Meanwhile, a month before the inauguration of the Prithviraj Memorial, the Qutub Golf Course reopened as an 18-hole golf course. A
few months before this, the board of the Delhi Golf Club, the much
older, more central and far from 'public' golf course, had a meeting.

The Delhi Golf Club's extraordinary general meeting on Saturday,
January 12, 2002, is expected to be a stormy one. There are two

schools of thought. One section is in favour of change of lease terms while another is vehemently opposed to it. The existing lease terms, signed in 1996, are valid until 2010.

If the resolution, signed by more than 100 members, is thrown away, the club will be open to offer membership to 125 government officials. These officials, 'bestowed' membership out-of-turn, will be exempted from paying entrance fee.

The Delhi Development Authority (DDA) has developed a course at Lado Sarai. It will soon be an 18-hole course. The government officials, interested in golf, should seek membership here instead of over-crowding the DGC, which is one of the most prestigious clubs in the country.... (*The Tribune* 2002)

At the Lado Sarai Golf Course, playing rights for life for government officials were available for Rs 20,000. For DDA officials, the figure was Rs 10,000.[6] A children's playground had been promised for Lado Sarai village, but has not yet been developed.

LADO SARAI

The narrative of Prithviraj Chauhan and the invader Mohammad Ghori as told in the village of Lado Sarai is slightly different. This story begins with the good but childless king Anang Pal Tomar of Delhi, the last of the line of the mythical Pandavas.

One day, in his old age, the good king Tomar decided to go on long pilgrimage and leave the kingdom in the care of two relatives, Prithviraj and Jaichand. Prithviraj was given custody of Delhi and Ajmer, while Jaichand, the king of the 'Jat belt', took care of Kannauj.

Prithviraj told Anang Pal that his custody was useless unless he had authority which other kings would believe in. 'Give it to me in writing', he said. 'No king can enter Delhi without the permission of Prithviraj'. So Anang Pal gave it to him in writing, and went off on his pilgrimage. Not much later, when he returned to his city, the gates were closed to him. No king could enter Delhi without the permission of Prithviraj. And so it was that Prithviraj came to rule Delhi.

Flashback. A trader from Afghanistan decided to start trading with India and thus expand his business and his profits. So he loaded his goods on camels and came to India, and to the court of the vigorous but childless king, Anang Pal Tomar, along with his beautiful daughter. He offered Anang Pal his daughter in marriage, saying, 'I know that you will have children with her'.

The marriage was consummated, the child was conceived, but the older, childless queen was jealous. While the younger queen was pregnant, she forbade Anang Pal from meeting her, and when the child was born, she threw him out on a garbage pile, *ghor,* in Sanskrit.

The child was picked up by a passing childless potter, who then brought him up as his own. When the child was seven years old, king Anang Pal passed a judgement which dissatisfied his people. The potter's son suggested another way in which judgement could be passed. The news spread like wildfire and reached the palace. Fearing the king's wrath, a servant from the palace went and told the potter who his son really was, and asked him to send the child off to Afghanistan, to his grandfather.

Years later Mohammad Ghori marched to Delhi to reclaim his inheritance, and Jaichand joined him. Prithviraj was defeated. Lad Singh, a soldier in Jaichand's army, settled in what was to become Lado Sarai village. His four sons lived in four domed structures, four gumbads, which existed there prior to their settlement, and around these domes the village of Lado Sarai grew.

Karan Pal Singh, about 70 years old, who told me this story, also told me:

> There are three kinds of history. One is those written in school books. This is written by those in power, and cannot be trusted. Then there is the history by the person who sits with books and tries to make sense of the past for himself. The third is oral tradition, what people remember from what ancestors tell them. There is some truth in both of these.

Whether the Jats who dominate the village of Lado Sarai remember coming with the armies of Jaichand or with those of Raja Surajmal a few 100 years later, the story always remembers them coming as soldiers and camping here, among these domes, surrounded by the traces of a past that was not theirs. By the early 20th century, at any rate, the Jat settler's relation to these traces of the past was eminently pragmatic. The 'Zafar Hasan List' found 16 'Pathan' monuments on the lands of Lado Sarai, most of which were being used as houses, cattle sheds, fodder stores or as common land. Zafar Hasan considered the preservation of most of these 'unnecessary'.

During the 1947 violence, villagers from Lado Sarai gave shelter to their neighbours, Muslims from the village of Hauz Rani. Cordial relations have been maintained between the villages till this day. After Partition, the attitude towards traces of the village's 'Muslim' past shifted. Many graves, which had been lying undisturbed earlier, were effaced to make way for the expansion of buildings and farmland. In 1955, the villagers started building a girls high school on the grounds of a large wall mosque on the western side of the village, which the Zafar Hasan list remembers as waqf land, 'The mosque has a spacious courtyard enclosed by a battlemented rubble wall and entered through a doorway on the east. It is strewn with numerous graves and is overgrown with trees and vegetation...' (Hasan 1997 [1920]: 115). Today, outside the high walls of the girls school, traces of the rubble wall surrounding the courtyard and the entrance gate to the mosque can still be seen. On the walls of the school is written, 'Do not piss here, this is a memorial to your father' (see Figure 8.4).The writing on the wall is an in-joke, remembering the graves buried under the school.

There are many Muslims in the village now. They are migrants from Uttar Pradesh and Bihar, who work in metal machining, which is now a big industry within Lado Sarai, operating out of single rooms in rented premises. Since the acquisition of Lado Sarai's agricultural land by the DDA, the whole economy of the village has shifted to a rent economy, exempt from zoning laws. So there are Internet cafés, metal machining and security services in the interiors of the village, and facing the main roads, there are carpet showrooms and lounge bars. Tenants far outnumber the house owners in Lado Sarai, and unlike more regulated parts of Delhi, there seems to be no special animosity or aversion reserved for Muslim tenants.

These narratives of Lado Sarai's past are choppy and contradictory. For, 'the Muslim' in these stories, to take an example, is not a stable descriptive category, unified over space and time. The 'Muslim past' and the 'Muslim neighbour' are different Muslims. So are the 'Muslim

**Figure 8.4   The boundary wall of the Government Girls
Higher Secondary School, Lado Sarai, built on the
site of a medieval wall mosque**

tenant' and the 'Muslim invader'. The national and global histories
landscaped onto the lands of Lado Sarai are very different, to make an
understatement, from the local histories of Lado Sarai.

EPILOGUE

About 50 metres from the Prithviraj Memorial, barely 10 metres from
the entrance to the park, the manicured lawn that stretches from here
through the golf course all the way to the Mehrauli Badarpur Road,
ends. Instead there is unkempt grass and, beyond a whitewashed platform, thick undergrowth. This is the Dargah Hazrat Sayyid, which could
be a 16th century structure, but with a history of veneration not much
older than a decade (see Figure 8.5).

This land, sold to the DDA by a third party, is claimed by the Waqf
Board as its own, and a family from Old Delhi claims it as their ancestral

Figure 8.5   The Dargah Hazrat Sayyid, close to the
Prithviraj statue

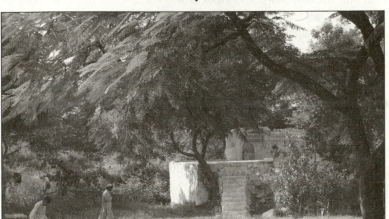

property. Twelve years ago, the family sent the younger son to physically squat on the disputed land. Anzar, the son, told me that his ancestor, the Sayyid, had come to India a little before Babur. Rather than Lado Sarai, he linked his genealogy to the nearby village of Saidulajab, which according to him was a village of Sayyids, descendants of the prophet. Despite his reputation as a goonda and squatting on the land, people started coming to the cleaned and whitewashed grave platform. And as the descendant of the Sayyid, he also became a bit of a faith healer. Six years ago, he got people from the Tablighi Jamaat to set up a small madarsa (a temporary structure because of the disputes) to handle the religious aspects of the shrine. It is an uneasy alliance between the fundamentalist reformers of the Tablighi Jamaat, who have an uncomfortable relationship with grave veneration, and a Muslim who is not very religious, but it has ensured a steady trickle of visitors to the shrine, bestowed it religious legitimacy, and kept the DDA and Jagmohan at bay.

It is possible to reconstruct a 'history' of these traces of the past— despite the violent histories of changing land use, duplicity and dispossession that Delhi's villages have seen—by looking at patwari records, court disputes, waqf grants, and the land/property records of the pre-colonial, colonial and post-colonial states. It is also possible to preserve the 'built heritage' of these monuments, through preservation and the stopping of 'encroachments'. But even these histories of 'ownership' and architecture would not give us the far more multiple histories of 'usage'—of how people interact with these monuments in their daily lives; of the way these monuments are, and have become, important to the memories of those who live around them; and how local histories cling to these traces of the past. Stories of migration and displacement, being and belonging. These are the claims ignored and erased by the discourses of built heritage and the promotion of tourism. Thus are local histories forgotten and global histories imposed by those in power.

The undulating green lawns of Jagmohan's imagination, the monuments without any histories except those imposed by power, remind me of a certain gentleman who used to live in these parts 150 years ago. An English sahib who imposed a rolling English parkland on hundreds of acres of Mehrauli, and dotted his estate with kiosks and pavilions which looked old and weathered and suitably medieval, but which were constructed on his orders to beautify his landscape. Ruins without claims to history.

The man was Thomas Metcalfe, then British resident of Delhi. The structures were called 'follies'.[7]

Notes

1. All photographs are by the author except where mentioned otherwise.
2. The 1999 Listing has five structures listed for Lado Sarai village. As a point of contrast, the Zafar Hasan List, 70 years older, had 16 structures listed.
3. Medieval Delhi is popularly believed to be a series of seven successive cities. The first of which was Mehrauli/Lal Kot/Qila Rai Pithora, dating from the early 11th century onwards, which is associated with the Rajput dynasties of the Tomars and Chauhans, and the Turkish 'Slave' dynasty.
4. For an account of the gentrification of cinema spaces in Delhi, see Taneja (2005a).
5. See, for example, *The Times of India* (2003). For a larger history of planning and dispossession around the Purana Qila, which casts an interesting light on events at Lado Sarai, see Taneja (2005b).
6. This has since been revised upwards to Rs 40,000 and Rs 20,000, respectively, with effect from 1 May 2006. See http://www.dda.org.in/sports/golf_course.htm#. By contrast, playing rights for life for others (non-service members) is Rs 1,75,000.
7. See Roberts (1998). Details of 'Metcalfe's Follies' can be found in Nanda et al. (1999: 232, 313, 337).

References

Hasan, Maulvi Zafar. 1997 (1920). *Monuments of Delhi—Lasting Splendour of the Great Mughals and Others*, Vol. II, Delhi Zail. Delhi: Aryan Books International.

Nanda, Ratish, Narayani Gupta and O.P. Jain. 1999. *Delhi The Built Heritage: A Listing*, Vol. 2. Delhi: Indian National Trust For Art And Cultural Heritage (INTACH).

Shri Jagmohan. 2000. 'Statement of Minister for Urban Development and Poverty Alleviation Shri Jagmohan in the Rajya Sabha Regarding Development of Prithviraj Chauhan's Qila Rai Pithora in South Delhi'. Available online at http://pib.nic.in/archieve/lreleng/lyr2000/rdec2000/r21122000.html.

Taneja, Anand Vivek. 2005a. 'Begum Samru and the Security Guard', in *Sarai Reader 05: Bare Acts*. Delhi: Centre for the Study of Developing Societies.

————. 2005b. 'Puratatv ka Myth, Myth ka Puratatv: Purane Qile ke Ateet aur Aaj', in *Deewan-e-Sarai 02: Sherhernama*. Delhi: Centre For the Study of Developing Societies. (Available in English as 'The Archaeology of Myth, the Myth of Archaeology: The Pasts and Present of the Purana Qila' at http://www.mit.edu/~shekhar/urban-media/taneja_archaeology_myth.pdf)

The Times of India. 2003. 'Jagmohan Invites the Pandavas to Old Fort', *The Times of India*, 5 August.

The Hindu. 2002. 'Retaliation If Infiltration Does Not Stop', *The Hindu* (Delhi), 8 June.

The Tribune. 2002. 'DGC Meeting May Be Stormy', *The Tribune* (Chandigarh), 12 January.

9

Eat, Drink and Sing, and Be Modern and Global: Food, Karaoke and 'Middle Class' Consumers in China

XUN ZHOU

INTRODUCTION: THE 'MIDDLE CLASS' DREAM

In all human societies, consumption is central to the cultural as well as material reproduction of social lives and relationships. In *Consumer Culture and Modernity* (1997), Don Slater argues that 'consumer culture is a motif threaded through the texture of modernity, a motif that recapitulates the preoccupations and characteristic styles of thought of the modern west.'

Since the beginning of the 1990s, a growing number of aspiring Chinese middle income consumers have been the driving force in changing the economic, social and political landscape of their country. Increasingly they are being referred to as the Chinese 'middle class', partly because like young, urban middle classes anywhere in the world, they are sophisticated, lead sophisticated lifestyles and want sophisticated products and services. Like the middle class in other Asian countries, they are looking for quality as part of a self-conscious search for identity. However, the definition of 'middle class' in China is somehow problematic.

According to a recent poll by the Chinese Academy of Social Science (CASS), no less than 46.8 per cent of the Chinese now believe they belong to the middle class. Li Chunling (n.d.), a researcher at the Sociology Institute of CASS, argues that the Chinese middle class only materialized in the mid-1990s and the concept is a media-fabrication. There is no doubt that the illusion of middle class success is relentlessly reinforced by the advertising industry in order to fuel mass consumption. For instance, Chinese TV is flooded with commercial advertisements, occasionally interrupted by soap operas, news and sports. For serial shoppers in big urban cities, desire is indeed reality. A report by CASS, on the other hand, considers five categories of middle class—Party cadres, business managers, chief executive officers in the private sector, qualified technicians and office staff. In terms of revenue, CASS researchers selected people with a higher revenue than the average local monthly salary. This, however, varies a great deal from region to region. In terms of lifestyle and consumer preferences, the researchers identified four groups of products and attributed points to their ownership—from indispensable items such as colour TVs, refrigerators and washing machines to luxury goods such as computers and private cars.

When many in the Chinese press applied the CASS criteria to the 2000 Chinese census, they came up with only 2.8 per cent of the Chinese population that could be counted as middle class. If this figure is anything to go by, then the 'middle class' does not represent a middle class, but an 'elite culture'. Although small in numbers, according to Li Chunling (n.d.), they nevertheless make their mark in big cities like Shanghai and are relentlessly glorified by the media—'the members of the middle class considerably influence the rest of the population with their lifestyle'. Certainly in big cities like Shanghai, Beijing, Guangzhou and Shenzhen, the huge number of malls, cars and packaged holidays in China as well as overseas conveys the impression of a middle class bubble (Xin Zhigang 2004).

Advertisements have indeed helped to invent the Chinese middle class bubble. This is further confirmed by a survey by Beijing-based CTR Market Research, a leading market research company in China.

The survey polled 340,000 senior executives, owners of enterprises and heads of key departments in four major cities including Beijing, Shanghai, Guangzhou and Shenzhen. Half of the executives said that advertisements 'enhanced their confidence' and influenced their choice of brands (Iyengar 2004). In other words, through advertisements they find favourite brands with which they want to reflect their social status.

'As an integral part of modern culture', Llewellyn-Watson and Kopachevsky (1996) argue, 'advertising's main function is twofold: one, to serve as a discourse about objects, symbols and ideas, as a template for erecting monuments to consumption and self-indulgence; and, two, to persuade people that only in consumption can they find not only satisfaction, but also mental and physical health, social status, happiness, rest, regeneration and contentment'. However, as pointed out by Michael Shudson (1986: xix), advertising also cultivates desires and needs, including 'freedom, fulfilment, and personal transformation', that are never quite fulfilled by purchasing goods. By generating a never-ending search for happiness and contentment through consumption, advertising underpins capitalism, which is dependent on continued acquisition.

In China, food, medicine and leisure activities are some of the most advertised products. Television and the advertising industry have become powerful tools in expanding materialistic values to stimulate consumption. These powerful symbolic messages spreading through the mass media have also contributed to the change in attitudes towards work and leisure, as well as consumers' idea of the 'self'. A survey by the Far Eastern Economic Review showed that 60 per cent of working men and women from Asian countries opted for more leisure—that is, spending less time at work—to improve their enjoyment of life. This enjoyment of life is expressed through consumption of leisure. This chapter will examine food and eating, as well as Karaoke—two of the most consumed products in contemporary China—with regard to their consumption patterns in contemporary China and their consumers. It will show how consumption of such activities provides a social alternative; by participating in them, aspiring consumers are not only able to define their individual status and identities, but also transformed into a desired social collective— the 'middle class'.

EAT 'GLOBAL', EAT 'MODERN' AND EAT 'HEALTHY'

In her study on food rationing and the politics of domesticity in the United States, Amy Bentley (1998: 85) shows that food consumption is much more than ingesting nutrients for biological survival. Acquiring, preparing and consuming food have become intimately woven into societies' cultural practices and beliefs. The consumption of food is an extraordinary social activity laden with complex and shifting layers of meaning.

In China, food has an intrinsic value. It is the epitome of Chinese culture and it sits deeply in the consciousness of the Chinese people. Historical sources show that already in the 16th century, eating had become much more than just filling the stomach. Food was a form of display, a status symbol and a fashion. This trend continued into the 19th century. The increase in material wealth since 1820 saw the widespread culture of conspicuous consumption. Food, a previously highly appreciated form of art, was reconfigured and transformed into highly valued good, a commodity. For the next century, with the emergence and proliferation of the advertisement industry, food was to play an integral part in the life of Chinese consumers. The advent of 'modernity' created a consumer market for 'modern' food, namely, imported food, sugary food, manufactured refined food, dairy food, processed food and tinned food. For the majority of wealthy and middle class consumers in China, the brand name was as important, if not more, as the quality of food.[1]

The first 30 years of Communism, from the early 1950s to the early 1980s, however, destroyed the rich and colourful food culture in China. While food became highly politicized, eating became a basic necessity and even a struggle for the majority of people. The economic reforms since the 1980s saw food shortages and starvation becoming a thing of the past for petty urbanites, though it continues to this day in many rural regions. Once more, food is given a central importance in defining class status and value, as well as 'modernity'. In a rapidly changing society, for many middle salary consumers, food has also become an embodiment of stability, a solace and a substitute for otherwise unfulfilled desires or dreams, as well as a sign of health in an age of anxiety, fear and stress.

Although food is often seen as the aspect of life in China least permeable to foreign influence, reality shows that increasingly—for a large number of aspiring middle income consumers—eating 'global foods', either imported or locally produced, is considered a sign of prosperity. In particular, milk products, breads, pastries and 'British' oats have appeared at the breakfast tables of the middle class, though oats have been a staple for the peasant population in northern China for centuries. A recent report by economists Fred Gale and Thomas Reardon shows that imported goods are now widely available in Chinese supermarkets, from Washington apples, California oranges and wines to lychees from Thailand, butter from New Zealand and cheese from France. Supermarkets also feature many international brands—such as Kellogg's cereals, Hormel sausages and hot dogs, Lay's potato chips, Nestlé and Danone milk products, McCormick jellies, Skippy peanut butter and major western chocolate brands including Nestlé and Cadbury, many of which are manufactured locally in China—partly responding to an ever increasing consumer demand. An estimated 200–300 million people out of 1.3 billion are consumers of these 'global goods' (Gale and Reardon 2004: 7).

Such a phenomenon is not only propelled by an increasing purchasing power amongst middle income consumers in China, but also has its roots in the culture of the 'modern'. In the 19th century, as elites around the world came to locate modernity in Europe, all things 'local' were increasingly rejected as signifiers of backwardness, while imported goods from France, England or Germany were embraced as prestige symbols. Dominant groups in Asia, Africa and South America believed that modernity had to be brought home in order to propel one's country into the universe of 'civilized' nations and join the universal march towards a better future. 'Foreign' stood for 'modern' and Europe was viewed as the fountainhead of a new world of progress. Foreign, in and out of Europe, was no longer merely exotic—to buy foreign was to be modern. After World War II, however, the location of 'modern' began to shift from Europe, first to America and then to the 'global'.

Global goods in general (for example, global fast food like Mac Burgers, KFC and Pizza Hut) have revolutionized consumption patterns in China, as well as in many other parts of world such as in Latin America and Southeast Asia. The key to their success in these parts of the world was their identification with modernity and the 'good life', contrary to their 'cheap' and 'unhealthy' images in Europe. The first KFC opened at the south side of Tiananmen Square in 1988. It made headlines in the Chinese capital and was a novelty for the majority of people living in Beijing. At the time the 'middle class' was yet unknown, and 'imported' fried chicken wings were certainly beyond the reach of the salaried Chinese. In 1990, one year after the Tiananmen incident, Beijing hosted the 11th Asian Games. The Chinese government seized the opportunity to reinstate China's image on the world stage—after the 4 June incident, many countries in the West had terminated trade relationships with China in protest. Suddenly, Beijing saw a number of foreign restaurants and bars opening up, thus signalling that China was becoming more modern and more global. Foreign food was also advertised on state television as healthier and more hygienic, as well as a source of personal happiness; at the same time, some western edu-cated and well travelled young professionals felt that local banquets were wasteful. Western-style set meals with a starter, main course and dessert became popular in big urban cities such as Shanghai and Beijing. KFC and McDonald's became ever more fashionable amongst middle income consumers. In a way, many 'western' style restaurants or bars did look cleaner than most ordinary local eateries. Bright and nicely decorated, with slightly more comfortable chairs rather than stools to squat on, they attracted the growing middle income urbanites who took pride in following the more 'civilized' ways appropriate to an era of modernity.

Some middle class families embraced not only 'western' food, but also adopted the usage of knives and forks which bespoke the foreign. Chopsticks never disappeared, yet more 'modern' ways of eating altered the rituals around the table. Some middle class families would even sit around a table covered with a white cloth; although the dishes would be traditional Chinese, these would be served the 'modern' way, each with its own chopstick and spoon, as the same sticks were no longer used to put food into the mouth as well as serve oneself from the common dishes placed at the centre. As new norms of hygiene gradu-ally disseminated among the middle class, the habit of sharing several plates at dinner parties was no longer considered to be sanitary.

Health concern is also a key to the supermarket boom and the rising popularity of organic foods in recent years. As shown in Gale and Reardon's report (2004), in 1990 there was only one supermarket outlet in China, but by 2003 there were approximately 60,000 stores with an estimated sale of US$ 71 billion. In many big cities, supermarkets have gradually replaced the traditional wet market as they offer superior quality and better sanitation. The supermarkets' success is in packaged foods and processed foods. In China, food was traditionally sold loose and weighed by the seller. From the 1990s, however, China witnessed an explosion in branded food, many with expensive packaging. Canned food, packaged biscuits and wrapped sweets become popular not only for reasons of taste, but also because they were considered to be more hygienic and modern. Tinned or wrapped food, moreover, are convenient to carry around, handy to use when travelling and ideal as gifts. Besides hygiene and convenience, the style conscious urban consumers and the profit seeking producers are the driving force behind the ever changing and growing packaging industry. Packaging can change far quickly and easily than food. With every new packaging, there may be an increase in the sales. Packaging can also represent the personality and status of the purchaser, and packaging can pack in many middle class aspirations. The best example of this is that during the mid-autumn festival season, middle class families no longer just buy any box of moon cake to celebrate—the brand of moon cake and the kind of package are far more important than the taste of the cake.

Eating at western restaurants and drinking in western bars have also become a status symbol. By the end of the 1990s, aspiring young elites with a fair amount of disposable income found restaurants such as the Courtyard in Beijing or M on the Bund in Shanghai as the ultimate place to be seen. Consumerism had inevitably brought a bewildering array of choices. As China boasts a prominent place in the global market, Beijing as the capital of China is full of global goods. As a pop song goes:

> On the side of the Boulevard of Eternal Peace, there are many, many bottles. The bottles are full of coloured liquors. Red, blue, purple and green…many, many colours. There are also bitter coffee and sweet juice, as well as bitter and sweet beers: from Carona to Carlsberg. You can drink and drink until you've had enough….

By consuming them, many Chinese middle salary consumers are being transformed to the 'middle class' in a global sense.

KARAOKE

Karaoke may initially have been a Japanese product, but it is undoubtedly a global phenomenon in modern times. Today, from Paris to Toronto, from Iceland to Brazil, as well as in the heights of the Pyrenees, people are passionate about Karaoke. In terms of time and space, Karaoke can mean very different things to different people. It is a machine, a tangible object, a cool thing to have and do, a status symbol. It is an illusion, a fantasy dream in an artificial chamber. While it encourages egalitarianism in countries like America, in cultures based on a hierarchical system such as East Asia, it serves as an instrument of homemade democracy. There, it is even used as a method for picking up foreign languages and to improve literacy. Recently in China, Karaoke inspired a 'mini novel' contest. Amateur writers were encouraged to submit a 350 word novel by text message. According to Yu Hua, the well known Chinese writer:

> To hold the competition is like bringing Karaoke to literature. Before the invention of Karaoke, there were only few people who could or would sing in public. Thanks to Karaoke, anyone and everyone can sing in public whenever they feel like it. Now thanks to the mobile phone, the same is true with writing (Michelle Zhang 2005).

As a popular media, Karaoke can also be an illicit activity or a state-sponsored event. It may be used as a tool for organizational propaganda and, at the same time, as a means for self expression. It is a mass culture without being 'mainstream'; there are a few 'Karaoke celebrities', yet all who participate are stars. It may be an entertainment, or a way of life; a pleasure, or a real pain. While some argue that as a modern technological tool, the Karaoke machine can enslave individuals and create alienation, others say Karaoke has liberated them from the DVD screen and computer desk, and made them social animals. In China, where a large percentage of the population has spent much of its time watching DVDs, the past few years has seen a resurgence of the Karaoke culture, as people feel that Karaoke is a more sociable thing to do.

The Karaoke boom in China took place during the advent of the economic boom in the early 1990s. It soon became an overnight hit.

Suddenly the Karaoke machine became the dream toy for millions of Chinese families. From night clubs to hotels, restaurants, bars, even in remote shanty towns, Karaoke has become a ubiquitous feature, as the hand-painted advertisements, which adorn pagodas, street corners and toilet-styled tiled houses. For urban dwellers in big cities, being without KTV (Karaoke TV) at home is almost a disgrace; for the villager in the remote hinterland, the magic tunes produced by the giant Karaoke machine sound 'scientific' and 'modern'. For them, to be 'scientific', was to be out of the village. Having been used to listening to Marxist jargon through loudspeakers, Karaoke has become the new media for the new dogma of consumerism. Syrupy pop songs, video footages of girls in long white dresses and young men in tuxedos running in slow motion through clouds of dry ice, or romping through the tourist sites of Taiwan, Hong Kong or Paris, have become the new definition of 'Communism with Chinese characteristics'. But the best thing about Karaoke is that the ordinary Chinese can also enjoy the privilege of holding the remote control and the microphone. With Karaoke and consumerism, 'Communism with Chinese characteristics' does indeed provide the illusion of 'equality'.

'Whether happy or sad, Karaoke is always ok', as a song goes. Indeed, today Karaoke has become a main feature in the consumer based Chinese society. For petty urbanites, it has become a way to redefine aspects of daily life—from self to love, misunderstanding, relaxation, work and even losing weight. After graduation, Yuanmei began working in a bank. She found the repetitive and boring work suffocating. She wanted to quit but did not have the courage to do so. One day a few friends invited her to a Karaoke, where she discovered her singing talent, boosted her self-image and found courage. Karaoke with friends has become a joy in her life. She has since decided to pursue a new and happier life. She is now working in a newspaper, while pursuing a course on fashion design. Of course, she continues to sing Karaoke. Ronan is a shy 21-year-old, who has been secretly in love with Ruby for a while. To help him express his love, his friends planned a Karaoke night for him and Ruby. At a private room, with a bunch of flowers and a big box of chocolate, Ronan sang his heart out and won the heart of his beloved Ruby. Years ago, Leon and Ruitong became enemies after falling in love with the same girl. Years later they met again at a KTV party—their shared love for singing has helped them forget the past and become Karaoke pals. Yuanye had become overly stressed by work and a hectic city life. He became silent. One day a friend took him to a KTV, where he suddenly belted out songs. After a whole hour of shouting to himself, he felt very good. 'I have learnt to relax and to live', says Yuanye, and Karaoke has now become a weekly activity for him. After a promotion, Adam has been finding colleagues at his team treating him differently. Many had become jealous and resentful. At the recommendation of a friend, Adam invited the entire team to a Karaoke night. Holding the microphone, Adam deliberately sung out of tune to make a fool of himself. It immediately lightened up the atmosphere and everybody suddenly became relaxed and friendly. The night turned out to be a great success and Karaoke became a regular night out for the team members.

In big cities such as Beijing and Shanghai, losing weight has become the latest frenzy amongst the young and fashionable. A recent report claimed that singing can help one lose weight and be slim. Overnight, 20- and 30-year-olds rushed to KTV. Cash Box KTV (*qiangui*), one of the biggest KTV joints throughout China and Taiwan, even has songs listed that are especially good for losing weight— with fast beats, requiring physical action. Now some Karaoke venues also have slimming fire pots or buffets for lunchtime and late night singers. As a matter of fact, KTVs have become popular lunchtime venues in Chinese cities. In China, eating at restaurants is essentially a social experience; turning up without company is regarded as 'socially unacceptable'. However, increasingly, office workers have to take turns for lunch as they are sick of seeing the faces of their colleagues. To escape the embarrassment, many have opted for KTV, where it is 'socially acceptable' for strangers to share a microphone or to listen to each other singing. Besides the price is usually low and it includes food and drink and unlimited songs.

Karaoke has also provided sustenance for many Chinese in an age full of uncertainty— the microphone has become the only thing they can hold on to. Post-1989, billions of Chinese have been dreaming about getting rich quickly. For the majority of them, however, this may well be a nightmare. Consuming seems to be the only light at the end of the dark tunnel, and if the future seemed uncertain, in the virtual and artificial space of Disneyland or Karaoke, every dream comes true— an experience of the glorious past, a journey to the West, a future into the fantasy land, and a song of unfulfilled love and ambition.

Disneyfication thus goes hand in hand with the Karaoke frenzy. As China is turning into the world's biggest Disneyland, Karaoke has become the centre of Chinese lives. Many posh Karaoke venues have been turned into Disneyland with 'high Chinese kitsch', including fake Carrara marble slabs as well as huge dragon and deer *bassorilievi* dotted by several golden cornucopias. Some even have a large water feature with fat auspicious carps swimming in it, conveying the message of good fortune and a prosperous future.

The 'New Chinatown' (*Tangren jie*) in Beijing is quintessentially the Disneyland of Karaoke palaces. This huge theme park has a main street in mock Tang dynasty façade. Inside, there is a red tinted room with a bar, reminiscent of *Cabaret* and *Boogie Nights*, manned by seated and sleeveless bar beauties. In the background, there is a bowling alley, a disco chamber, and a warmly lit and glitzy club with more than 60 comfortable, spacious and affordable Karaoke rooms. If 'New Chinatown' is too affordable, a venue accessible to average Beijing consumers, there is also the exclusive made-in-China French château, the Zhang-Laffitte. In the early 1990s, Zhang Yuchen, a former Red Guard shifted to real-estate development and built the first high-class villas in the suburbs of Beijing. To promote his new 1,000-villa complex, Zhang came up with the brilliant idea of copying a 17th century French château, Maisons-Laffitte. With help from the Chinese architect Liu Peirong, the Zhang-Laffitte turned out to be Disneyland China at its best—a French château with Vatican colonnades and two symmetrical alleys 'borrowed' from the famous Fontainebleau castle. The interior consists of a golden *faux* baroque with a giant Karaoke next to the wine cellar.

In Shanghai, Karaoke is intertwined with the fabric of the city's nightlife. According to a regular of the upmarket Karaoke night scene in Shanghai—an assiduous Karaoke practitioner and a business man from Hong Kong in his early forties—in the summer of 2004, there were at least 300 luxury Karaoke establishments scattered throughout the city. No ordinary Chinese person would be able to afford spending a night in such places. The clientele here are wealthy Chinese men and other East Asian males from Taiwan, Hong Kong and Korea, many of whom are permanent residents of Shanghai, or businessmen spending some time in the city. Offering a night to potential business partners at an expensive Karaoke place is *de rigueur* for guaranteeing the success of most high-level economic transactions in China. The cost of such evenings can run high. In 2004, the rental fee for a luxury Karaoke box amounted to 1,500 RMB (about US$ 40), about half the monthly salary of an ordinary clerk. On top of that, it was customary for the host to provide several bottles of whisky or other imported spirits, each costing 500 or 600 RMB per bottle, together with expensive tea, snacks of dry meats and fruits, and several boxes of imported cigarettes. At least 300 RMB (around US$ 35) is necessary to 'hire' a female hostess. These women are known in Chinese as *sanpei xiaojie*, literally 'three-accompaniments miss', with reference to their accompaniment in singing establishments, dancing establishments and eating establishments. Despite China's ban on prostitution and occasional crackdowns in cities throughout the country, entertainment venues from Karaoke bars to five star hotels continue to offer under-the-table services to wealthy male clients.

Karaoke is indeed big business in China. On 1 March 2004, operators of some 12,000 entertainment outlets, mostly Karaoke bars and clubs in over 50 cities across China, received a letter issued by two law firms in Beijing. On behalf of more than 50 music clients in China and abroad, including EMI, Warner, Universal, Sony and Rock Records, they demanded the named outlets pay compensation for using music material without authorization. A few months earlier, New Chinatown and Melody bar in Beijing and an outlet of Cashbox—a giant Karaoke chain in Southeast Asia—were amongst the first to face legal action brought by various recording companies. The story hit the news headlines; it became an issue about intellectual property. The upcoming ruling could decide the fate of the KTV industry nationwide. In December 2003, the Beijing No. 2 Intermediate People's Court ruled that Chinatown had infringed upon the plaintiff's copyright and awarded 38,000 yuan (US$ 4,578) as compensation, thus setting a precedent. Warner had demanded 300,000 yuan (US$ 36,000) for economic damages and 50,000 yuan (US$ 6,000) for litigation expenses. Meanwhile, New Chinatown appealed to the Beijing Higher People's Court, believing that even if music TV, music video and the Chinese edition of Karaoke are the creative works of Warner Music, their expenses had long been paid when it purchased the entire music collection years ago for 1.2 million yuan (US$ 140,000), including machines and equipment. Others such as a spokesman for Cashbox in Beijing argued that:

> KTV and the music industry are complementary, like fish and water, counting on each other for upcoming consumers. If everything goes well this time, it's a good beginning to raise awareness for copyrights. However, if mediation efforts fail and litigation starts, it will be harmful to both (*China Daily* 2004).

Public reaction was sympathetic towards the accused, arguing that KTV is a new technology and it should be treated differently from printed publications and patented products. Furthermore, there was no history in China of any record companies having charged for using songs. The conclusion was that China is different from the rest of the world. China is unique.

Indeed, in an economy that thrived on counterfeits, the legal challenge seemed pointless. Besides, the international music industry seemed to have forgotten that, prior to KTV, there was no music industry in post-revolutionary China. In the erstwhile centrally planned economy, music was owned by the state, it was a voice of the Party and a tool of propaganda. From the late 1980s and early 1990s, the KTV business facilitated the growth of the Chinese music industry, and hardly any pop music stars in China today would have had a career had it not been for KTV or MTV.

Unlike in Europe or in many other parts of the world, pop concerts were a rarity in China and government censorship meant the dissemination of pop music was extremely restricted.[2] KTV, however, allowed a privileged relationship between individuals and artists. It also provided a new mode, the Karaoke machine, by which popular songs were produced and consumed and became truly popular in China. And it was through Karaoke albums that many 'controversial' Chinese and western pop stars became known in China. For instance, even if the Chinese government does not quite approve of Madonna's songs, she can still appear on the screen of KTV with Communist revolutionary songs such as 'Oh Party, forever our loving mother' as the lyrics. While the music industry is on the decline in many parts of the world because of file sharing, in China it is on the rise, mainly because of the consumers of Karaoke.

A symbol of personal wealth and a sign of modernity, as well as an aspect of modern consumer life, Karaoke is featured everywhere in China today. Signs of KTV are seen on huge billboards placed on many city skyscrapers. They are often inscribed with calligraphies of famous celebrities, rich entrepreneurs as well as high ranking officials—one more means for them to show off besides holding the microphone. The continuous popularity of Karaoke in a constantly changing society such as China is largely due to its flexibility, adaptability and variety. A popular KTV venue today is very different from the Karaoke bar of the 1990s. A Karaoke box in the city is very different from a Karaoke hall in the countryside. Even in one Karaoke venue, there are hundreds of different rooms creating different atmospheres catering to different customers. At a Karaoke, in one night, a person can have many different experiences—from Japanese style Karaoke to Sicilian style and Bangkok style, whereas the music can be a sad melody, hard rock or syrupy pop. As one Chinese writer noted 'No one can get bored in a Karaoke, there is something for everybody in a Karaoke' (Liu Jianmei 2002: 191). As China is globalizing, for millions of Chinese consumers, Karaoke has become a way to experience the 'global'.

CONCLUSION

Food or Karaoke, consumerism has become the new religion[3] or the new dogma in China. Through consumption, aspiring Chinese consumers are able to construct social identities and relations out of a wider social environment. Thus consumption is central to the cultural reproduction of the everyday world. By consuming, each consumer can also find out his or her moral and social value, and discover his or her individual identity. The popularity of 'foreign' or 'global' food and Karaoke amongst Chinese consumers shows that consumerism plays an integral part in creating new identities as well as sustaining old ones. While the former gives consumers a 'taste for modernity', the latter provides consumers an 'experience of global'. By consuming them, individual Chinese consumers have been transformed into the global 'middle class' and 'modern citizen'. At the same time, 'foreign' or 'global' food and Karaoke have been transformed to become 'Chinese' to sustain 'traditions' as well as to provide individual consumers with a sense of stability in a rapidly changing society.

In China today, while spending amongst 'middle class' consumers is rising steadily and there seems to be an ever wider choice of consumer goods, poverty levels are also growing. With an estimated current rate of unemployment at over 8 per cent, the gap between the 'middle class' and the rest of population is deepening. Social unrest and crime are two major concerns of Chinese society today. While living in fear and behind walls in its highly secure compounds, the Chinese 'middle class' is also facing several dilemmas:

1. Where will the next vacation/travel destination be?
2. Should they invest in stocks or foreign currencies?
3. How to choose among so many apartments?
4. It is easy to get fat and hard to stay slim.
5. The next generation will have no sense of the hardship of the past.
6. It is easy to communicate but difficult to see each other.
7. Middle class homes are filled with consumer electronics.

Purchase does not buy contentment—it leads to disillusionment and longing for ever new products. This is not only the dilemma of the Chinese 'middle class' consumers; this is a main characteristic of contemporary consumerism all over the world. In this sense, Chinese consumers have truly become 'global'.

Notes

1. For further reading, see Dikötter (2007).
2. For further readings, see Lee (1995).
3. In China today, even religion is to be consumed.

References

Bentley, Amy. 1998. *Eating for Victory: Food Rationing and the Politics of Domesticity.* Urbana and Chicago: University of Illinois Press.
China Daily. 2004. 'What's a Sing-along Video Worth?', *China Daily*, 24 March.
Dikötter, Frank. 2007.*Things Modern: Material Culture and Everyday Life in China.* London: Hurst and Company.

Gale, Fred and Thomas Reardon. 2004. 'China's Modernising Supermarket Sector Presents Major Opportunities for U.S. Agriculture Exporters', *AgExporter*, November.

Iyengar, Jayanthi. 2004. 'In China Say It With Consumer Goods', *Asia Times Online*, 14 May.

Lee, George B. 1995. '"The East Is Red" Goes Pop: Commodification, Hybridity and Nationalism in Chinese Popular Song and Its Tele-visual Performance', *Popular Music*, 14(1): 95–110.

Li Chunling. n.d. 'Zhongguo dangdai zhongchan jieceng de goucheng ji bili' (The composition and percentage of China's contemporary middle stratum), in *Shehuixue renleixue Zhongguowang*. Available at http://www.sachina.edu.cn/Htmldata/article/2005/09/289.html.

Liu Jianmei, 2002. *Bainian zhongguo shehui tupu: cong chuantong xiaoqian dao xiandai yule* (An illustrated history of Chinese society in the past hundred years: From traditional pastime to modern entertainment). Chengdu: Sichuan Renminchubanshe.

Llewellyn-Watson, G. and J.P. Kopachevsky. 1996. 'Interpretations of Tourism as Commodity', in Y. Apostolopoulos, A. Leivadi and A. Yiannakis (eds), *The Sociology of Tourism*. London: Routledge, pp. 281–300. (This also appeared in *Annals of Tourism Research*, 21(3): 643–60.)

Michelle Zhang. 2005. 'Make Short Work of a Novel', *Shanghai Daily*, 15 September.

Shudson, Michael. 1986. *Advertising, the Uneasy Persuasion*. New York: Basic Books.

Slater, Don. 1997. *Consumer Culture and Modernity*. Cambridge: Polity Press.

Xin Zhigang. 2004. 'Dissecting China's Middle Class', *China Daily*, 27 October.

10

Transnational and Transcultural Circulation and Consumption of East Asian Television Drama*

CHUA BENG HUAT

INTRODUCTION

For media industries in East Asia, the entire region constitutes one highly integrated market. Pop cultures—movies, television programmes and pop music—from different countries flow and cross porous national and cultural boundaries routinely and are distributed throughout the entire region (Chua 2004); 'pop' is used to designate media generated popular culture rather than the larger popular cultural sphere that encompasses the everyday life of the masses, in contradistinction to elite culture. Within the larger region, the locations that are predominantly ethnic Chinese—the People's Republic of China (PRC), Taiwan, Hong Kong and Singapore, which in spite of its Southeast Asian

* This paper was presented at the International Conference on Consumerism and the Emerging Middle Class: Comparative Perspective from India and China, India International Centre, New Delhi, 7–9 November 2005.

geographical location should be included—share a long history of ebbs and flows of the pop cultures based on Chinese languages, truncated or disrupted by political developments, but at no time totally severed. This may be referred to as 'Pop Culture China' (Chua 2001).

Within Pop Culture China, Hong Kong is the dominant location for films and television dramas and, until the late 1980s, for Cantonese pop (*Cantopop*). As Mandarin pop became the money-spinner for Chinese singers because of the opening up of the PRC market, Taiwan has emerged, since the 1990s, as the dominant location for Mandarin pop music. The PRC produces but exports a very small number of both films and television dramas. Since the 1980s, a few film directors have become well known, first, in the film-festival circuits and, then increasingly, in international commercial markets. Export of television dramas has been limited to historical period dramas or serialization of Chinese literary classics, such as *Shui Hu Chuan* (*All Men Are Brothers*)[1] and the widely read and repetitively remade *wuxia* (martial arts action) novels. Singapore has a very small film industry that produces a few full-length commercial and art-house feature films per year in English and Chinese; the English language films have greater opportunities for international film festival circuits while the latter genre are almost exclusively for the domestic audience. Its homegrown, state-owned television stations do produce drama series but these are seldom exported. Singapore is essentially a consumption space that imports a steady stream of films and television drama series from the entire East Asian region, while PRC imports films largely from Hong Kong.

In the 1960s, Japanese action movies were popular in East Asia; the *Blind Swordsman* film series was much studied and emulated in the Hong Kong *wuxia* movies (Yau 2005). After a long lapse of time, Japanese TV dramas became popular in East Asia in the 1990s—the typical romance and melodramatic narratives, featuring beautiful young professionals in trendy urban settings of upscale consumerism in and around Tokyo, were generically known as 'trendy' drama (Iwabuchi 2004: 73).[2] This was a serendipitous development for the Japanese producers. They were, at the time, not keen to tap into the regional market because the booming 'bubble' economy at home was able to sustain production profitably, in spite of the very high cost of production. Importation and screening of Japanese trendy drama by satellite stations in Taiwan, for example, were often done without licence, using copies brought over from Japan by small entrepreneurs. A similar process of smuggling of Japanese pop culture took place in South Korea, where for reasons of resentment for its colonization by Japan, importing of all Japanese cultural products was officially banned until 1998, with the Joint Declaration of the New 21st Century Korea–Japan Partnership. However, long before that, Japanese pop culture was 'copied', 'partially integrated', 'plagiarized' and 'reproduced' into Korean products. According to sociologist Kim Hyun Mee, 'Japanese [pop] culture in Korea has already set its roots deep into the emotional structure of Koreans' (2004: 4).

The latest entry—in early 2000—into the regional pop culture scene was what has come to be known as the 'Korean Wave'. In the mid-1990s, the South Korean government decided to make 'pop culture' an export industry, after discovering that the successful Hollywood film *Jurassic Park* 'generated, with all its spin-off sales, revenue worth foreign sales of 1.5 million Hyundai cars' and 'since Hyundai Motors' annual foreign sales numbered about 6,40,000 autos, a well-made film could be worth more than two years' of Hyundai's car exports' (Shim 2002: 340). The consequent inundation of Korean films, television dramas and pop music has created what ethnic Chinese fans quickly dubbed as the 'Hanliu' ('Korean Wave'). As one enthusiast proclaims, 'South Korean cinema is finding its place in the sun' (Stringer 2005: 1), reflecting the international reach of Korean films. South Korean television drama, on the other hand, has a more East Asian rather than global presence, arriving just when Japanese television drama waned in production and export (Iwabuchi 2002).

The flows of pop culture within both the larger region and Pop Culture China are unequal. At the larger regional level, Japan is predominantly an exporter of television drama and pop music, importing very little from elsewhere. Korea is also a regional net exporter of films, television drama and, to a lesser extent, pop music, making greater inroads into Japan in the late 1990s. Pop Culture China is a net importer from these two exporting countries and within it, Hong Kong and Taiwan are exporters compared to PRC and Singapore. In this chapter, I want to map out, partly as a research agenda, some aspects of the transnational and transcultural dimensions of East Asian pop culture production, distribution and consumption, and the character of its larger community of consumers.

PRODUCTION

The multi-level economic integration of the East Asian pop culture industry into one single market for production and distribution is visible in various ways. For the consumer, it is most visible in the increasingly common co-starring of actors from different locations in films. Some examples from the past few years are the 2003 PRC produced *Warriors of Heaven and Earth* which star Japanese actor Nakai Kindi; and the 2001 Korean produced *Musa* which stars PRC actress, Zhang Ziyi. When one takes into consideration producers, directors, actors, actresses and other technical professionals and consultants, the border crossing collaborations are even more complex. For example, the 2004 PRC/Hong Kong produced *House of Flying Daggers* had a PRC director Zhang Yimou and featured the Hong Kong actor, Andy Lau, the Taiwan-born Japanese actor Takeshi Kaneshiro [3] and PRC actress Zhang Ziyi. Going beyond the boundaries of East Asia is the 2005 Jackie Chan directed film, *The Myth*, which stars Chan himself and Tony Leung Kai Fee, both from Hong Kong, Korean actress Kim Hee-Seon and Indian Bollywood actress Mallika Sherawat.

Potential collaborations and border crossings are infinite but not random. The combinations are guided almost exclusively by the box office potentials of the directors, actors and actresses for their respective regional and local audiences. For example, featuring Zhang Ziyi in a Korean film potentially draws in the Chinese-language audience; similarly featuring the Korean actress Kim Hee-Seon is aimed at the Korean audience.[4] This may explain the fact that such collaborative 'pan-East Asian' films are increasingly multilingual and subtitled rather than dubbed into a single Asian language for a specific local audience. This obviously better reflects the complexities of social, cultural and political exchanges within Asia rather than homogenizing the complexities through a common language.

While some of these 'pan-East Asian' collaborations have met with great box-office successes, others have more qualified achievements. For example, Zhang Yimou's *Hero*—a co-production of PRC and Hong Kong, with a major investment from Miramax, US—is the top-grossing movie in the PRC to date, with box office receipts in excess of US$ 40 million, beating the Hollywood blockbuster *Titanic*, which had made US$ 38.6 million. Zhang's *House of Flying Daggers* was a great box office success as the top grossing movie in the PRC for 2004.[5] Of greater conceptual consequence are the different receptions such films might have from the regional and western audiences. For example, the Ang Lee directed film, *Crouching Tiger, Hidden Dragon*, in 2000, was hugely successful internationally but was poorly received in the PRC and Hong Kong (Teo 2005). There are several plausible explanations. First is the aesthetics of the film. According to a Hong Kong film critic:

> [making] Chinese aesthetics, culture, calligraphy and choreography accessible to the global market is the main strategy adopted by Lee. There are practically no untranslatable local data of any sort in the film; the director has made sure that the spectacular action flights are rendered both aesthetically and culturally approachable. The whole point is to popularise a new transnational genre (Chan 2005: 76–77).

This 'internationalization' is made possible by the relative ignorance of the global audience of what Teo (2005: 200–03) calls the Chinese conventions of the *wuxia* (martial-chivalry) genre. The 'knowledge-able' Chinese audience probably did not take well to the film's explicit subversion of the conventions. Here, the stoic machismo of the male hero characteristic of the genre was subverted by a 'dispirited' *wushu* (martial arts) Master Li (played by Hong Kong actor, Chow Yun-Fat) from the very opening sequence of the film. The film opens with Master Li arriving to make a gift of his sword to a friend/official. Within the conventions of the genre, this is tantamount to leaving the *wuxia* world. After that, throughout the entire film, his life leading up to his ultimate demise was dominated by the three female characters, giving the film its overall 'feminist' reading, more in tune, perhaps, with the sentiments of its global, especially US, audience.

Regional and international box office returns become an even more serious consideration for movie production in locations which have a small domestic market. This is most obvious in the case of Singapore. The major commercial film production company in Singapore is Raintree Pictures, in which the state is a majority shareholder through its media company, Media Corp. Given the small domestic market, the company can hardly afford to finance films catering strictly to a domestic audience. Consequently, almost all of its endeavours are collaborative efforts. An example is the financially successful *Infernal Affairs II* in 2002, which was made in collaboration with Hong Kong producers. However, given Singapore's geographic location, Raintree Pictures also collaborates with Southeast Asian players; its 2005 box office successful film, *The Maid*, directed by Singaporean Kevin Tong, stars a Filipino actress in the lead.

Co-production and co-financing arrangements among different parties unavoidably has its effect on commercial films. One of the serious consequences of co-financing is particular to Chinese language films. Within Pop Culture China, it has been a common practice for cinema-theatre owners with film exhibition capacities to invest in the production of Chinese films. One of the co-financing instruments is the so-called 'pre-sale' practice in which potential distributors/exhibitors of a film pay for the rights to distribute/exhibit in advance of the making of the film (Lii 1998: 129). Such an arrangement allows exhibitor-investors in different locations to specify, if not dictate, the development of parts of the film to suit not only the sentiments of the local audience but also comply with local political and censorship authorities, especially in more authoritarian polities in the region such as the PRC and Singapore. It is, therefore, common to find Hong Kong films, in particular, with two different endings for different locations; for example, in the first instalment of the trilogy, *Infernal Affairs*, the film ends with the success of the gangland mole embedding himself within the Hong Kong police department for all audiences except those in the PRC, where the gangland mole was killed by the police that exposed him.

Beyond cinema, collaboration in production is less common but not completely absent. Again, the size of the domestic consumer market matters. For example, during the late 1990s, Singapore television station tried to enhance the popularity of its programmes at home and expand the potential audience overseas by engaging popular Hong Kong actors and actresses as main characters in situation comedies and television dramas. Similar arrangements were also struck with Taiwanese artistes. The limited success of this approach is evident in the infrequency of such arrangements. All the other East Asian locations seem not only to be able to sustain their own television programmes but also export these, especially TV dramas.

DISTRIBUTION

The distribution of films within East Asia is not remarkable as it is conducted in an orderly manner by film production and exhibition enterprises. However, this is not the case with television drama series. Within Pop Culture China, there have always been steady streams of TV drama serials exported from Hong Kong and, to a lesser extent, Taiwan to the other Chinese communities. For example, Singaporeans were introduced to the now famous star, Chow Yung Fatt, in his lead role in the TV drama series *Man in the Net*, which had Singaporeans glued to the television set every night in the late 1970s. Alongside this routine stream of Chinese language TV dramas, as mentioned earlier, the Japanese 'trendy drama' series became popular throughout the region in the 1980s.

As mentioned earlier, since the domestic market yielded sufficient profit, Japanese television stations initially did not give much consideration to any export market and, initially, Japanese TV drama series were 'smuggled' into Korea and Taiwan by individual entrepreneurs who would travel to Japan and return with copies of the drama as personal luggage. In Korea, as a result of the formal ban on Japanese cultural material, Japanese TV dramas came in through underground channels. In the words of a Korean cultural commentator:

> We firmly lock and bar front doors but leave our back doors wide open. With our left hands we indignantly slap away any offers but we are busy snatching at any opportunities with our right. This has been our society's attitude toward popular Japanese culture during the last 30 years (Do Jung Il quoted in Kim 2002).

After the signing of the Joint Declaration of the New 21st Century Korea–Japan Partnership in 1989, cultural products criss-crossed national boundaries. This also paved the way for the joint production between a Japanese and a Korean television station of a drama series, *Friends* (2002), a tale of romance between a Japanese woman and a Korean man, who struggles against and overcomes social prejudices. Finally, in 2004, to prop up its falling audience rate, an NHK satellite station 'experimented' with the screening of the first Korean TV drama in Japan, *Winter Sonata*, in its late night broadcast slot. The popularity of this series caused it to be repeated in the same year and in the following year, and it is to be broadcast yet again, this time on free-to-air territorial station. The overwhelmingly Japanese, middle-aged housewife-audience 'discovered' Korea through this TV drama and Korean men through the lead actor, Bae Yung Joon, who came to be honoured as *Yung Sama*, Lord Yung.

In Taiwan, in the early 1990s, after the lifting of martial law, satellite stations sprouted like mushrooms after the rain, without any government regulations. Pirated Japanese TV dramas, dubbed into Mandarin, were broadcast on cable television stations without any licensing arrangement with anyone, including the Japanese producers. The dramas were reproduced into DVDs. Once this was done, the pirated drama serials could easily flow into and circulate within the greater Pop Culture China. 'Taiwan is acknowledged as possessing the richest sources for distributing Japanese TV drama, and has taken the strongest lead in the enthusiastic pirating of Japanese TV dramas of all the Asian societies' (Hu 2005: 171). The spread of DVD circulation within East Asia is difficult to estimate; nevertheless, its circulation suggests that the size of the consumer population far exceeds any statistics one can obtain from any official sources. Significantly, it should be noted that the pirating of Japanese dramas is in part driven by the reluctance of Japanese producers to market the rights of their products to the rest of the region, making it difficult and creating undue delays for consumers to access the programmes. Impatience drives the eager consumers to pirated products (Hu 2005: 172).

One peculiar aspect of the distribution circuit of Korean and Japanese films and TV drama series within Pop Culture China should be noted. Within Pop Culture China, different Chinese languages dominate in different locations: Mandarin in PRC and Singapore, in the latter because all Chinese languages other than Mandarin are banned from mass media; Cantonese in Hong Kong; and Mandarin and Minnan/Taiwanese, a language of Fujian province, in southern PRC. The three main Chinese languages may be mutually incomprehensible to monolingual ethnic-Chinese. This accounts for the 'peculiar' phenomenon of having subtitles in the Chinese written script for all Chinese language(s) films and TV programmes for the benefit of ethnic-Chinese audiences. This is because if a viewer does not understand the dialogue, he/she might be able to read the subtitles, given the 'shared' ideographic written script. However, if one were never schooled and thus cannot read, one will not understand the dialogue at all.[6]

Furthermore, the written script is itself differentiated in two ways. First, the PRC has simplified the ideograms radically to make it more accessible to the masses, and Singapore has adopted this simplified script. Taiwan, for the obvious political desire to differentiate itself from PRC, has retained the old, complex script. Hong Kong also continues to use this older script. The two different scripts now demand that books need to be published in both scripts to reach a larger potential market. Second, since 1997, Hong Kong has adopted Cantonese as the language of instruction in schools. There are Cantonese words that cannot be rendered in the existing Chinese written ideograms. So new ideograms are created which are not necessarily comprehensible to non-Cantonese speakers/readers. At other times, even if an ideogram were recognizable, it has to be read in Cantonese rather than Mandarin, as its appearance in a specific speech-location within a line of dialogue would be nonsensical if read in Mandarin. In these instances, the recognizable ideogram is used only for its 'Cantonese' sound and not its conventional semantics or pragmatics. The same is happening in Taiwan, with the Taiwanese using Chinese ideograms for reading in the Minnan language.

As a result, it is entirely possible to be watching a film that is dubbed in one Chinese language and subtitled in another. For example, in Singapore, where all Chinese languages are banned in the mass media, a film will be dubbed in Mandarin, with subtitles in Cantonese. This gives rise to the puzzle of which route the film has travelled within Pop Culture China: it could have first been imported to Taiwan and, therefore, dubbed in Mandarin, then re-exported to Hong Kong, where the Mandarin dialogue remains but subtitles in Cantonese are added, and then re-exported to Singapore. It could have been dubbed and subtitled in Hong Kong at the same time, in order to cater to not only the Hong Kong Cantonese audience but also the increasing number of Mandarin speaking mainlanders on the island. Or, it could have been imported to Singapore, where the importer had dubbed it into Mandarin and subtitled in Cantonese, in preparation for re-export to Hong Kong and the rest of Chinese 'diaspora' across the globe. Two observations can be made here. First, there is no way for an audience anywhere within Pop Culture China to know the route the film has travelled. Second, the possibility of circulating the film throughout Pop Culture China as one huge market is the primary reason why Korean and Japanese films and TV dramas are more likely to be dubbed and translated into Chinese rather than vice versa. This also explains the unequal flow of pop cultural products from Japan and Korea into Pop Culture China rather than from the latter to the two former locations. Finally, with increasingly formal licensing arrangements, partly as a result of increasing pressure of intellectual property protection laws, TV dramas are often broadcast in 'dual sound', allowing the audience to choose between the dubbed local language or the original language with local language subtitles.

CONSUMPTION

Of the three pop culture genres of film, TV dramas and pop music, the genre that generates a more lasting influence on the everyday life of their respective audience/consumers is TV drama. Pop music has the most limited transnational capability because translation is impossible. Consumers without the necessary proficiency in the original foreign language will not understand the lyrics; consequently, pop music that is transnationally successful is, overwhelmingly, music that can be danced to and where lyrics are secondary. At best, the same tune can be re-recorded in another language; for example, it is very common for Chinese singers to record pop songs from other languages, such as English or Japanese, with Chinese lyrics. Although foreign language is not a problem due to the possibility of dubbing, films make limited demands on the audience in terms of sustained commitment. Engagement with both the on-screen characters and the film narrative is limited to the duration of the screening time, thus, severely limiting the influence of a particular film on the audience. This is reflected in the general absence of audience reception research in academic film studies, which is dominated by the analysis of film texts and their symbolic and ideological significance.

In contrast, TV drama serials demand sustained viewing at regular intervals, either every evening at the same time or at least one episode a week at a fixed time. Many other activities need to be displaced or even sacrificed in order to watch every episode of a TV drama. Efforts have to be made to video-record an episode that has been missed and time has to be found to watch the recording before the next episode is screened the following day or the following week. Succumbing to these demands results in an active engagement with what is on screen. The drama narrative draws the committed audience into an intimate virtual relationship with the on-screen characters and their respective fates. Beyond the actual watching, viewer interest is sustained at the personal level with fellow viewers, who are ready to dissect the narrative of the entire series or of a particularly 'meaningful' episode or character and, finally, share in their collective anticipation of the next and future episodes. Such sustained audience engagement is the necessary condition that has enabled audience-reception analysis of TV dramas.[7]

Obviously, TV consumers throughout the East Asian region watch both local and imported programmes. Indeed, as a rule, the local audience tends to favour local programmes, as identification with on-screen events and characters is often instantaneous. It is like watching oneself on the screen. For analytical purposes, cross-cultural consumption of imported TV dramas, either dubbed or subtitled, is the more interesting and significant question. A detailed discussion or analysis of a particular drama series is beyond the scope of this chapter. What follows is thus a set of general observations that are derived from ongoing research and published materials.[8]

Those TV dramas that are successfully exported are the overwhelmingly romantic ones set in urban areas. For example, Japanese trendy dramas have typical romance and melodramatic narratives, featuring beautiful young professionals living on their own in well appointed apartments, and dining and shopping regularly in upscale establishments in the most trendy consumption districts in and around the major cities such as Tokyo or Osaka. In contrast, Korean TV dramas tend to feature characters of a younger age group, including characters in their late teens who are still in school. Therefore, the institution of the family continues to feature prominently in these dramas, although the same demand for beautiful actors and actresses applies. The different framings have drawn different audiences. Japanese trendy dramas tend to have younger audiences than the more family-based, if not family-oriented,

Korean dramas, which have a large number of middle-aged housewives as fans. One can observe generally that the trials and tribulations of urban living are intimately familiar to and, therefore, easy to identify with for the largely urban audience throughout East Asia.

However, consumers of imported TV dramas not only desire to watch the 'familiar', but also 'foreignness', which is a very significant part of the viewing pleasure. Viewing pleasure is significantly derived from looking at a different 'world', distinct from one's mundane routines. This is more than the conventional understanding of watching TV dramas as being escapist or based on fantasy—watching imported dramas is a vicarious entry into the lives of foreigners which can be contrasted with our own. In many East Asian locations, this implicit comparison derived from TV watching is recognized in the frequently expressed 'fear' of unwholesome influences of American TV programmes on local populations; American TV is almost always cited as a source of value corruption in the cultural-political discourse in Asia. Television dramas from Asian producers are seldom tarred with similar accusations but are not entirely exempt.

As foreignness gives pleasure, foreignness must be recognizable to the audience. Language can, of course, serve as a marker of foreignness; however, dubbing destabilizes it for this purpose. The most reliable marker of foreignness is outdoor scenery. Given the relative similarity of East Asian physiognomy, it is very difficult to identify the source of a TV drama from an indoor, close-up sequence, unless one is familiar with the actors and actresses themselves. Consequently, a very large part of TV dramas are shot outdoors at sites with widely known icons of the city, for example, the Tokyo Tower. Or, in a less obvious manner, the writings on the ubiquitous urban sign boards, including names of shops and restaurants, such as Korean scripts on neon signs on buildings, which signify the 'national' in the drama. These sceneries transport the audience into a 'foreign' space and place; together they constitute a mode of 'visual tourism'. Indeed, the audience becomes so enamoured by the on-screen locations that it is but a short step for tourist agencies to transform 'screen-sights' to 'tourist-sites'.

At the peak of their popularity, Taiwanese and Singaporean tourist companies routinely organized tours to the sites featured in Japanese trendy dramas (Lee 2004). Similarly, since the late 1990s, South Korean tourist agencies have been featuring locations (for example,

Jeju Island) where popular drama series are shot on their posters as vacation destinations. Korean TV dramas have outperformed every conceivable contributing cultural element in promoting Korean tourism. The snow scenes in *Winter Sonata* have contributed greatly to sell Korea as a winter holiday destination—especially with its ski resorts— to Singaporeans, for whom due to living in the permanent tropical heat, snow is intrinsically 'romantic' and the layering of clothes to keep warm a 'fashion' statement. *Winter Sonata* has radically transformed Korea from a business and sex-tourism site for Japanese men to a 'cultural' tour destination for Japanese middle-aged women and families, who like visiting the sites where the drama series was shot.

At a more conceptual level, the popularity of urban romance with a high capitalist-consumerist culture appears to have a larger underlying logic. An important element that analyses of cross-border consumption have found is the relative degree of 'capitalist modernization' of a location within East Asia. Different countries can be placed loosely on a continuum of developing to developed capitalist economies. At the apex of capitalist economic development is, of course, Japan. At the other end would be the PRC or other parts of Southeast Asia. In the middle are Singapore, Taiwan, Hong Kong and Korea, which are comparable in their positions in global capitalism. This three level structure appears to structure the 'identification' of imported TV dramas to audiences at different locations.

Japanese TV dramas have penetrated every market in Asia. These narratives of urban romances, with beautiful male and female actors cast as young professionals, with the most upscale consumerist lifestyles, away from the constraints of families, is a world that is deeply desired by audiences located where advanced consumer culture is absent. Thus for the Vietnamese youth, Japanese TV dramas provide an imaginary future that they aim to achieve (Thomas 2002). Similarly, for Taiwanese youth, 'metropolitan Tokyo is represented as the locus where the individuals pursue freedom, love and careers; the imagery of "Tokyo" is a *visual place* that mediates between reality and dreams' (Ko 2004: 123, emphasis original). From their context of living with their families until marriage, due to the government's pro-family housing policy, the young Singaporean audience desires the independent, high consumption lifestyles projected in Japanese trendy dramas. One can thus generalize these observations as: the audience in Asian locations, which are economically 'behind' Japan, consume Japanese TV dramas through a 'desire for the future'. Here, the actual contact with the 'real' Japan, as through the drama-tours, often has a sobering effect, which has more than one outcome. It can either reduce or intensify a fan-tourist's desire for the future imagined through Japanese consumerist modernity (Lee 2004).

Conversely, standing at the apex of economic development, the Japanese audience tends to treat all imported pop cultures from the rest of East Asia as being from 'less developed' places, where 'Japan used to be'. The narratives and characters on screen are thus viewed by the Japanese audience as 'reminders' of 'Japan's past', as narratives of a time when Japan was full of energy in forging its future. Popular TV dramas imported from the rest of Asia, which show the energetic struggles of people to achieve a better life, thus, evoke a sense of 'nostalgia' among the Japanese audience for 'their lost purity, energy and dreams' (Iwabuchi 2004: 154).

This nostalgia takes on a more personal note in the case of Japanese consumption of Korean TV dramas. The structure of sentiment is less about the Japanese nation's loss of its economic vitality and more about the personal loss of love and concern towards family members. Middle-aged housewives, who form the majority of the fans of *Winter Sonata*, turned up in the thousands at the airport on the arrival of the male star of the show, Bae Yung Jun, and created an instant media event.[9] They claim to be attracted by the simple and single-mindedness of the love between the two main on-screen characters, and by the care and concern of every on-screen character towards each other, regardless of the complexities and difficulties in their familial and romantic relationships.[10] They lament not only their own lost love and youth but also of a Japan that has become too capitalist and 'western' to retain the personal sentiments so apparently and abundantly portrayed in Korean TV dramas.

The structure of identification is more complex when the local audience does not concede to being 'behind' or 'ahead' of but 'coeval' with the capitalist economic culture of the location that produced the imported TV drama. Reception tends to be a mixture of sentiments, alternating between identification and distancing, between 'like us' and 'unlike us', depending on the context on screen. Significantly, there is a general tendency for audience identification to be elevated to a higher level of abstraction beyond nationality and local culture. Moments of identification are often rendered either as 'we are all humans' and, therefore, I can identify with the on-screen character, or 'as an Asian' I can understand why the on-screen character acts as he/she does. Conversely, moments of distancing, of 'unlike us', tend to be framed in nationalist-cultural terms, for example, 'that is typical of Korean male chauvinism', unlike us. Overall there is perhaps much less emotional and intellectual engagement with the drama text, and the audience regards it as 'just entertainment'.

If the structure of identification and distancing by an 'in situ' audience at different locations with on-screen characters and narratives of TV dramas has a logical structure that is constructed on a continuum on the road to capitalist modernization, and if the viewing of imported TV dramas contributes to the formation of self-identity, then, the identity of the audience is one of a participant in the modern capitalist consumerist culture, rather than in the nationalist culture of the production locations, which would have, for instance, involved being 'Koreanized' or 'Japanized'.

COMMUNITY

Questions around emergent identity among media consumers are not only of academic interest but also 'nationalist' cultural interest. For example, given the US dominance in global media entertainment, almost every location in Asia has some discursive version of 'anti-Americanism' in local media-and-ideology debates. Such a moralizing discourse is best seen as serving the narrow interests of the nationalist-cultural industry players and conservative nationalist politicians, or other conservative moral gate-keepers who would like to shut the gate on globalizing pop cultural tendencies. My own position is that such concerns with 'identity' are too simplistic. Identity formation is substantively an unending process in which different sources and inputs layer and interact with each other to result in an 'identity' that is always multiple and complex. Although the earliest cultural socialization might be more foundational, it is by no means hegemonic to the point of reducing and simplifying the identity to a single dimension. All claims to 'single' dimension identity are made for political and ideological purposes rather than being reflective of identity as such. In the case of pop culture consumption, both the products and consumer affections are short-lived and ephemeral, changing rapidly with the latest trends and icons, such that any suggestion of 'identity' formation based on pop culture consumption is unavoidably far-fetched.

While the impact of pop culture consumption on identity may be over exaggerated, identification with an artiste, a particular TV drama or a particular genre is always a possibility. This is reflected in the establishment of fan clubs which are essentially communities of consumers who share affections for a particular artiste or a genre of programmes. However, a pop culture may be considered 'popular' when it has a wide reach into the consumer market beyond avid aficionados. The large number and geographically widely dispersed consumers potentially constitute an 'imagined' community of consumers of a particular pop culture item. Beyond the fan clubs, consumption is the only qualification for 'membership' in this potential 'community of consumers'. Neither the individual nor the community at large is subjected to any institutional authority nor bounded by geographic boundaries. Its 'composition' is transnational and transcultural. Nevertheless, it is not completely without public social and cultural institutions, which assist in its realization and manifestation.

Among the public institutions that make visible and thus enable the realization of the potential community of consumers are the different constituent parts of the media industry, such as newspapers and lifestyle magazines. Take the entertainment section of any newspaper in East Asia as an illustration. The page-space can be conceptualized as a 'community' space for the entire East Asian pop culture industry. Geographically, this community space is defined by the places that appear regularly in the page-space, namely, the production centres of East Asian pop culture—Seoul, Tokyo, Shanghai, Beijing, Hong Kong, Taipei and, very occasionally, Singapore. The page-space is peopled daily with images and information of artistes from these cities: the likes of Bae Yung Jun in Seoul, Faye Wong in Shanghai, Wong Kai Wei in Hong Kong and Jay Chou in Taipei. The artistes inhabit the page-space at irregular intervals, more frequently in the rising phases of their careers, with diminishing presence when they are on the way out. Outside the pages are the readers, who are not necessarily known to each other, let alone regularly engage each other in face-to-face interactions. A 'community of consumers' is instantly manifest should two or more readers who happen to be present at an occasion/event, as part of free flowing conversation, exchange comments on the artistes reported in the pages. Such instances demonstrate the 'community of consumers' of East Asian pop culture as an 'occasioned' and 'occasional' community, befitting the practices of the overwhelming majority of consumers, where consumption is leisure and entertainment, rather than a primary focus of everyday life.[11]

However, the presence of fan clubs suggests that pop culture consumption can be of greater consuming passion than an occasional leisure activity that fills out the day. Avid consumers often seek ways to intensify the pleasure of consumption through active exchanges and engagements with others similarly disposed, using whatever means at their disposal. In the contemporary world, the Internet, the latest transnational communication technology, has been harnessed for this purpose. As mentioned earlier, Japanese TV drama producers are often disinterested in marketing their products in the rest of East Asia for a number of reasons, including the weakness of intellectual property rights protection in these areas, but primarily because the domestic market is sufficiently profitable. This creates frustration among fans in the region, who are impatient in their desire to get the weekly broadcast episode of a popular series. As recounted by Hu (2005: 177–78), the following is a summary of what happened to the series *Pride*:

> In January 2004, a Hong Kong fan, R, who is a skilled Japanese speaker, did the Chinese subtitling for *Pride*, a few days after the original broadcast in Japan. Her subtitling is an individual display of her mastery of language in articulation of her love for the drama. She thanks T and A for their supplies of the raw material, and online fans for their support and suggestions by constructing herself a fan persona, which interacts with those of other fans. Even when she made a mistake in the subtitling, she took care to insert a correction by thanking another fan for pointing out the mistake.

Significantly, pirated businesses cannot compete with such immediacy since they usually copy a Japanese TV drama into a complete set of VCDs instead of selling each episode at a time. Furthermore, R's version of Chinese subtitling of *Pride* was so popular and widely circulated among Chinese fans through online circulation that it threatened the marketing of another version of *Pride* produced by a leading Taiwan-based pirated-Japanese-VCD company.

Obviously, there is nothing accidental or occasional with this online community in which a few language and technology savvy members take the lead in constantly and passionately doing the painstaking work of initiating and amending the translation/subtitling of their favourite drama series. All these activities are done for the benefit of the other members of the fan community in cyberspace, beyond the clutches of profit-oriented market players and the legal constraints of the nation-state, and without the necessity of face-to-face interactions that are conventionally seen as absolutely essential to the life of a 'community'. That there is a community is indubitable. Nevertheless, membership will always remain unstable and ever changing. As one fan grows out of it, a new one is voluntarily inducted in quick succession, often following the rise and fall of a particular artiste as a personal 'idol', through consumption of pop culture products, with no other qualifications required. The duration of 'fandom' is often too short and culturally ephemeral for it to contribute to the long process of self-identity formation.

CONCLUSION

In East Asia, production, circulation and consumption of media pop culture have become progressively integrated into one market network. Given the very significant differences in national histories, languages and local cultures within the region, intriguing questions of how this integration is achieved need to be posed. Although market economic considerations are fundamental, the integration of flows and consumption of media pop culture must be facilitated by social and cultural processes executed by the variously located audiences. To the extent that pop culture products have very short shelf-lives, analytic attention must be focused on these social and cultural processes rather than on specific cultural objects or particular artistes. In this chapter, I have attempted to analyze some aspects of the production, circulation and consumption of pop culture and the potential emergence of communities of consumers of such cultural products in the region. These aspects, by no means exhaustive, are nothing but building blocks of the total picture of the transnational and transcultural phenomenon, which needs to be mapped out through multi-sited collaborative research.

Notes

1. *All Men Are Brothers*, 1939, trans. by Pearl S. Buck. London: Metheun.
2. According to a successful Japanese trendy drama producer, trendy drama is "'package drama", which weighs the setting, cast and music more heavily than the content' and 'they would feature fashion, music and trendy places where [attractive young women who are the primary target audience] would want to go on a date' (Ota Toru in Iwabuchi 2004: 73).
3. The case of Kaneshiro Takeshi demonstrates the transnational and transcultural character of East Asian pop culture through his career across the region (Tsai 2005).
4. Beyond East Asian regional spaces, some of the East Asian artistes have reached international stardom and are able to draw global audiences, particularly in the lucrative English-speaking US market, for example, Jackie Chan's Hollywood action-comedy movies and the New York based Taiwanese director, Ang Lee, who won the Hollywood Academy Award for best director in 2006 for the American movie, *Brokeback Mountain*.
5. The ticket sales figures are obtained from *Straits Times* (Singapore), 6 April 2006.
6. It is interesting to note the politics of language in this multi-lingual Chinese community. This has been discussed in terms of the general issue of Chinese identity (Ang 2001; Chun 1996) and specifically in relation to pop culture consumption (Chua 2003).
7. A path breaking work is Ien Ang's (1985) analysis of the American prime time soap opera, *Dallas*.
8. Over the past few years, I have benefited from participation in several conferences focusing on East Asian pop culture such as the international conference on 'Feeling Asia's Modernities: TV Drama Consumption in East/Southeast Asia', International Christian University, Tokyo, 23–25 November 2001; Workshop on East Asian Pop Culture: Transnational Japanese and Korean TV Dramas, Asia Research Institute, National University of Singapore, 8–9 December 2004; and International Conference, Cultural Space and Public Space in Asia, Asia's Future Initiative and Institute of Communication Arts and Technology, Hallym University, 15–16 March 2006.
9. The popularity of Bae Yung Jun with middle class, middle-aged housewives have led to his being labelled in Singapore as an 'auntie slayer' and in Hong Kong and Taiwan as 'shi nai ou xiang' (middle-age women's idol)'.
10. The findings reported here are drawn from papers presented during the Workshop on East Asian Pop Culture: Transnational Japanese and Korean TV Dramas, Asia Research Institute, National University of Singapore, 8–9 December 2004. The papers are being prepared for publication.

11. The concept of the newspaper entertainment 'page-space' as imaginary geography of East Asian pop culture is developed in greater detail in another essay (see Chua 2006).

References

Ang, Ien. 1985. *Watching Dallas: Soap Opera and the Melodramatic Imagination*. London and New York: Methuen.

———. 2001. *On Not Speaking Chinese: Living between Asia and the West*. London: Routledge.

Chan, Ching-kiu Stephen. 2005. 'The Fighting Condition in Hong Kong Cinema: Local Icons and Cultural Antidotes for the Global Popular', in Meaghan Morris, Siu Leung Li and Stephen Chan (eds), *Hong Kong Connections: Transnational Imagination in Action Cinema*. Hong Kong and Durham: Hong Kong University Press and Duke University Press, pp. 63–80.

Chua Beng Huat. 2001. 'Pop Culture China', *Singapore Journal of Tropical Geography*, 22(2): 113–21.

———. 2003. 'Taiwan's Future/Singapore's Past: *Hokkien* Films in-between', in *Life is Not Complete without Shopping*. Singapore: Singapore University Press, pp. 156–76.

———. 2004. 'Conceptualizing an East Asian Popular Culture', *Inter-Asia Cultural Studies*, 5(2): 200–221.

———. 2006. 'Gossip About Stars: Newspapers and Pop Culture China', in Wanning Sun (ed.), *Media and the Chinese Diaspora: Community, Communication and Commerce*. London and New York: Routledge Curzon, pp. 75–90.

Chun, Allen. 1996. 'Fuck Chineseness: On the Ambiguities of Ethnicity as Culture and as Identity', *Boundary*, 23(2): 111–38.

Han, Seung Mi. 2000. 'Consuming the Modern: Globalizations, Things Japanese, and the Politics of Cultural Identity in Korea', *Journal of Pacific Asia*, 6: 7–26.

Hu, Kelly. 2005. 'The Power of Circulation: Digital Technologies and the Online Chinese Fans of Japanese TV Drama', *Inter-Asia Cultural Studies*, 6(2): 158–70.

Iwabuchi, Koichi. 2002. *Recentering Globalization: Popular Culture and Japanese Transnationalism*. Durham: Duke University Press.

———. 2004. 'Time and the Neighbour: Japanese Media Consumption of Asia in the 1990s', in K. Iwabuchi, S. Muecke and Mandy Thomas (eds), *Rogue Flows: Trans-Asian Cultural Traffic*. Hong Kong: Hong Kong University Press, pp. 151–74.

Kim, Hyun Mee. 2002. 'The Inflow of Japanese Culture and the Historical Construction of "Fandom" in South Korea'. Paper presented at the International Conference on Culture in the Age of Informatization: East Asia into 21st Century, Institute of East and West Studies, Yonsei University, Korea, 16 November.

Ko, Yu-fen. 2004. 'The Desired Form: Japanese Idol Dramas in Taiwan', in K. Iwabuchi (ed.), *Feeling Asian Modernities: Transnational Consumption of Japanese TV Dramas*. Hong Kong: Hong Kong University Press, pp. 107–28.

Lee, Ming-tsung. 2004. 'Travelling with Japanese TV Dramas: Cross-cultural Orienta-
   tion and the Flowing Identification of Contemporary Taiwanese Youth', in
   K. Iwabuchi (ed.), *Feeling Asian Modernities: Transnational Consumption of
   Japanese TV Dramas*. Hong Kong: Hong Kong University Press, pp. 129–54.
Lii, Ding-Tzann. 1998. 'A Colonized Empire: Reflections on the Expansion of Hong
   Kong Films in Asian Countries', in Chen Kuan-hsing (ed.), *Trajectories: Inter-Asia
   Cultural Studies*. London: Routledge, pp. 122–41.
Shim, Doboo. 2002. 'South Korean Media Industry in the 1990s and the Economic
   Crisis', *Prometheus*, 20: 337–50.
Streeter, Thomas. 2003. 'The Romantic Self and the Politics of Internet Commercial-
   ization', *Cultural Studies*, 17(5): 648–68.
Stringer, Julian. 2005. 'Introduction', in Chi-Yun Shin and Julian Stringer (eds), *New
   Korean Cinema*. Edinburgh: Edinburgh University Press, pp. 1–14.
Teo, Stephen. 2005. 'Wuxia Redux: Crouching Tiger, Hidden Dragon as a Model of Late
   Transnational Production', in Morris, Li and Chan (eds), *Hong Kong Connections:
   Transnational Imagination in Action Cinema*. Hong Kong and Durham: Hong
   Kong University Press and Duke University Press, pp. 191–204.
Thomas, Mandy. 2002. 'East Asian Cultural Traces in Post-socialist Vietnam', in Iwabuchi,
   Muecke and Thomas (eds), *Rogue Flows: Trans-Asian Cultural Traffic*. Hong Kong:
   Hong Kong University Press, pp. 177–96.
Tsai, Eva. 2005. 'Kanesiro Takeshi: Transnational Stardom and the Media and Cultural
   Industries in Asia's Global/Postcolonial Age', *Modern Chinese Literature and
   Culture*. 100–132.
Wilson, Rob. 2001. 'Korean Cinema on the Road to Globalization: Tracking Global/
   Local Dynamics or Why Im Kwan-Taek is Ang Lee', *Inter-Asia Cultural Studies*,
   2(2): 307–18.
Yau, Kinnia Shuk-ting. 2005. 'Interactions Between Japanese and Hong Kong Action
   Cinemas', in Meaghan Morris, Siu Leung Li and Stephen Chan Ching-kiu (eds),
   Hong Kong Connections: Transnational Imagination in Action Cinema. Hong Kong
   and Durham, Hong Kong University Press and Duke University Press, pp. 35–48.

11

Sex, Television and the
Middle Class in China

JACQUELINE ELFICK

INTRODUCTION

You're foreign aren't you? Do you like 'Sex and the City', my friends
and I have watched every single episode?...Last year was great, my
world changed. I bought my first car, went on my first trip to Japan,
and had sex with a foreigner for the first time.... (Mei, 28 years)

These revealing comments were made at a barbecue at the beginning
of the Shenzhen fieldwork and immediately brought a number of
questions to mind. What kind of work does this young woman do?
How did this surprising level of sexual frankness come about? Was
the American television series *Sex and the City*, responsible? How
much sexual freedom does the average Chinese woman have? What
type of public discourse shapes it? And lastly, why did she categorize a
particular type of sexual experience together with purchasing a car
and travelling overseas?

Initially, Mei's micro-skirt, expensive designer bag and immaculate
grooming gave the impression that she was a high-end sex worker.

In Shenzhen, it is not unusual to meet sex workers and mistresses at private parties in people's homes. Prostitution was abolished when the People's Republic of China (PRC) was founded in 1949. However, the economic reforms introduced since the 1980s have seen a resurgence—it is estimated that China now has over five million male and female sex workers.

The main reasons for the revival of prostitution are economic. Young women from rural areas are attracted to urban areas by the higher living standards. Some of these women become sex workers with the aim of earning fast money so they can return home and start their own business. However, many women, having tasted sophisticated urban life that their wealth gives them access to, stay on permanently. Sex workers range from the mistresses of wealthy men to women who primarily have poor migrant workers as their clients.

As one of China's wealthiest cities, Shenzhen has a high number of sex workers. It was designated as one of the four special economic zones in the 1980s by Deng Xiaoping. Originally a fishing village, it has become an economic boomtown with a population of around 11 million. Shenzhen now has the fourth highest GDP in China after Shanghai, Beijing and Guangzhou.

Eventually, it transpired that Mei was not a high-end sex worker but an accountant with a multinational firm. The fieldwork subsequently revealed that Mei's comments were not unusual among a particular type of middle class women and in time I came to hear them frequently.

This chapter takes Mei's comments as its starting point and examines the relationship between consumption practices and social identity among young Chinese professionals. In particular, the role of television in establishing the consumption of sexual experience as a marker of middle class identity in China is examined. This is done by placing sexual behaviour and the extraordinary manner of recounting it, as encountered during the Shenzhen fieldwork, in the context of existing explanations for China's ongoing sexual revolution. Several explanations are examined, the most popular being the relaxation of sexual repression by the state.

This chapter argues that existing explanations for China's sexual revolution are insufficient to fully explain what was encountered during the Shenzhen fieldwork, and that other elements are at work. These elements are class formation, media and specific fieldwork location.

Much has been made of the link between economic reforms and sexual behaviour. The Chinese media teems with images of immoral women who willingly become sex workers for materialistic reasons. My research, like that of Farrer and Sun (2003), is grounded in the idea that not all sexual relations in urban China can be reduced to economic exchange. This chapter focuses on sexual behaviour that is non-commercial by nature.

The concept of sex as an experience that can be consumed by women is a relatively new concept in China. This chapter maintains that this notion is still evolving and is subscribed to by young professional women in China's large cities. Although the number of individuals who hold this belief is small, it is likely that it will be adopted by a larger number of individuals in the near future. As the middle class grows in China, more people aspire to join it and will adopt its values and behaviours.

THEORETICAL CONTEXT AND FOCUS

This chapter views modernity as an experience of multiple, often contradictory, epistemological styles. This approach builds upon the work of other scholars such as Liechty (2002) and aims to bridge the ethnographic gap between local experience and translocal cultural forces. It is especially concerned with how new ways of seeing the world— through goods, images and experiences—promote new ways of being in the world.

The broad theoretical context of the chapter is postmodernism, which maintains that consumption is a determinant of everyday life (Featherstone 1991). Mass media phenomena such as advertising have lead to an endless search for new experiences and sensations. A number of scholars have already examined the consumption of goods as communicators that signify taste and lifestyle (Bourdieu 1984). Rather than being simple utensils, material goods are consumed as communicators and are valued as signifiers of taste and lifestyle (Featherstone 1991).

Consumption has often been studied as an important way of reproducing class. Objects of consumption have always been used to culturally reproduce social identities (Slater 1997). The idea is that consumption patterns are deeply embedded in class habits and politics of distinction. In China, an ongoing process is resulting in the crumbling of the old class system based on the Party elite and workers, and a new class system is emerging that is largely based on individual wealth. China is still undergoing social transformation and will continue to do so for some time. As China's new social order is still evolving, consumption cannot be studied as a tool for reproducing existing classes. Instead, consumption should be viewed as a means of negotiating new social identities.

In China a new openness about sex has accompanied the economic reforms of the 1980s. Discussions regarding changing sexual attitudes and practices have become prominent features of popular culture. Sex in post-reform China has also been a popular topic for researchers. It has been studied through many lenses ranging from sexual attitudes and private morality (Farrer 2003) to sex and the elderly (Shea 2005). This chapter also focuses on sexual attitudes and behaviour but views these through the lenses of consumption and class formation.

RESEARCH METHODS

The chapter is based upon 38 in-depth interviews among middle class professionals conducted in Shenzhen in 2004 and 2005. These interviews are supplemented by socializing with informants and ongoing relationships with some of them, media reports and short interviews with 12 professionals including psychologists who have frequent contact with middle class individuals through their work. The chapter also draws on surveys of nearly 700 students and middle class professionals conducted in Beijing, Shanghai and Shenzhen between 2001 and 2005. It has four main sections apart from the introduction and conclusion:

1. Research findings
2. China's sexual revolution
3. Existing explanations for new sexual behaviour
4. Towards new explanations: (*a*) Class formation (*b*) Media (*c*) Shenzhen

RESEARCH FINDINGS

The initial aim of the Shenzhen fieldwork was to study the role of consumption practices and the mass media in forming social identities among young Chinese professionals, and to provide a detailed account of the practices that make up contemporary middle class life. Existing literature pointed to material goods as the key to understanding consumption (Douglas and Isherwood 1979). Bearing this in mind, fieldwork interviews were designed to focus on the acquirement or aspiration to acquire material goods such as houses and cars.

This focus changed during the course of the research when it became clear that female informants had another topic on their minds—the consumption of experiences. Interviews designed to elicit information about financial and career goals from young professional women, quickly turned into sessions where subjects proudly displayed their worldliness by recounting experiences that they described as modern, crazy, excessive or 'rock and roll lifestyle'. The following account is typical.

> I'm exhausted; I spent last night out with friends in a five star hotel. We were really crazy. We jumped up and danced on the bar and broke RMB 1,200 worth of bottles. It was all expensive imported alcohol. The barman said this had never happened before, he couldn't believe that women could do something like this. Look, here are the photos (shows photos in mobile phone). There were lots of guys watching me and my friends. One of them was cute so I went home with him, I can't remember his name though (Lilly, advertising executive, 32 years).

These accounts often had the following ingredients: behaviour that was considered novel or daring by mainstream standards, an exclusive location, the consumption of luxury items like alcohol or food, and sometimes sex.

Socializing with subjects revealed that many women engaged in one-upmanship in group situations. These exchanges centred on conspicuous consumption—the lavish dinner the night before, exotic holiday destinations, the exclusive location, and so on. An unspoken competition was taking place; the aim was to consume as many experiences as possible. Points were scored based on the type of experience, was it novel/modern/excessive, where it took place (overseas was best) and how much it cost.

I was constantly probed for information about my own recreational experiences in the West. What was it like to drink vodka in Iceland, had I driven a Ferrari, were French men good lovers, and so on. Many questions were related to sexual experiences. It was not unusual for subjects to ask long and detailed questions about subjects such as infidelity, homosexuality, specific types of unusual sexual activity and sexual experimentation. The assumption was made that as a foreigner, I would have experienced all these things.

My lack of expertise in all areas was disappointing to some individuals who, undeterred, directed their questions at other foreigners at social gatherings. It was not uncommon for subjects to ask visitors intimate questions related to unusual sexual practices within five minutes of being introduced. When stunned acquaintances were unable to answer these questions, subjects were very surprised. It was obvious that many subjects had a strong mental model of foreigners and that this was not being lived up to.

Women were not just interested in talking about hypersexual activity; many of them also practised it. Sexual experiences were like honour badges; the more you collected, the more status you had. Individuals sometimes boasted that they were more open-minded than western women,[1] even the female characters in Sex and the City.

Interestingly, many references were made to this television series when discussing sexual behaviour, marriage and career goals. Women often likened themselves to one of the four female characters or referred to a specific scene from a particular episode. All of the 38 subjects had watched at least half of the Sex in the City series and 29 had watched every episode. The series' sophisticated representations of the social and professional status of single women, as well as the dilemmas of independence, were clearly very appealing. The character that subjects liked the most in Sex and the City was Samantha, an attractive slightly older woman who scorns marriage and motherhood. Samantha prides herself on 'being like a man'—preferring sex to romance and afraid of commitment.

The Shenzhen fieldwork showed that a small group of young professional women strove to consume many types of new experiences, which they label using terms such as 'modern'; that sexual behaviour has changed dramatically; and that openness has become normal. The next section looks at China's unfolding sexual revolution.

China's Sexual Revolution

Chinese media brims with talk of the nation's new sexual revolution, ranging from a lament about the decline in morals to pride in the new liberal attitudes towards sex. Everyone appears to have an opinion about sex—whether it is psychologists dispensing advice on phone-in radio shows or private citizens venting in chat rooms.

Pre-reform Views of Marriage and Sex

Traditionally, marriage was almost universal in China. Sex only took place within marriage for the purpose of having children. Marriage was viewed as an economic transaction and was arranged by the parents according to the social rules of that time. Sex was seen as threatening to the power structure of the family. The most important social ties were based on filial piety. Strong sexual ties between husband and wife were discouraged as they could possibly undermine the important relationship between the man and his parents.

After the establishment of the PRC in 1949, the state identified sexuality as a site of political control (Evans 1995). It applied a code of normative sexual and gender expectations to sexuality that was legitimized by pseudo-scientific authority. The 'technology of sex' (Foucault 1978) was a means of ordering marital, familial and social relationships. It was achieved through a variety of medical, social and political discourses. Arranged marriages were outlawed and the only form of marriage recognized was that based on the free choice of partner. Concubinage and prostitution were also prohibited and divorce was made easier. In this period, sexual behaviour and romantic love were deemed to be 'shamefully illicit or as a manifestation of bourgeois idealism and thus detrimental to collective welfare' (Evans 1995).

During the Cultural Revolution, any expression of sexuality was repressed. Men and women wore the same types of clothes and any attention paid to one's physical appearance like elaborate hair and make-up was viewed as bourgeois. Sex education was limited to official government pamphlets, contraceptive information (restricted to married women) and regular Party pronouncements on morality. Outside these official discourses, all things sexual were perceived to be taboo. To summarize, all forms of overt sexuality were discouraged in pre-reform China. Men and women were usually segregated during group activities, and displays of public affection between couples were prohibited.

Recent Transformation of Sexual Practices

During the last two decades, sex has exploded into popular culture in China. Public discourse about sex can be found in magazines, newspapers, on the Internet, on television and radio programmes, and in government publications. The subject matter ranges from tips on how to be more seductive to advice for individuals who suspect their lovers are cheating on them. This new openness has its roots in the economic reforms that started in the 1980s. It represents far-reaching change and contrasts sharply with the secrecy surrounding sex during previous decades.

This openness in the media about sex has been accompanied by a transformation in sexual practices in urban areas. Although the countryside still remains conservative, premarital sex, extramarital affairs, cohabitation before marriage and casual sex have become increasingly common in large towns and cities. A growing number of young men and women subscribe to a new youth sex culture based on romance, leisure and free choice (Farrer 2002).

New Sexual Freedom and the State Agenda

Another interesting development has been the new sexual freedom for women. Traditionally women were viewed as passive second-class citizens whose place was in the home. The Confucian doctrine reinforced such ideas with teachings such as 'the virtue of a woman lies in the three obediences: obedience to the father, husband and son' and 'the virtue of a woman lies in the lack of talent'.

The only sexual activity that public morality permitted women to engage in was for reproductive purposes. A woman's primary duty was to produce a son to continue her husband's lineage and not doing so constituted grounds for divorce. Women were valued according to their fertility, ability to do household chores and chastity. Although Chinese society still expects women to take on supportive and self-sacrificing roles, less pressure is placed on women to marry in urban areas. The previous requirement of sexual purity on the part of women is less strict now. In urban areas, divorced women and women who live together with partners before marriage are no longer ostracized.

Chinese media takes an ambivalent stance towards female sexuality. On the one hand, local media often portrays sexually active women as money-hungry marriage wreckers or as psychologically unstable individuals who pose a danger to everyone. On the other hand, the same media revels in the new sexual freedom of women. During the past 12 months, the results of a number of sex surveys of Chinese women were published with great fanfare in national newspapers. These surveys claimed that 90 per cent of women students approved of pre-marital sex (*China Daily* 2004) and that Chinese women were lining up to test female Viagra (*People's Daily* 2004). Other articles reported that according to the '2003 Durex Global Sex Survey', globally males regard Chinese women as the most sexy in the world (*China Daily* 2004); and, that a new trend is emerging in some cities—divorces instigated by men whose wives have been unfaithful. This was previously unheard of and is seen as a reflection of the growing economic independence of women.

The state agenda concerning sexual behaviour is now largely confined to enforcing the one-child policy. The previous control of sexuality within the private sphere has almost completely disappeared. Pre-marital cohabitation has been enabled by changes in the household registration laws, which previously favoured married couples, and by revision of the marriage law. The old marriage law prohibited cohabitation with the opposite sex and adultery was punishable throughout the pre-reform era (Farrer 2003). It is now illegal only if an individual resides with someone of the opposite sex while married to a third party.

EXISTING EXPLANATIONS FOR
NEW SEXUAL BEHAVIOUR

The Chinese media, scholars and the public at large attribute the recent sexual revolution to a number of developments—all engendered by China's transition from a centrally planned economy to a market economy. These developments can be categorized into three basic types.

The first is political. The reform period was accompanied by the relaxation of regulation of many aspects of private life, including sexual behaviour. The traditional Chinese extended family declined; large-scale migration from rural to urban areas occurred; and small nuclear families emerged in urban apartments. All these factors led to the loss of social control (Pan 1993). It is interesting that the sexual revolution is sometimes compared to the country's economic reforms—'the country is in the midst of wholesale privatization'.

The second is economic. New market forces have brought about economic empowerment and greater individual freedom and choice, especially for women. Economic empowerment also means that a growing number of people now have access to foreign media content and to western values regarding love and sex. The Chinese themselves describe these changes as an 'opening up' in response to foreign influences and increased westernization (Farrer 2002).

The third is social. New individualism and personal liberation mean that Chinese society now has a greater tolerance toward sexual openness. Popular soap operas such as *Divorce Chinese Style* (*Zhongguoshi Lihun*), *Big Sister* (*Dajie*), *Mother-in-Law* (*Popo*) and *Romantic Things* (*Langman De Shi*) deal with topics such as infidelity and divorce and attribute their success to their relevance.

Farrer points out that communism provided much of the momentum for China's sexual revolution (2002). It was the gender equality promoted by the Party that helped pave the way to greater sexual freedom, especially for women.

TOWARDS NEW EXPLANATIONS

Class Formation

This chapter acknowledges the important role of market economics and foreign influence in the loosening of China's previously strict sexual morals. However, these elements alone are insufficient to account for the new sexual behaviour and ways of recounting it as encountered during the Shenzhen fieldwork. The chapter argues that other forces are at work—the most important being class formation.

After the establishment of the PRC, Mao eradicated pre-revolution social identity and divided society into four classes: the workers, the peasants, the petite bourgeoisie and the national-capitalists. Between 1952 and 1958, private ownership of productive assets was gradually eliminated (Whyte 1975 and Kraus 1981 cited in Bian 2002). Farming was collectivized and the urban economy was consolidated into the state. This state socialist economy engendered a rigid status hierarchy. The reform period has seen this fixed hierarchy transform into an open, evolving class system (Davis 2000).

Defining the Term 'Middle Class'

The middle class is often defined according to its relations to the means of production. Karl Marx used the relations of production to classify a society. Marx maintains that classes are political forces based on the relations of property and power. According to this vision, a society consists of two main classes, the rulers and the ruled. This chapter does not take this view. Instead, it defines the middle class according to the ability of individuals to access resources (Tomba 2004).

This chapter's definition of the new middle class is similar to the term 'salaried middle class' as commonly used in China. Middle class individuals can be characterized as home owners, highly educated and able to allocate substantial resources for education, and usually employed in positions that entail some level of responsibility—whether it be managerial, technical or administrative—in either the private or public sector. Middle class status and identity is increasingly shaped around a new set of collective interests, especially in their modes of consumption and access to resources.

China's Middle Class

Everyone is excited by the prospect of China's new middle class. Western nations widely expect China's middle class to regenerate flailing economies through its purchasing power and to be the agents of democracy. Ironically, the Chinese government expects this purchasing power of the new middle class to improve rather than undermine social and political stability. The creation of a highly consumer-oriented professional middle class has been an important objective of the economic reforms in recent years (Tomba 2004). Class is now largely determined by how individuals fare in a market-style economy. Occupational mobility has become a significant factor due to the newly emerging labour markets. Public policies, economic conditions and the allocation of resources have all contributed to the rapid upward socio-economic mobility of professionals.

Privatization of the Chinese economy and growing unemployment has meant downward mobility for much of the working class. Their working situation is no longer formalized as it once was. Job security has disappeared for most and guaranteed benefits are shrinking. Unlike the working class, well educated salaried professionals are in a good position to benefit from the state's efforts to create a consumer society. Cities such as Beijing, Shanghai and Shenzhen have benefited greatly from the influx of foreign investment and now have large populations of white collar workers.

Consumption and Middle Class Identity

With shifting social identities in China, people have become extremely class conscious. Consumption has become the single most important form of expressing social identity. Recreational activities are particularly significant. The type of recreation that a person engages in is viewed as an expression of his/her status and wealth. As such, young professionals are anxious to participate in as many recreational activities as they can afford.

Most subjects interviewed went out four–six evenings per week. Favourite activities were dining out, salsa classes, exercising at the gym, polishing public speaking skills at Toastmasters, singing Karaoke or dancing in nightclubs. Socializing on a week night until 2 a.m. was not rare. During the weekend, high-end night clubs are usually packed to maximum capacity until closing time at around 4 a.m.

Having a busy social schedule is imperative and no expense is spared. Salsa classes are around RMB 500 for 20 lessons and the membership of a fashionable downtown gym is usually RMB 400 per month for unlimited use. Most money is spent in nightclubs where drinks cost between RMB 20–40, which is expensive considering that an average professional salary is RMB 6,000 (€600) per month. Individuals often treat their friends by purchasing a whole bottle of spirits in a club for RMB 250.

New experiences that are seen as prestigious are attending classical music concerts; learning music, painting or other art forms; and visiting exhibitions, art galleries and museums. A new type of popular experience-based activity is visiting theme bars. These tend to be small establishments that educate their patrons in a specialized area—like wine or tea appreciation—by hosting events and providing supporting materials. The décor is specifically designed to reinforce the experience and experts are often invited to come and give talks. Theme bars are not limited to culinary experiences. Some focus on activities such as literature and handicrafts, and even psychological well-being.

Tourism is an essential middle class experience. Individuals travel to domestic destinations such as Beijing, Nanjing, Hangzhou, Suzhou and Xian. Enormous social prestige is derived from travelling overseas especially if done on an individual basis rather than as part of a tour group.

Bed Hopping and Middle Class Identity

People who drive good cars and travel abroad are open-minded. Most of them understand that women can enjoy sex too. It's not just something to please your husband. My parents don't know anything about romance and passion; they're from the countryside and didn't go to university. Everyone I know has had sex before marriage; some even have one night stands. None of them are ashamed of this, it's because they're well-educated. A taxi driver wouldn't share these same ideas (Jinlin, 32 years, PR associate).

The way subjects spoke of their professional and personal lives indicated that financial resources and the willingness to consume a wide variety of experiences enhance social status. Experiences, especially novel and unusual ones, are highly valued tokens that are proof of modern character traits such as open-mindedness and daring. It is interesting to note that these personal characteristics are being rewarded in China's new professional milieu, especially by foreign companies which have the most financially rewarding and prestigious jobs.

Informants relished recounting their sexual experiences. Women boasted about the number of sexual partners, variety of locations, unusual sexual practices, emotional indifference to sex partners and, in some cases, infidelity. Although these women were unmarried, some had steady partners whom they were unfaithful to. A favourite saying was 'what's outside the home is more attractive' (*jiawai caiqi piaopiao*). Significantly, subjects always pointed out that their experiences were extraordinary by Chinese standards.

Media

The Media in China

The media in China has functioned as the ideological apparatus of the state since 1949 and is referred to as the 'throat of the Party' in official publications. The reform period has seen a growing diversity in media content. This can be attributed to the following factors. First, state media is now largely expected to fund itself through advertising. In addition to promoting state policy, content also has to appeal to large audiences in order to secure advertising revenue. To this end, the state vigorously encourages competition between media outlets. Second, although the state has clearly defined restrictions relating to content in both state-owned and private media, new technologies such as text messaging mean that media control is increasingly less effective. Third, the Chinese media market has been opened, allowing the establishment of privately funded newspapers, magazines and websites—some of which are owned by foreign publishers.

A growing number of individuals have direct access to foreign media. People who live in the southern coastal cities are able to access Taiwanese and Hong Kong television and radio. This is done using short wave radio, a simple television antenna, cable television, which is available for a fee, and inexpensive satellite dishes. Residents in coastal cities often have relatives in Taiwan and Hong Kong who travel back and forth, bringing foreign magazines and newspapers with them. In addition to this, much of the foreign media content can be accessed via the Internet and the thriving trade in pirated DVD copies of films and television programmes. All of this means that the state is no longer the only source of public discourse.

The Allure of International Media

Access to foreign media content means that people now view Chinese media in a new light. Higher production budgets mean that foreign media content is often glossier and visually appealing. Most developed countries now have a film rating system that determines the suitability of a film for minors by categorizing films in terms of sex, violence and bad language. The lack of such a film rating system in China means that films have to be appropriate for all age groups including young children. Therefore, local film productions are very limited in their choice of topics.

Informants felt that international media content was more sophisticated, less condescending and more truthful than the Chinese media, whether state or privately owned. Chinese media is still considered as an instrument of the state or as being controlled by it. Foreign media is often viewed as inherently truthful, simply by nature of being foreign. This is especially the case with young professionals. This belief in foreign media is part of the growing cynicism towards the state.

Having experienced new forms of management and learnt new skills at work, young professionals are painfully aware of how inadequately the Chinese education system has prepared them for work in the new China. Skills like independent thinking, creative problem solving, being able to individually interpret information and the ability to work independently are not part of the national curriculum. Young professionals prize these skills as well as values such as open-mindedness, self-development and meritocracy. Life outside China as depicted in foreign media content is perceived to embody and encourage these skills and values.

Transnational Consumer Culture

Since the reform period began, the Chinese middle class have embraced transnational consumer culture. Visiting foreign fast food restaurants such as McDonald's and KFC are popular experiences. Many people prefer Hollywood to domestically produced films. Foreign goods are generally viewed as reliable, well-designed and innovative, and foreign media content is seen as exciting and untainted by state censorship. Those who can afford to consume foreign goods and experiences, invariably do. Although many people have yet to travel overseas, individuals go to great lengths to display their knowledge of global culture and values, whether it is through products they buy or values that they advocate. Linking oneself with transnational culture, whether it is through the consumption of foreign goods or experiences, yields status and implies sophistication.

This fondness of foreign things also extends to cultural events. Although the Spring Festival is universally observed in China, the urban middle class is now celebrating Christmas and Valentine's Day in growing numbers at the expense of some of the traditional celebrations such as the Dragon Boat Festival. Foreign goods and experiences are strongly linked with being modern. However, this does not mean that individuals are keen to emulate all western lifestyles and values.

New wealth, less stringent moral control by the state, open markets, and improved access to mass media and communication technologies may have enabled individuals to connect with a transnational consumer identity. Although urban, highly educated groups in many countries increasingly share common aspirations and beliefs, the transnational identity as described in this chapter is not homogeneous. In other words, it is not a single pre-existing identity complete with fixed values that is imported wholesale and unquestioningly from the West. Rather, it refers to a collection of local perceptions and interpretations of what transnational consumer culture is and what participation in it entails. In China, it is the middle class—especially highly paid professionals—who engage with aspects of transnational consumer culture, interpreting and transforming them in the process. The resulting beliefs and behaviours are then emulated by individuals who aspire to belong to its ranks.

The Role of Television

For the past six years, the middle class in China has had access to foreign content television programmes in the form of satellite television and pirated DVDs. Foreign programmes with explicit sexual themes such as *Sex and the City* have become common viewing in large cities and inspired tamer imitations such as *Pink Ladies (Fenhong Nulang)*. As mentioned earlier, informants frequently referred to *Sex and the City* when talking about sex or recounting their own recent exploits.

In contrast to the print media which leaves a lot to the imagination of the reader, television is distinctive because it presents fully envisaged situations. However, rather than just acting as a do-it-yourself (DIY) sex manual, *Sex and the City* had several important functions for the women that I interviewed.

First, the series portrayed the personal dilemmas of being a young educated single woman living on her own in a big city. Interview subjects could relate to this and treated the series as a self-help manual that could provide solutions to complicated problems, sexual and emotional, which were otherwise not being addressed. As one informant put it 'Americans have the Bible and we have *Sex and the City*.'

Second, it functioned as a template of how informants could lead their lives professionally. Women often discussed aspects of the series such as how much personal information you should reveal to colleagues, what to do if you were being bullied at work and how to handle sexual harassment in the workplace.

Third, *Sex and the City* spelled out in detail what being a glamorous transnational consumer entails. The four female characters in the series not only have an international perspective on shopping, clothes, food, men of many nationalities and the most fashionable places to holiday, but are also able to handle themselves confidently, whether in New York or Paris.

Many of the episodes in this series feature consumption. The four characters shop a lot, purchasing designer shoes, clothes and furniture on a regular basis. And, most importantly, the characters are open to new experiences—whether it is going to see a movie on one's own or participating in unusual sexual behaviour. One of the underlying messages that comes across is that being a modern single woman means not being overly concerned by what others think and having the confidence to try out as many new things as possible. By the end of the series, the four characters have racked up an astonishing breadth of culinary, recreational, emotional and sexual experiences.

This exposure to transnational consumer culture is also facilitated by other American television series such as *Friends*, and the numerous Japanese and Korean soap operas available on cable and pirate DVDs.

Subjects found *Sex and the City* appealing mainly because they could identify closely with the characters. In many cases, their most important relationships in Shenzhen were with other single professional women. They too had moved to a new city to pursue careers and, in doing so, left their social networks behind. This meant many lonely evenings after work unless you consciously filled your social agenda. However, leaving your social network behind meant that you were free to behave in any way you pleased.

Informants described the series as 'based on reality' unlike most of the locally produced copycat shows. The sexual revolution which is taking place in China's cities and its negative aspects—as faced by young single women on a daily basis, such as infidelity and unwanted pregnancies—are simply not reflected in Chinese television productions.

By referring to *Sex and the City* in conversations, subjects attempted to establish a common frame of reference that would make communication easier. By doing this, they also placed themselves in a sophisticated light by associating themselves with the glamorous transnational consumer identity as depicted in the series. These were Mei's intentions during our exchange at the barbecue. Grouping a particular type of sexual experience together with purchasing a car and travelling overseas was logical and made sense as these were all aspects of a type of transnational consumer identity that she wished to be linked with.

Television has played a significant role in establishing the consumption of sexual experiences as a marker of middle class identity. This has been achieved by introducing a transnational consumer culture with an emphasis on the consumption of goods and experiences, including sexual ones.

Shenzhen

Anonymity

Shenzhen is a new city and its original population of Cantonese speakers is minute. It is rare to meet people who are true locals. The majority of the city's inhabitants come from other places in China. People pour in from all over the country for work and many leave just after a few years, armed with new skills and valuable experiences. Shenzhen is unique in that it has a disproportionately large middle class. It is a city of aspiration and high achievers. Every year, tens of thousands of bright individuals arrive armed with university degrees, eventually leaving as polished middle class sophisticates. Although many of these individuals have lived in large cities while studying at universities, most have done so as poor students. Shenzhen is where careers start, earning power kicks in and upward mobility rules.

Most Shenzhen residents arrive in the city without their social network of family and friends. Many people leave the city after just a few years to set up a business in their home town or because their company transfers them. The lack of social networks and the transient nature of the population mean that there is very little social control. This relative anonymity means that people feel free to try out new social identities and experiences, and to behave in ways that they would not at home. Part of my initial suspicion that Mei was a high-end sex worker stemmed from previous occasions where acquaintances arrived at social functions with sex workers as their dates. These companions ranged from sophisticated young women, who drove expensive foreign cars and lived in luxury apartments, with no visible source of income, to handsome young men who worked full-time as live-in chauffeurs for wealthy older women. It was interesting that companions of this type were conspicuously absent when relatives came to town to visit.

Recklessness

The words that characterize much of young professional life in Shenzhen are recklessness and one-upmanship. People take pleasure in describing their own lives or that of people around them as excessive (*guofen*). Binge drinking, consumption of drugs such as ecstasy and amphetamine, and casual sex are common. Although these behaviours can be observed in other large Chinese cities, they occur in less extreme forms and are limited to small sections of the population.

Having studied conscientiously for years to get into prestigious universities and obtain good jobs, young professionals are out to enjoy themselves. As one foreign academic put it, 'Shenzhen is one non-stop freshman year'. People abscond from work, arrive late while still intoxicated or under the influence of drugs from the night before, poach clients from friends' companies and change jobs frequently. The reasons for job-hopping are higher wages, opportunities for career development, better prospects for promotion, a bad relationship with a superior at work and simple short-term thinking. Young professionals are not concerned with job security as they expect the economy to keep growing.

Job-hopping for just a slight wage increase is surprisingly common. Many individuals have large debts and have difficulty in curbing their spending. It is not unusual to have spent one's monthly salary within a fortnight of pay day. Disputes with friends and colleagues are often about borrowed money.

Class Formation

As mentioned earlier, consumption in China is a means of negotiating new social identities. It has become the single most important manner of expressing status and class. Shenzhen is a demographic anomaly. There are few elderly people and young children. It is a city where young adults come of age and transform themselves as they build their careers and make their fortunes. An absence of a traditional social hierarchy, on the one hand, and high salaries that facilitate conspicuous consumption, on the other, mean that the process of social mobility is accelerated here. As one of China's coastal cities near Hong Kong, Shenzhen has easy access to international media content and imagery of the transnational consumer identity described earlier. The elements of consumerism, class issues, media and transnational consumer identity, all combine to make the drama of class formation in Shenzhen especially intense.

CONCLUSION

The objective of this chapter was to examine the role of television in establishing the consumption of sexual experience as a marker of middle class identity in China. This was achieved by placing sexual behaviour and the extraordinary manner of recounting it, as discovered in Shenzhen, in the context of existing explanations for China's ongoing sexual revolution. These explanations were found to be insufficient when it came to fully explaining the responses of interview subjects. It was clear that there were other elements at work—class formation, media and fieldwork location.

First, research showed that the consumption of experiences served as a marker of middle class identity and that class formation sometimes took on extreme forms. Second, new media content has made a growing number of people in China aware of a type of transnational consumer identity. This identity emphasized the consumption of goods and experiences. Sex, rather than being the result of years of sexual repression by the state, is just one of many experiences that can be consumed. Being linked with this social identity implies status and sophistication, and is something that many middle class professionals in China aspire to. Third, the special type of sexual openness as encountered during the research is pronounced in Shenzhen where the drama of class formation and the presence of international media content are especially intense.

Note

1. Westerners are often perceived as promiscuous in China.

References

Appadurai, Arjun. 1996. *Modernity at Large: Cultural Dimensions of Globalization*. Minneapolis, Minnesota: University of Minnesota Press.

Bian Yanjie. 2002. 'Chinese Social Stratification and Social Mobility', *Annual Review of Sociology*, 28(1): 91–116.

Bo, Z. and G. Wenxiu. 1992. 'Sexuality in Urban China', *The Australian Journal of Chinese Affairs*, 28(July): 1–20.

Bourdieu, Pierre. 1984. *Distinction: A Social Critique of the Judgement of Taste*. Cambridge, MA: Harvard University Press.

Caplan, Pat (ed.). 1987. *The Cultural Construction of Sexuality*. London: Tavistock Publications.

Chao, Linda and Ramon H. Myers. 1998. 'China's Consumer Revolution: the 1990s and Beyond', *Journal of Contemporary China*, 7(18): 351–68.

China Daily. 2004. 'Durex Sex Survey Another Promotion Stunt', *China Daily,* 11 November.
————. 2004. '90% of Women Students Approve Premarital Sex: Survey', *China Daily,* 19 December.
Davis, Deborah S. (ed.). 2000. *The Consumer Revolution in Urban China.* Berkeley: University of California Press.
Diamant, Neil J. 2000. *Revolutionizing the Family: Politics, Love, and Divorce in Urban and Rural China, 1949–1968.* Berkeley: University of California Press.
Dikotter, Frank. 1995. *Sex, Culture and Modernity in China: Medical Science and the Construction of Sexual Identities in the Early Republican Period.* Hong Kong: Hong Kong University Press.
Douglas, Mary and Baron Isherwood. 1979. *The World of Goods: Towards Anthropology of Consumption.* London: Allen Lane.
Evans, Harriet. 1995. 'Defining Difference: The "Scientific" Construction of Sexuality and Gender in the People's Republic of China', *Signs,* 20(2): 357–94.
————. 1997. *Women and Sexuality in China: Female Sexuality and Gender Since 1949.* New York: Continuum.
Farrer, James. 2002. *Opening Up: Youth Sex Culture and Market Reform in Shanghai.* Chicago, London: University of Chicago Press.
Farrer, James and Sun Zhongxin. 2003. 'Extramarital Love in Shanghai', *The China Journal,* 50(July): 1–36.
Farquhar, Judith. 2002. *Appetites: Food and Sex in Post-Socialist China.* Durham, London: Duke University Press.
Featherstone, Mike. 1991. *Consumer Culture and Postmodernism.* London: Sage Publications.
Foucault, Michel. 1978. *The History of Sexuality,* Volume 1: An Introduction. New York: Pantheon.
Goodman, David S. 1999. 'The New Middle Class', in Merle Goldman and Roderick MacFacquhar (eds), *The Paradox of China's Post-Mao Reforms.* Cambridge: Cambridge University Press, pp. 241–61.
He Li. 2003. 'Middle Class: Friends or Foes to Beijing's New Leadership', *Journal of Chinese Political Science,* 8(1&2): 87–100.
Kraus, R. C. 1981. *Class and Class Conflict in Contemporary China.* New York: Columbia Univ. Press.
Liechty Mark. 2002. *Suitably Modern: Making Middle-Class Culture in a New Consumer Society.* Princeton, N.J.: Princeton University Press.
Larson, Wendy. 1999. 'Never So Wild: Sexing the Cultural Revolution', *Modern China,* 25(4): 423–50.
Link, Perry, Richard P. Madsen and Paul G. Pickowicz (eds). 2002. *Popular China: Unofficial Culture in a Globalizing Society.* Lanham: Rowman & Littlefield Publishers.
Pan, S.M. 1993. 'A Sex Revolution in Current China', *Journal of Psychology and Human Sexuality,* 6(2): 1–14.
People's Daily. 2004. 'Chinese Women Line Up to Test Female Viagra', *People's Daily,* 7 September.

Shea, Jeanne L. 2005. 'Sexual "Liberation" and the Older Woman in Contemporary Mainland China', *Modern China*, 31(1): 115–47.

Slater, Don. 1997. *Consumer Culture and Modernity*. Oxford, UK: Polity Press.

Tomba, Luigi. 2004. 'Creating an Urban Middle Class: Social Engineering in Beijing', *The China Journal*, 51: 1–26.

Whyte, MK. 1975. 'Inequality and Stratification in China', *China Quaterly*, 65: 684–711.

Yang, Mayfair Mei-Hui. 1999. 'From Gender Erasure to Gender Difference: State Feminism, Consumer Sexuality, and Women's Public Sphere in China', in Mayfair Mei-Hui Yang (ed.), *Spaces of Their Own: Women's Public Sphere in Transnational China*. Minneapolis: Univ. of Minnesota Press, pp. 35–67.

12

Aspirational Weddings: The Bridal Magazine and the Canons of 'Decent Marriage'*

PATRICIA UBEROI

THE PECUNIARY CULTURE AND CONSPICUOUS CONSUMPTION

Thorstein Veblen's *The Theory of the Leisure Class* (first published in 1899) merits re-reading. Discounting his flights of fancy—most painful for the anthropologist—on the historical evolution of mankind through the stages of peaceful barbarism to predatory modern times, or his curious bio-genetic theories of the contrasting roles of the *dolichocephalic-blond*, the *brachycephalic-brunette* and the *Mediterranean* types in the formation of the modern culture of 'pecuniary emulation' (1957 [1925]: 15), Veblen's description of the consolidation of 'the leisure class' as an economic institution rings uncannily true for the

* This chapter is part of a larger project on 'modern marriage' in post-liberalization India, looking at new sites for the renegotiation of the cultural meaning of conjugality. I am grateful to Anuja Agrawal, Christiane Brosius and Zoe Uberoi for help in locating sources, and to Sanjay Srivastava for his comments on an earlier draft of this chapter.

exploding market economies of India and China today, as it did over a
century ago for the US. 'The basis on which a good repute in any highly
organized industrial community ultimately rests', Veblen wrote (1957
[1925]: 84), 'is pecuniary strength; and the means of showing pecuniary
strength, and so of gaining or retaining a good name, are *leisure* (that is,
exemption from productive work) *and the conspicuous consumption of
goods*' (emphasis added). The common factor in both types of consumption, Veblen explained, was the principle of '*conspicuous waste*'. 'In the
one case it is a waste of time and effort, in the other a waste of goods.
Both are methods of demonstrating the possession of wealth, and the
two are conventionally accepted as equivalents' (ibid.: 85).

Veblen provided many wry examples of the typical 'pecuniary canons of taste' of the leisure class of his time—indeed, a lifestyle manual
of 'punctilious discrimination' in religious rituals and festivities, in
food and drinks and narcotics, in gems and ornaments, in dress and
fashion, in flowers, parks and gardens, in pedigreed pets, in expensive
hand-crafted goods, in sports and entertainment, and so on. He also
commented perspicaciously on the gendered division of labour in conspicuous consumption and waste, between the not-quite-top-drawer
middle class man, obliged to earn a living in some occupation, and his
wife who, through her conspicuous consumption of leisure and goods,
bears vicarious witness to his enviable economic and social status.[1]
But in all this, Veblen ignored what in the South Asian region is the
most visible site of conspicuous consumption and conspicuous waste—
weddings. The omission is curious—and *not only* from a South Asian
perspective, one might add—for marriages must surely have been great
occasions for status display and invidious competition in the American society of his day. But Veblen tucks away his only mention of
'weddings and funerals, and the like honorific events' (Veblen 1957
[1925]: 327) in a chapter otherwise concerned with *conspicuous piety*.
He is not alone in this neglect of the obvious, whether it be Vance
Packard's incisive analysis of 'the status seekers' in post-War America
(1959) or Pierre Bourdieu's very detailed description (1984 [1979]) of
the indices of social distinction and taste in France in the 1960s and
1970s (to name but two of the very influential contributors to the
science of social snobbery), and it is only comparatively recently that
feminist authors have sought to lift the veil of secrecy that envelops the
lavish 'white wedding' in late-capitalist society to reveal the symbolic-

ideological and material dimensions of the contemporary 'wedding industrial complex'.[2]

Throughout the colonial period in India, British administrators such as Sir Malcolm Darling, the celebrated author of *The Punjab Peasant in Prosperity and Debt* (1947 [1925]), had deplored the Indian peasantry's extravagant and improvident expenditure on marriages (as well as funerals and other social ceremonies), such that:

> [i]n a good year his [the cultivator's] ignorance and improvidence make him spend the whole of his surplus on marriages and festivities and his extravagance on such occasions often leads him even in good years to the doors of the money-lender. A ryot would stop at no extravagance in marrying one of his children or performing any funeral or social ceremony *to show more ostentation than his fellows* (quoted in Darling 1947: 52, emphasis added).

In the Punjab, where the sex ratio was woefully skewed in favour of males, Darling noted, the exorbitant costs of marriage included three components: (*i*) the cost of 'buying' a wife (for the peasantry), or of securing a high status and wealthy husband (for the well-off and the higher castes); (*ii*) the costs of the ceremonials and feasting; and (*iii*) the expenditure on jewellery (Darling 1947: 55–67). The latter expenditure, which he estimated as perhaps one-half to two-thirds of the total marriage expenditure, was what accounted for India's 'ceaseless absorption' of precious metals, such that 'the wealth that should have been the means of financing every kind of development has been largely applied to the adornment of ear, nose, neck, arm, ankle and wrist' (ibid.: 57). Education (especially for girls), new economic institutions and opportunities, and puritanical social reform movements *might* work to modify this passion for ornament, Darling hazarded cautiously; but, on the other hand, a longer term view supported the seemingly paradoxical proposition that *prosperity* was a major cause of extravagance and, in turn, of rural debt: 'The greatest cause of extravagance is prosperity', Darling concluded (ibid.: 67), and

> [i]t is this combination of prosperity and extravagance which helps to explain the high prices given for brides, the mass of gold converted every year into ornaments, the excessive prices paid for land,

the large consumption of liquor in the more prosperous districts, and the ever-increasing number of [law] suits.

In the ideology of the post-liberalized economic regime of India since the 1990s, habits of conspicuous consumption and competitive emulation and the incurring of debt on this account are no longer the moral issues that they were in Darling's day, when they were seen to simultaneously impoverish the hard-working peasantry and thwart the extractive designs of the colonial state. Nor—so long as the economy keeps growing and the taxman gets his cut—are they counter-posed against the goals of productive development, as they were during the first three or four decades after Indian Independence. Indeed, they are read now as both the measure and the motor of national development on a global scale, led by a burgeoning 'new' middle class of dedicated consumers.[3] As Satish Deshpande has written:

> If there is one class for whom the benefits of globalization seem to clearly outweigh the costs, it is the middle class, particularly its upper (managerial-professional) segment. This class segment is today interpellated by globalization in the same (or perhaps more intense) way that, a generation or two ago, it identified itself with development. Indeed, much of the celebratory rhetoric about globalization emanates from and is aimed at this group. Having consolidated its social, economic and political standing on the basis of the developmental state, this group is now ready to kick it away as the ladder it no longer needs (1997: 310).

For this emerging and growing class, as for those lower down on the social ladder who seek to emulate them, weddings (though not perhaps funerals, these days) continue to be, as they were in Darling's time, a most important site for staking claims to social and economic—not to say *political*—status, as well as for the staging of major 'lifestyle' exhibitions. The anti-dowry legislation, initially instituted in 1960, and the 'guest control' orders of the Emergency period (1975–77), always flouted more than honoured, appear increasingly and quixotically irrelevant: what is the use of wealth unless it is spent, and spent conspicuously? But in weddings now, as in all else, the crucial question from the perspective of social reckoning is not only *how much* is spent, though size certainly does matter, but *in what way* it is spent—a question of *taste*.[4]

This chapter is concerned with one small domain for the cultivation of national taste in the matter of wedding celebrations—the Indian 'bridal magazine'. It should be emphasized, however, that this exercise is not only about the differentiation of class fragments through distinctions of taste in the goods and services pertaining to weddings, and the converse obliteration of all but the faintest traces of the caste system, which provided the traditional basis of Hindu social hierarchy.[5] It is also, simultaneously, about the negotiation of ethnic identity on a national scale, the assertion of national identity on a global stage, and the remaking of gender and family relations under the regime of economic liberalization. It is the latter concern—specifically, the active renegotiation of the meaning of marriage—that will be our special focus here.

THE INDIAN BRIDAL MAGAZINE

A prominent feature of the post-liberalization media scene in India since the 1990s has been the growth in the number of glossy magazines available throughout the country, whether these be expensive imported magazines, the cheaper Indian editions of foreign magazines, or magazines published in India to international standards for local sale or export. Originally identified as 'niche' magazines for market segments that were neglected in the staple, run-of-the mill news, women's, film and sports magazines, such magazines are now touted as 'lifestyle' magazines, providing new 'canons of taste' for those aspiring to attain or maintain grounds of social distinction vis-à-vis their neighbours. Indeed, so great is the appeal of lifestyle magazines (or so remunerative their advertising revenues), that many newsmagazines are now themselves partnered by lifestyle supplements, and even the daily newspapers—already revamped to publicize the social shenanigans of the rich and famous at home and abroad—have added new lifestyle pull-outs devoted to travel, cuisine, entertainment, leisure, décor, fashion, health, beauty, shopping, and so on. The bridal magazine typically incorporates all these features, in specific relation to weddings.

Of course, women's magazines in India (as elsewhere) have always devoted considerable attention to weddings and bridal costumes. But there is a difference. First, the new bridal magazines are *themselves* markers of social distinction, being relatively expensive objects of visual attraction and consumption. (This is particularly true of the glossy South Asian bridal magazines produced abroad.) Second, as remarked, they double as lifestyle magazines—as guides to the discriminating purchase, tasteful display or motivated gifting of elegant market commodities, or to the pursuit of travel, adventure and leisure activities. Third, they are an aspect of an emerging service industry, known as 'event management', in which—and this is not widely advertised—the wedding industry is a major, perhaps *the* major, component (see Trehan 2004).

This latter feature calls for some comment. Until relatively recently, to present a rather over-simplified picture, weddings were largely a family and community affair, the main events of which were held at the family homes of the brides and grooms. Senior family members (especially women) and community elders, according to status and ability, were in charge of matchmaking, hospitality and ceremonies, assisted by ritual and caste-based specialists, along with professional caterers, providers of 'tents', furniture and equipment, photographers and videographers, wedding bands and musicians, and so on. These various roles, functions and services have gradually been professionalized, commercialized and centralized (cf. Kaur 2004; Trehan 2004). 'Banquet halls' and hotels now provide a range of wedding services under one roof, while event management firms make a business of coordinating the many separate ritual and ceremonial activities that are involved in the staging of a socially notable wedding. This industrialization of the marriage business is no doubt connected with the multiplication of public occasions of display now associated with weddings (some five to seven functions may be expected, some of them almost rivalling the scale of the actual marriage reception); with the influence of popular cinema and television portrayals of marriages;[6] as well as with the social and spatial mobility of the professional Indian middle class and its increasingly transnational location across continents.

The overall format of the bridal magazine is fairly standardized globally and, following the general formula of the global publishing industry,[7] many features appear to be translations or transpositions of materials from international bridal magazines, well- or ill-adapted to local tastes and expectations. In the Chinese and Indian 'bridals' that I have looked at, many of the advertisements are for international brands of luxury items—cosmetics, perfumes, jewellery, watches, cars, and so on—often advertised by Caucasian models against international backdrops. Chinese brides dress up in white, Victorian-styled bridal gowns and veils for their wedding photographs (though white is traditionally the *funeral* colour in China), and Indian couples are invited to shop for romantic 'honeymoon packages', indicating the consolidation of the conjugal 'couple' rather than the incorporation of the new bride into her husband's lineage (which is the central emphasis in traditional South Asian marriage rituals). Such transformations suggest the emergence, at least for the more affluent classes, of a new, global culture of conjugality, supplemented by authorized local touches. The reality, as this chapter will seek to indicate, is rather more complex. Global models are not so easily domesticated, and pleasurable fantasy worlds are compromised by not-so-pleasurable realities that refuse to go away.

There are quite a number of Indian bridal/wedding magazines available in the market today, jostling for attention with 'Asian' bridal magazines from UK and Pakistan—the former rather expensive by Indian standards, the latter the subject of fervent voyeurism (if one goes by the sales talk of the local vendor). There are, of course, differences of style and emphasis between them but, as local variants of bridal magazines produced elsewhere, they follow a rather similar format in presentation and content. They are, first of all, typical 'glossies', meaning that visual display (in features and advertisements) predominates over text, with design, production values and visuals to international standards. All are priced in rupees, dollars and pounds sterling, suggesting that, as with many big-banner popular films since the early 1990s, the Non-Resident Indian (NRI) market is kept high in mind. Fashion and jewellery are especially showcased including the designs of the best-known Indian fashion designers who clearly continue to earn their bread-and-butter in bridal trousseaus and other wedding attire. Furniture, décor and home-making features are prominent—reportedly, a deliberate choice on the part of the publishers, who see these features as ensuring a longer shelf life as well as attracting a wider audience for the bridal magazine. Gift-giving is highlighted as an important social activity requiring discrimination and continued alertness to new, unusual and exclusive 'gift ideas'—not only for brides and grooms, it might be said, but even for 'grandmothers'. Product prices, especially of designer wear and high-end jewellery and accessories, are typically huge (a wedding outfit can easily cost as much as a new car[8]), though this may well be true of wedding-related items globally: sometimes a certain coy mystery is added by the words 'price on request'. 'Wedding planning', logistic and financial, is a stock feature, repeated in every issue: it is meant to take the 'stress' out of the event. Some attention is also given to food and feasting—with mouth-watering recipes to match—and to the layout of banquets. Health and beauty sections (especially the latter) are robust, and travel and tourism are incorporated through magazine sections on exotic/romantic 'honeymoon destinations' in India and abroad. By the international standards of bridal magazines, it seems that Indian grooms are comparatively well attended to—in fashion, accessories, gifts and (let us not pun) even grooming.

In seeking to tease out the many social meanings that are imbricated in the Indian bridal magazine, I will take up a particular instance, the magazine *Bride and Home* (*B&H*, subtitled 'The Magazine for Indian Brides'), which was launched at the end of 1997 as 'India's first bridal magazine'. Indeed, it was the entrepreneurial talent of its founders that recognized and labelled this market segment as a 'niche' to be exploited, thereby professionalizing a domain of social and ritual activity that, as noted, had previously been largely a family and community (and in this sense relatively *private*) affair. I will first attempt to decode *Bride and Home*'s inaugural editorial, and the promotional material that accompanied its high profile launch as a 'niche' and 'lifestyle' magazine produced for both a local and a transnational clientele, paying attention to positive statements of intention, as well as to silences and erasures. I will then follow *B&H* through to its aptly titled and celebratory 'first anniversary' issue by which time, in response to readers' queries and feedback, some of the areas of silence and repression were finally and frontally addressed. Clearly, the intervening period was a story of struggle over the meaning of marriage which, judging by readers' responses, could not after all be reduced to a mere shopping list of aspirational luxury and lifestyle commodities. In fact, *B&H* readers were actively pleading for addressing 'relationships'.

In analyzing and interpreting this material from the perspective of the sociology of the family, I did not, I must confess, find the standard anthropological and sociological literature on Indian marriage very helpful. Despite the wealth of ethnographic material on lifecycle rituals, ceremonial gift-giving, matchmaking and affinal relations, there is near silence on 'modern marriage' as this is presented in the idiom of the Indian bridal magazine (cf. Ingraham 1999: 3). Conversely, the magazine fails to address the themes on which Indian sociologists have lavished most attention. Instead, and in line with the orientation of this volume, I turn for inspiration to a recent ethnographic account of a comparable segment of the 'bridal industry' in contemporary Taiwan, Bonnie Adrian's *Framing the Bride: Globalizing Beauty and Romance in Taiwan's Bridal Industry* (2003),[9] which similarly seeks to interpret the unreal 'fantasy' world that the typical bridal magazine seeks to promote. Serendipitously, I was able to back up Adrian's Taiwan ethnography with some informal fieldwork in Taiwanese-owned bridal photography shops in Beijing's central shopping area on Qidan Road, from where I also acquired some glossy Chinese bridal magazines.[10]

READING BRIDE AND HOME

Bride and Home, begun with an initial investment of 1 crore rupees,[11] was reportedly modelled on the successful British bridal magazine *Brides and Setting up Home* and was published by a new company— Heathcliff Publications—expressly set up for the purpose.[12] Its editors were two young 'expatriate' women (so identified): one, a Peruvian-born London barrister and, the other, a British-bred NRI anthropologist-turned-real estate manager. The former was married to Arjun Oberoi, described as 'the scion' of the socially prominent Oberoi Hotels family,[13] and the latter, engaged to Oberoi's old school friend, was planning a 'traditional' wedding in historic/romantic Rajasthan. In a very short time in India, both young women had reportedly come to appreciate that, while 'marriage is one of the biggest social events in the calendar of an Indian family' and 'millions of Indian couples get married every year', there was still no dedicated magazine to advise them on how to go about it. Positioned as a 'niche' and 'lifestyle' magazine, *B&H* was pitched not only to an upper income group in the metros, with sufficient disposable income to afford the relatively expensive products advertised, but also to those who aspired to this style. It hoped to sell 20,000 copies in all the metros initially, and 50,000 by the end of the year, targeting the foreign (NRI) market in particular. The project was reportedly backed by preliminary market research with '30 or 40 women', which concluded that 'Indian women liked to read (articles) about India written by Indians, and would be willing to spend on a magazine that would give them a host of useful ideas on weddings, gifts to choose, how to plan their homes, and for practical tips on how to finance your home and car and so on'.[14] The initial issue advertised 'How to plan the perfect wedding', 'Heavenly jewellery', 'Bed essentials' (linen, that is, not sexual advice!),[15] 'Fabulous bridal fashion', 'Gift ideas', and 'Great honeymoon destinations'. An interesting feature was an astrological column by J.N. Sharma, providing not only detailed astrological predictions but also answers to readers' queries on matters connected with marriage ('when will I get married?', 'are we astrologically compatible?', and so on) and also, conspicuously, on careers.

B&H's inaugural editorial makes interesting reading, both for what it *says,* and also for what it *avoids saying.* Referring to the 50th anniversary of Indian Independence the same year, it begins by reminding its readers of the 'tremendous changes' that have been seen in India over the last several years, particularly in the media. India has finally come of age, and the mark of this maturity is the possibility of *choice.* 'There are now over 20 satellite channels to choose from', and a huge variety of glossy magazines on all manner of subjects—fashion, computers, cooking, travel, jewellery and lifestyle. In all this profusion, there was a 'surprising gap'—a 'wedding magazine'. I quote the remainder of the editorial in full:

Arranging a wedding in India has been traditionally a family affair, and so it should remain; but it is to offer choice that *Bride and Home* steps in and gives young couples a freedom to partake in the most important decision of their lives: marriage.

Dreams, wedding expectations and fears all come together as you begin to plan your wedding. It is both an adventure and a period of discovery for you as a couple, or as parents, to chart this special day of celebrations. Cultural and family wedding traditions, a breath-taking reception site, a colourful flower choice and a romantic honeymoon will already be on your 'must have' list, but much of what you will choose will come from your explorations over the next few months, as we bring you not only what is available or new, but what is right for you.

We endeavour to seek out and feature the very best of Indian weddings and homes; from fabulous wedding *lehengas* to stunning bridal jewellery, from exciting wedding venues to inspirational interiors. Different customs and religions will also be featured so as to cover India's extensive cultural diversity.

Bride and Home celebrates India's love of weddings and it is our hope that we will spark ideas for you wherever you are and put you in touch with the resources you need to convert your wedding dreams into a joyous occasion.[16]

There are a number of observations one might tease out of this inaugural statement. First, the editorial is explicitly framed in the neo-liberal vocabulary of *choice*. Being modern, being global, and now—at last—being Indian, means the *freedom to choose* in all spheres of consumption (Munshi 1997: 39–40). Lifestyle magazines can provide the information necessary to exercise that choice with taste, in emulation of those for whom discriminating consumption is *habitus*; they 'put you in touch with the resources you need' to transform aspirations into reality. Nonetheless, *B&H* is faced with a delicate situation in attempting to lay down the canons of national taste and pecuniary emulation, for in India marriage has 'traditionally' been a family and community affair: '*and so it should remain*', say the editors firmly. The conceptual challenge, therefore, is to redefine the boundaries between the localized, private and ritual aspects of marriage ceremonies and the public and secular domain and, as it were, drag more of the former into the latter (cf. Booth 2005: 207–08).

One way of doing this (in tribute to 'India's extensive cultural diversity') is ethnicization, that is, turning private ceremony into the ethnic display of different regional and religious marriage customs (cf. Kaur 2004: 118–19; Sheel 2005: 341–43). For the time being, this plurality is effectively 'ascribed', not 'achieved' (to mimic the sociologist's jargon); but ultimately the principle of choice can enable one to 'choose' an 'ethnic' wedding from a catalogue, for instance, *B&H* editor, Sanjit Dhillon (British-born Jat Sikh [?]) was planning to wed her Christian fiancé Matthew 'in the traditional way' in Rajasthan (Neemrana Fort, perhaps?), 'keeping the good old traditions alive', even as *B&H* offers 'refreshing new ideas for a honeymoon in Hawaii'. One may merely note here, alert to absences and erasures as well as positive and pre-scriptive statements, that 'caste' customs are not generally acknow-ledged,[17] though these are, ethnographically speaking, exceedingly well-documented—it appears that caste is not one of the 'good old traditions' that the architects of modern marriage wish to 'celebrate' and 'keep alive', even if it continues to be a significant *habitus* of their readers in real life.

Second, it is clear that the 'freedom' referred to in the inaugural homily is the freedom to choose the commercial products and services associated with marriage and *not* the freedom to choose the partner. In fact, spousal choice is a matter on which *B&H* is strangely silent, taking care, it would seem, neither to condemn nor applaud the hoary insti-tution of arranged marriage.[18] Indeed, the 'Wedding Album' section of the magazine, which features the 'real life weddings' of the socially prominent (political personages, royalty, big business families), has examples of both self-arranged marriages (often inter-community, inter-caste, inter-regional), and also arranged marriages that are, by all appearances, political and dynastic alliances and/or business mergers.

Third, it is not clear from the editorial who is the intended addressee, the privileged subject of the new freedom to choose. In western bridal magazines (and in the segment of the Chinese [PRC and Taiwan] bridal industry, to which we will refer shortly), the addressee is primarily *the bride*, and to some extent the affianced couple. In the opening issue of *B&H*, the bride is herself the cover attraction and prominently visible in features and advertisements,[19] but editorial address is *first* to the naturalized couple, now given 'a freedom to partake in the most im-portant decision of their lives'. Then, as something of an afterthought (and risking some infelicity of expression), *B&H* addresses *the parents* as well as the couple, promising the parents, too, 'an adventure and a period of discovery...to chart this special day of celebrations'![20]

The privileging of the bride as the primary object of attention and visual attraction is a signature of bridal magazines globally,[21] but it is a phenomenon that nonetheless calls for interrogation, as several feminist writers have cautioned (Adrian 2003; Currie 1993; Ingraham 1999; Otnes and Pleck 2003). First, the bride's self-presentation is dependent on the transformative power of a 'makeover', a preparatory regimen of diet, exercise, weight-loss, and skin and hair care, and then professionally executed make-up for the wedding itself, to transform the 'girl-next-door' into a picture-perfect 'bride'. A Givenchy 'celebrity make-up artist' is called in 'to reveal some of his top beauty secrets and [make] up his first Indian bride exclusively for *Bride and Home*': being French, his philosophy is that '[i]t is love that makes [the bride] beautiful and not the make-up artist. She's the star and has to look like a dream, her face translucent, soft, and glowing', and she 'must always look young'.[22] Local artists ignore the rhetoric of 'love' and seek practical make-up formulae for different types of brides—'Kashmiri', 'Punjabi' and 'south Indian' (a proxy for skin colour from fair to dark).[23] It's nice, too, if grooms can *look*, and importantly *smell*, good on their wedding day.[24]

While the bride is the *nominal* addressee of the Indian bridal magazine, and the wedding *her* 'special day', the bride's struggle for recognition of her autonomous selfhood is manifest in several domains. For instance, in some, so-called 'orthodox', cases, she may not be consulted at all in the fixing of her marriage. In such an event, *B&H* advises that she could try to persuade her parents to let her get to know the young man in the hope that he may not be so bad after all; *but*, if she is financially dependent on her parents, she 'may have to concede to their wishes' and thence prepare to 'enter the marriage with an open mind'.[25] In the case of self-arranged or 'love' marriage, the woman's choice of spouse is also clearly constrained by parental approval on both sides. Thus, *B&H* warns young women seeking to marry in the face of parental hostility that 'your choice of partner will be your responsibility to carry through your marriage, and you will not be able to expect much support from your parents should your marriage fail later on.'[26] It also sympathizes with the parents of a young man who wants to marry a divorcee against their wishes: 'From their point of view', the adviser tells the young divorcee, 'you are not what they feel would be a suitable wife, given the fact that you failed to remain married to your husband'; her only hope is that her boyfriend will be able to persuade his parents 'that he loves [her] enough to want to marry [her] in spite of [her] failed previous marriage.'[27] Similarly, a bride-to-be has little say in the scale of wedding that her parents want to host for her: 'ultimately, it is your parent's decision what they want to spend', even if this is really beyond their means.[28] A young woman whose parents are planning an 'extravagant wedding' for her but who would really prefer a quiet and intimate ceremony is reminded of a number of compelling considerations:

> Your question very much depends on whether you are an only daughter. If you have other sisters, you can reason with your parents to arrange a big, elaborate wedding for them and let you have a simpler one. *Of course, this will have to be discussed with your future in-laws' agreement. Should you be the only daughter of your parents, you may have to concede to their wishes* (emphasis added).[29]

Indeed, the bride is regularly reminded that she is the instrument of relations of alliance between two families, and not an independent actor scripting her own destiny (cf. Uberoi 1998). The jewellery given to a young woman by her natal family, a token of a father's love, is also a currency in this marital exchange[30] as well as 'the ultimate aphrodisiac' in the context of conjugal intimacy.[31]

In one issue, however, *B&H* defended the personal autonomy of the bride—particularly if she was in paid employment—and the autonomy of the couple vis-à-vis the larger family. This was the question of individual and joint financial assets. The second issue of *B&H* contained a feature on 'Home Loans', and the following issue a feature on 'Car Loans'. Numerous features advised young couples on setting up house and elegant interior decoration. And a year down the track, in response to readers' demands, an article in the 'Couple counsel' section, 'My money, your money',[32] tackled the money issue in a conjugal relation head-on:

> Unlike our mothers, who would have died of shame (rather) than raise the M word before marriage, many couples now discuss the nitty-gritty, the bread-and-butter details, before they step into matrimony....
>
> In this age of working women and decreasing happily-ever-after marriages, 'My money, your money' is a big issue. Women want separate accounts, clear divisions as well as joint assets. Smart couples

are realizing that it is important to achieve some clarity about money equations and learn ways of managing matrimonial finances.

Taking a cautious stand on the advisability of setting up of joint accounts,[33] the general advice was a three-way division of earnings— into household expenditures, savings and personal expenditure— but there was no suggestion at all that the couple would be expected to pool all or most of their earnings in the joint family fund, as is commonly reported in ethnographies (cf. Sharma 1986; Singh and Uberoi 1994).

SILENCES AND DISSONANCES

As we have seen, the main and stated purpose of *B&H* was to offer young couples (and their parents) 'choice' with respect to the goods and services required to stage a socially notable wedding, in effect substituting family 'custom' in this respect with orientation to the rapidly expanding consumer market for luxury goods. Judging by the published readers' letters[34] and the efflorescence of wedding magazines and bridal exhibitions that followed in the wake of *B&H*, the magazine did indeed succeed in its objective. Readers were appreciative of the magazine's glossy get-up, appropriate to the status-enhancing business of marriage. Sometimes they requested the expansion of certain features (the honeymoon section was obviously a great hit), address to issues that were neglected (banqueting was initially one of these) and information on stockists of display items in their region (*B&H* was originally strongly Delhi-centric). There were a number of complaints that the goods on display were excessively expensive: 'I enjoy reading your magazine but the only problem is that it caters to the rich. None of the clothes or items featured on your pages are for those with a medium budget'. *B&H* promised to make amends and feature wedding outfits for those with a limited budget.[35]

But this was clearly not enough. Right from the start, readers demanded address to issues of enormous concern to the eponymous *Bride* that could not, or could not *easily*, be commuted to a shopping-list of market commodities. The first of these was the question of how the new bride should adjust to her husband's family; the second, anxieties regarding the initiation of conjugal sexuality.

Patrivirilocal Marriage and its Discontents

As is well known, Indian kinship—like Chinese kinship in fact—is for the most part based on the patrilineal principle whereby descent, succession and inheritance are in the male line; post-marital residence is 'patrivirilocal' (in the anthropologist's terminology, that is, the newly-wed couple move in to live with the husband's patrilineal kin group); and authority resides with senior males of the family or lineage. However, the rules of marriage differ fundamentally between north and south India, creating what kinship scholars see as fundamentally contrasting kinship regions (see Karve 1965; Trautmann 1981); and there are also differences in kinship and marriage practices according to caste and class status, as well as by community affiliation.[36] There have, of course, been changes over the years in the system of kinship and marriage, as well as reformist legal interventions since the beginning of the colonial period aimed particularly at ameliorating the position of women in the family. While public attention has focused on the supposed nuclearization of the Indian joint family, many professional sociologists see changes in family composition as much more complex—restricted to particular social segments, and also balanced by trends in the opposite direction (see Uberoi 2003). Besides, the ideology or 'moral economy' of the joint family remains quite firmly in place, reinforced by the modern mass media,[37] notwithstanding the challenge of 'modern' notions of conjugality and family life since the late 19th century. The modern period has also seen increasing pressure for the homogenization of marital practices through law and social reform in the first instance,[38] and thereafter the gradual development of a new, *class*-based, 'glocal' culture of Indian kinship and marriage that effectively polarizes contemporary India between 'dual' cultures.[39] The modern mass media, and magazines like *B&H*, are both reflections and instruments of the consolidation of this new, cosmopolitan culture of Indian kinship and marriage, which is self-consciously both 'modern' and 'ethnic'. As one correspondent wrote approvingly, '*Bride and Home* is a wonderful and informative fusion of the traditional and the modern'.[40]

Given the salience of the idea of the 'couple' in modern (and western) conceptions of family life, a number of features of *B&H* address the conjugal couple in addition to the bride herself (who is, of course, the manifest object of attention in the bridal magazine). There are features, for instance, on how high-profile young couples set up and furnish their homes to create 'a home that's elegant, simple and which radiates the warmth and love that the couple share';[41] or on how newly-wed couples look back on their first year of marriage and on the little adjustments they have had to make.[42] Several readers sought advice on resolving conflicts over style and taste in home décor: *B&H* advised a bit of give-and-take in such matters:

> How about a compromise? You agree to have the bedroom in his style, and perhaps the study, too, since he will be spending more time in it than you will. He agrees to let you decorate the sitting and dining rooms in your taste.[43]

But a major problem, on which advice was repeatedly sought, was how to deal with in-laws, particularly (but not exclusively) the *mother-in-law*:

> I come from a nuclear family and will soon be getting married to a man who lives in a joint family. His mother is not supposed to be the easiest person in the world to get along with. How do I cope? Help![44]
>
> Please include articles on how a newly married bride can adjust to the new world of her husband in order to make a happy home and have a good relationship.[45]

The simple answer to the former request is 'wait and see—you may be pleasantly surprised by your in-laws' welcoming attitude towards you'. In response to the latter, *B&H* announced a new feature on 'Couple Counsel' which, on the magazine's first anniversary, addressed 'in-law anxieties' with the fourfold prescription: confront differences; respect your partner's family; avoid taking sides; and present a united front.

> Ultimately, every couple has to establish a healthy give and take relationship. While the extended family is important, it should not

be allowed to intrude upon the special bond that exists between a husband and wife. Focusing on this bond, and maintaining your perspective over family intrigues is particularly important.[46]

The Initiation of Conjugal Intimacy

Apart from the problem of the bride's 'adjustment' to her in-laws, a major source of anxiety was the occasion glossed as 'first night'. By the time of B&H's first anniversary, it was clear that readers would *not* be fobbed off with discussions of bed-linen, bedroom décor and lingerie for the 'first night', and a travel-guide to romantic honeymoon desti-nations in India and abroad, or with Calmpose and Alprax, 'available at all chemists' to quell 'wedding jitters':[47] they wanted urgently to know about sex (defloration) and contraception. B&H finally responded with a triptych of 'first-night advice': an article on setting the mood with linen, perfumes, soft lights, music, aromatherapy and the gifting of little presents, and so on;[48] a very clinical paradigm of the advantages and disadvantages of different types of contraception, 'since most newly wed couples don't want a baby right away';[49] and, *at last*, an article on the initiation of conjugal sex and love-making for couples for many of whom 'this is actually the first time they are completely alone with each other'.[50] Though *style* and *competitive consumption* are no longer at the forefront of attention, one suspects that this homely advice would have struck a responsive chord.

The Politics of the Gift

Marriages are great occasions everywhere for gift-giving and B&H, like bridal magazines globally, provides an extensive catalogue of expen-sive and stylish gifts (and beautiful wrappings) for all the occasions and events associated with marriage, and for all family members as well. Sometimes these gifts are specifically named—'Tikka (reception) gifts', 'Shagan (*shagun/shakun*—gift on an auspicious occasion) surprise', 'wedding gifts', and such like, and sometimes identified by a further gloss—'for your groom', 'for the woman you love', 'for the couple' or 'for the bride and groom', 'wonderful ways to show your new family you care', 'a grand bazaar for grandmothers', and so on. The items concerned appear surprisingly miscellaneous, ranging, for example, from Rs 200 coffee mugs and a Rs 300 subscription to *B&H* to a new Maruti Zen car (Rs 3,35,798).[51] Advertisements in the magazine for other items, including household furnishings and luxury items like silverware, saris, jewellery, perfumes and watches, are also clearly intended as 'gifts'. On the whole, the gifts that the bride and groom give each other are only a small fraction of this considerable exchange, just trinkets really, or, if more substantial, an item in the total calculus of the affinal exchange.[52]

Ethnographies of Indian marriage are rich in descriptions of gift-giving,[53] with each ritual act accompanied by the gifting of cash or kind to specific categories of people. These include gifts to the persons who perform specific ritual functions or who provide specific items for the ritual; to caste specialists whose function is to remove impurity or avert inauspiciousness; from specific categories of close kin (especially the mother's brother) to the bride or groom; to categories of relatives whose playful activities (like preventing the groom's horse from moving, or barring his entrance to the bride's home, or stealing his shoes after the ceremony) dramatize ritual changes in status; to the bride and the groom, individually and as a couple; and to their parents, siblings, affines and extended relatives of various types. Indeed, the bride *herself* is understood as a 'gift'—*kanyadān*, the purist and pre-eminent of the several types of *dān* (unrequited gifts) that are invoked in the course of the ritual cycle of marriage (Fruzzetti 1990; Trautmann 1981).

In common parlance, the gifts of cash and goods intended for the groom and his family, including the gifts that cement the engagement, the cost of the wedding reception, as well as gifts that continue to be sent back to the groom's kin every time the bride visits her natal home, are known as 'dowry' (*dān-dahej*). These highly asymmetrical exchanges between the intermarrying groups are subject to quite mercenary negotiation before the alliance can be finalized. But all this is occluded in *B&H*'s presentation of 'the gift' and left, largely, to the imagination. However, like any wedding video or photo-album, the real-life society weddings pictured in the final pages of each issue of *B&H* tell a different story, with fulsome coverage of rituals of welcome, blessing and gifting, and the omnipresence of the obligatory kin in these activities.

Speaking at the launch of *B&H* magazine, the editors were explicit that they would *not* address issues like 'dowry and marriage problems': 'These issues were better dealt with in *serious* magazines', they said. On the former, that is, the question of dowry, they kept strictly to their word![54]

BRIDAL PRACTICES IN TAIWAN:
A COMPARATIVE DIMENSION

Our reading of *B&H* through its first year of publication has underlined a number of features of the Indian bridal magazine that call for critical appraisal. The transformation of social relationships into tasteful shopping for goods and services is the *other* side of the evasion of real-life anxieties (the role of the incoming bride in the joint family, the etiquette of affinity, the sexualization of the virgin, and so on) and the erasure of the seedy side of gift-giving as the expression of asymmetrical relations between bride-givers and their bride-takers, the so-called 'demands' of the latter on the former. The fantasy of the beautiful bride and the amorous couple is played out against a discordant background that is only partially conceded by the editors and that seeps through the images of real-life weddings that occupy the final pages of each issue.

In many ways, interesting parallels can be drawn with the practice of bridal photography in present-day Taiwan, described by Bonnie Adrian in an exemplary monograph (2003). Increasingly through the last two decades, it has become *de rigueur* for Taiwanese brides to commission huge and very expensive bridal portraits for display in their homes and in the wedding albums that have now become very visible items of 'competitive emulation'. The fashion, which is linked to the production of bridal magazines as well, has also spread through Taiwanese entrepreneurs to China (PRC) where, in a remarkably short time, it has become established as an important segment of the local 'wedding industrial complex'.

Independent of the actual wedding ceremonies, which take place some time later, Taiwanese brides undergo an extensive 'makeover' to transform themselves into cover-girl beauties—often (usually) with little resemblance to their real selves. The brides are outfitted in a series of Victorian-style white wedding dresses and other décolleté gowns and evening dresses (supplied by the photo-studios), complete with tiaras, bouquets, veils and gloves, and so on. They are then photographed, with and without their tuxedo-clad grooms, through the course of an all-day photo-shoot in romantic settings and postures, indoors and outdoors. Oddly, this expensive, painful, time- and energy-consuming rite of passage to transform the girl-next-door into the exemplary beautiful bride takes place some time before the actual wedding rituals and banquet, and appears to be composed in a completely different semiotic register.

As with Indian marriage (and the two kinship systems are, as noted, structurally quite similar), the actual marriage ceremonies and the attendant secular rituals of conspicuous consumption involve the participation of numerous ritual specialists, extended kin and the community at large. Symbolically, they emphasize the transfer of the bride from one lineage to another, and her potential role in assuring the continuity of the family line. By contrast, the photo-shoot indexes the status-aspirations of the young couple—the groom's love for the bride and his commitment to the relationship (it is he who mostly foots the bill, and few grooms dare back out once the photo-shoot has been done)—and *especially* the salience of 'romance' as a sign of modernity: 'The photos represent the marriage as if it were about affect and personal pleasure, not about kinship and reproduction', notes the ethnographer (Adrian 2003: 66).

What, then, is the social function and meaning of the Taiwan practice of bridal photography? Why do young women so compulsively seek to transform themselves into conventionalized objects of visual attraction, quite unlike their natural selves? Why do they isolate this activity from the real-time events of a Taiwan wedding? Adrian's ethnography suggests several different, if not unrelated, explanations. On the one hand, there is a generational difference of attitude between young folk brought up in post-boom Taiwan and their more 'traditional' parents, who had seen much harder times:

Young people *prefer* the way the bridal industry sees their relationships, in individualistic and romantic terms rather than as part of the familial obligation to reproduce. *Bridal salons are often the only*

place where the view on marriage that young people prefer is enacted
(Adrian 2003: 22, emphasis added).[55]

Then, she further elaborates, the very fact that the extended kin group
are *absent* from the bridal photographs suggests that they are, in fact,
very much a complicating presence in the couples' real lives. The
untrammelled romantic couple is mere fantasy, wishful thinking,
as the *other* album of amateur and professional photographs of the
actual marriage ceremonies betrays. Finally, Adrian suggests, the
celebration of the bride (even *above* her groom) through the medium
of the bridal portrait 'contrasts with the widespread belief in Taiwan
that marriage constitutes a downward movement in status for women'
(ibid.: 10). Read against the relative self-indulgence of late-marrying,
salaried women who continue to enjoy the facilities of the parental
home before marriage, with minimal familial responsibilities, the bridal
photograph is 'the bride's "last time" to enjoy status as a young, attractive, independent woman before she becomes burdened by housework
and familial demands' (ibid.). Little wonder perhaps (and a sad commentary on modern marriage) that the bridal portrait is put to hang
so prominently over the marital bed, a reminder of lost beauty, youth
and freedom!

The same might be true for the upwardly mobile patrons of high-
end bridal photography establishments in the PRC and especially for
the trend-setting 'dragon ladies' working in foreign-owned enterprises, consumers *par excellence* of contemporary lifestyle products.[56]
Yet informants stress a somewhat different meaning in the PRC context. Here, the glamour of the 'white wedding' is experienced as an
important index of a new freedom for young people whose parents
had married in an era of colourless austerity (cf. Davis 2000). Indeed,
as remarked earlier, consumerism is now a value in itself in the PRC
where, under the regime of 'socialist market economy', the state
itself is caught in the awkward dilemma of deploring habits of conspicuous consumption on the one hand, and seeking to stimulate
the domestic market for white goods on the other (Chen 2004), of
critiquing the recrudescence of feudal customs yet welcoming the
market potential of customary and ceremonial obligations, particularly with reference to the provision of bridewealth.[57] And the same
phenomenon has an added dimension of significance for Muslim

(Hui) brides in Xi'an, in China's northwestern Shaanxi province (described by Maris Gillette [2000]), where the low-cut western-style wedding gown and veil (usually pink or red), and the 'white wedding' costume of the obligatory photo-shoot index both conformity to contemporary, consumerist fashion dictates and an expression of 'agency' by women, young and old, *contra* the state, the Party cadres, the mullahs and community memories of an impoverished past. In addition,

> [b]y donning such bridal attire, Hui women created images of themselves that contravened the parochial, backward, and 'primitive' stereotypes the state perpetuated on China's ethnic minorities. They carved out—for themselves, their families and their communities—identities that appeared prosperous, cosmopolitan, and modern (ibid.: 106).

SOME CONCLUDING REFLECTIONS

There are several ways of construing the dissonances and silences that we have noted in the course of our analysis of *B&H*'s first year of production, and in our comparative look at certain bridal practices in Taiwan and the PRC. The first is to interpret the fantasy of the beautiful bride and perfect wedding as a function of the operation, *via* the contemporary mass media, of society's dominant ideologies—sexist, classist and racist, as the case may be (cf. Ingraham 1999; Otnes and Pleck 2003). Certainly, the focus on the person of the bride invites such critical deconstruction.[58] As the object of feminine fantasy, desire, gratification and identification, bridal magazines might be seen as a fairy-tale compensation for the drabness and constraints of everyday life and the asymmetry of gender relations, even as they embody and promote normative expectations of feminine beauty, body-shape and self-presentation, and of the romance of mature heterosexuality and marriage (cf. Ingraham 1999).

Second, as is the case with bridal magazines globally, the bride of *B&H* is a conspicuous object of visual attraction, her well-toned body inviting inspection and emulation.[59] She is also the manifest addressee of the magazine, in partnership with her fiancé, and the potential object of romantic attention from 'her groom'. Yet, as we noted, her selfhood and autonomy of action are severely constrained by her circumstances, especially if she is financially dependent on her family. As the photo-documentation of real-life weddings indicates, the bride is rarely the stand-alone cynosure she appears in the fashion and costume pages of magazines such as *B&H*. Similarly, the conjugal couple are allowed brief, conventionalized moments of public togetherness— the *Jaimala* (exchange of garlands), feeding each other a morsel of sweets, perhaps cutting a cake together (western-style), and so on.[60] But for the most part in a real-life wedding, the couple must share visual space with their parents and numerous relatives on both sides, all of whom are carefully identified to the photographer in the course of the ceremonies and reception, and memorialized in the wedding album or video (see Sengupta 1999). After all, these kin are the people who, after hard-nosed negotiation on the mercenary terms of the alliance, ultimately call the shots on the scope and style of the wedding and the quantum of gift exchange.

In the Taiwan case, and in China too, the tension between the bride/ couple, on the one hand, and the kin network, on the other, is expressed in the institution of the bridal photo-shoot, which is quite separate from the wedding itself.[61] The narcissism invoked by the bridal photo-shoot is her last act of untrammelled self-indulgence, a final fling, before she settles down to the serious business of family reproduction; momentarily, too, the bride is the publicly affirmed object of the groom's romantic attention.

Critical commentary on the lavish 'white wedding' and the 'wedding industrial complex' in the West has focused especially on 'unveiling' the ideological role of the lavish wedding in sustaining what Otnes and Pleck (2003) describe as 'the two most sacred tenets of American culture', namely, romantic love and excessive consumption. In non-Western societies, the gap between not-so-pleasurable reality and pleasurable fantasy may have a different ambience, for it may also be construed as a manifestation of the transition or contestation between 'tradition' and 'modernity' in family life. Non-Western societies are expected, indeed actively seek, to implement what are seen to be 'modern' modes of family life as these are entailed in such features as nuclearization of the family, the endorsement of romantic love as the foundation of marriage, the discontinuation of dowry and bridewealth payments, and so on, even at the regrettable cost of an increase in rates of divorce, neglect of the elderly, and so on. In *B&H* we see both a tension between pre-existing, so-called 'orthodox', and new (=western) ideals of family life, as well as the selection of a number of features of costume and ceremony to represent the continued and reassuring presence of 'tradition'. This evocation appears to be particularly important not only for the diasporic community seeking to assert its Indian identity, but also, clearly, for those at home. *B&H*'s readers claimed to have appreciated the magazine's judicious mix of the traditional and the modern, requesting further coverage of different Indian 'marriage customs' and articles on the 'meaning' of various marriage rituals and ceremonies. 'Tradition' is thus detoxified *via* 'ethnicization', providing further scope for competitive emulation and informed choice in respect to wedding-related goods and services. Increasingly, wedding venues get transformed into 'theme parks'.[62]

Third, mass media genres like the bridal magazine can be seen as sites of the dialectic of global, regional and local cultural forces. Bridal magazines are a global phenomenon whose pattern was already well-established in the US in the post-World-War II period, if not before. These features are reproduced in contemporary bridal magazines now published elsewhere—in India, Taiwan and China, for instance (the particular cases discussed here)—whether through imitation (*B&H*), or active collaboration (*Xinniang*). In this sense such magazines represent and consolidate a global culture of bourgeois romantic marriage—with authorized local touches—backed by international brands of luxury goods. Yet appearances can be deceptive. The 'white wedding' bride who adorns the cover of a bridal magazine in US, China or India conveys different messages in each locale: let us say, convention and tradition in the first; modernity and freedom in the second; the identities of the Anglo-Indian or Christian communities in multi-cultural India in the third. The ideological or fantasy-function of the magazine, too, might be rather different in each locale. To sum up rather brusquely: The western bridal magazine affirms the value of the long-term romantic commitment of a couple in a society where in fact the likelihood of marital breakdown is quite high; the Indian bridal magazine seeks to establish the centrality of the bride herself and the privacy of the conjugal couple against the cacophonous presence of a wider family and the asymmetry of relations between bride-givers and bride-takers; the Taiwan bridal magazine and photo-shoot give the bride the opportunity for self-indulgent narcissism, before she belatedly settles down to the unglamorous responsibilities of family life; the up-market Chinese bridal magazine authorizes romance, glamour and luxury consumption, experienced as liberation; while Xi'an bridal practices allow women to cock a snoot at cadres, mullahs and community elders, and to affirm the practical modernity of a community otherwise labelled 'backward'. All in all, the comparative perspective reveals the density of local meanings in apparently homogenized global media phenomena.

In all this romanticization of the 'glocal', however, we should not forget the common theme of conspicuous consumption and competitive emulation that the bridal magazine represents, nurturing the social and material aspirations of one class, while providing wholesome fantasy on married bliss for all.

Notes

1. What Hannah Papanek (1990) has felicitously called 'family status production work'.
2. To use Chrys Ingraham's disparaging term (1999). See also Currie 1993; Otnes and Pleck 2003.
3. For a discussion of the new legitimacy of consumerism in China and its rationale to develop domestic consumption in the years following the Asian financial crisis, see Chen 2004; Davis 2000.
4. The matter of conspicuous consumption at weddings was recently debated in the popular NDTV programme, 'We, the people' (compere, Barkha Dutt). Taking a high moral stand, some speakers condemned lavish weddings as 'non-productive consumption' leading to the pauperization of those classes who lacked the means to emulate those above them, while others, contrariwise, sought to emphasize the employment that such extravaganzas generate. For those routinely featuring in 'Page Three' social events and those in the business of advertising, event management and wedding planning, the criterion of approval or disapproval of conspicuous consumption was based largely on the demonstration of 'taste' (refined or vulgar as the case may be), though ultimately they conceded that if you have the money, it is surely your business how you want to spend it.
5. That high caste status is a form of 'cultural' and 'social capital' facilitating the consolidation of high class status has been ably demonstrated by Satish Deshpande.
6. The 1994 Bollywood blockbuster, Hum Aapke Hain Koun...! set the pace (see Uberoi 2001b; also, Sengupta 1999: 290–91, 300–01).

7.   See for instance the Indian women's magazines *Elle* and *Cosmopolitan*.

8.   According to the manager of a company that manufactures trousseaus, up-market designer wedding *lehenga*s are in the range from Rs 80,000–Rs 2,50,000, though most of his customers opt for costumes within the Rs 1,00,000–Rs 1,50,000 bracket (Trehan 2004). In the issues of *B&H* that I consulted for this chapter, the most expensive *lehenga* was just under Rs 2,00,000. The items marked 'price on request' may well have been more expensive, or subject to negotiation with the dealers. Jewellery was comparably expensive. Given the several functions that comprise a wedding, the total cost of wedding outfits must be very considerable.

9.   The comparison with China is particularly apt, given the structural similarities of the Indian and Chinese systems of kinship and marriage (cf. Uberoi 2001c), and the rapid expansion of the consumer economies in both societies (albeit from different starting points). Bridal magazines are also produced in Taiwan and in China as an adjunct to the bridal photography business. I have with me an issue (November 2005) of the Chinese monthly *Modern Bride* (*Xinniang*) published in collaboration with the American *Modern Bride* magazine by China's state-run China Council for the Promotion of International Trade. (*Xinniang* appears to have commenced publication in mid-2002). Glossy advertising pullouts of this magazine, with comprehensive information on bridal industry retail outlets and services in Beijing, are presented to clients of the bridal photography establishments in Beijing's Qidan Road shopping area.

10.   November 2005. I am grateful to Hemant Adlakha who cheerfully accompanied me on this expedition, including visits to two of the most high-profile establishments, Figaro and New York.

11.   Information in this section of the chapter is drawn from a number of newspaper reports of *B&H's* launch: 'Now, a Mag for the "Good" Bride, *The Pioneer*, 7 October 1997; 'Brides in the Making', *The Pioneer*, 8 October 1997; 'Perfect Match', *The Indian Express* (New Delhi edn), 12 October 1997; 'Wedding Belles', *The Economic Times*, 12 October 1997.

12.   Whimsically, the publishing company was named after the 'dreamy-eyed' St. Bernard dog (said to be 'very nasty to strangers'), owned by one of the editors. It was reported that the first reader to 'spot' Heathcliff in *B&H* would win a honeymoon trip to Sri Lanka. (Frankly, I did not manage to spot him.) It was hoped that the company would subsequently publish 'some other high quality consumer magazines' in due course.

13.   Advertisements for the Oberoi luxury hotels feature prominently in *B&H* as ideal honeymoon destinations.

14.   Financial planning, beyond simple wedding budgeting, was an interesting aspect of the magazine, aptly demonstrating the link between bridal magazines and the new, post-liberalization consumerism. The second issue of *B&H* (Jan–Feb 1998) carried a feature article on home loans (pp. 89–90) which began:

> Gone are the days when young married couples waited until their mid thirties to make their dream of owning a house a reality. The spirit of freedom and choice of today brings in its wake multiple options.... Easy availability of legitimate financing schemes make your dreams come true...and even if there is a

prodigious price to be paid, it can be staggered out in manageable installments (p. 89).

'The crucial element that young couples should keep in mind', the article went on to elaborate, 'is that their joint income today can play a major role in getting a property' (*B&H*, Jan–Feb 1998, p. 90). A subsequent issue (March–April 1998) used the same arguments to advocate car loans.

15. The innuendo was not unintended, however, for pillowslips were emblazoned with texts such as 'Not tonight', 'Please, sir, I want some more' and 'She who must be obeyed'. In the following issue, the editors identified this particular 'home' feature as one on 'contemporary ideas on how one might create a suitably inviting atmosphere on the first night' (Jan/Feb 1998, p. 8).

16. *B&H*, Oct–Nov 1997, p. 8.

17. The exception is for 'Rajput' custom in relation to the several 'royal' marriages reported in the *B&H* 'Album' section on real-life weddings.

18. Indian women's magazines are similarly circumspect (see Uberoi 2001a).

19. The magazine later explicitly positioned itself in its publicity as 'the new magazine for Indian brides'.

20. It is not clear *whose* parents are referred to, the bride's, the groom's, or both, but one presumes that the bride's parents are the primary focus. An Australian bridal manual I consulted, by way of comparison (*The Bride's Diary*, New South Wales edition, 1999), reminds couples that it is important that they *remember* to inform their respective parents immediately that they have taken the decision to get married. Obviously, the days of the suitor formally asking the bride's father for her hand are long gone, though the occasion of 'the proposal' has meanwhile been greatly elaborated and romanticized (see Otnes and Pleck 2003: 71ff.).

21. As is the case also for women's magazines.

22. *B&H*, Jan–Feb 1998, pp. 36–37.

23. *B&H*, Jul–Aug 1998, pp. 30–32.

24. Article by reigning beauty expert, Shahnaz Hussain, *B&H*, May–June 1998, p. 32.

25. *B&H*, Jan–Feb 1998, p. 94.

26. *B&H*, Oct–Nov 1997, p. 84.

27. Ibid.

28. Ibid.

29. Ibid.

30. A De Beers' diamond advertisement prominently placed in the inaugural issue, shows a gamin-faced young woman with expensive-looking diamond earrings. The text reads:

> I wasn't born a princess. *But my father turned me into one.* There's something magical in the way diamonds transformed me. I wonder if it's their sparkle that makes me feel so special. Or the thought that I'm so loved, *so precious to my parents....* I was just another girl-next-door, but things changed, once I was touched by my diamond (*B&H*, Oct–Nov 1997, p. 5, emphasis added).

The history of De Beers' brilliantly orchestrated worldwide promotion of the diamond engagement ring is a story worth telling. See, e.g., Otnes and Pleck 2003: 63ff.

31. *B&H*, Oct–Nov 1997, p. 6, advertisement for Delhi-based Khanna Jewellers.

32. *B&H*, Nov–Dec 1998, p. 33.

33. Recent work by Supriya Singh (1997) on the new meaning of marriage in Australia, where live-in relationships are quite common, suggests that a couple's 'commitment' to each other in marital or non-marital partnership is measured by such marks of 'trust' as: (*i*) a joint bank account; (*ii*) the deposit on a house; and (*iii*) sharing of pin-codes and computer IDs.

34. One should be cautioned that since readers' letters are pre-selected for publication, they are not necessarily an accurate reflection of overall reader response.

35. *B&H*, Sept–Oct 1998, p. 10. Designer saris and *lehengas* so featured in this issue were mostly in the range of Rs 25,000 to Rs 40,000 where the price was given; other costumes offered 'price on request' (Also see n. 8). The same issue had a feature article, 'For Richer, For Poorer' on 'how to cut costs and save money on the big day, without sacrificing style' (pp. 40–41). For instance, *B&H* advised that it was not essential to honeymoon abroad: there are plenty of romantic places for a honeymoon in India.

36. See, e.g., Karve 1965. This is, of course, a very crude description of a complex phenomenon. There are also a number of matrilineal communities in India, in the southwest and northeast.

37. See Uberoi 2003. Elsewhere (Uberoi 2006: 29–33), I have described the 'moral economy' of the Indian family as based on ideals of selflessness and altruism, duty and sacrifice, as against the pursuit of individual self-interest and self-gratification. Among other things, this moral economy requires the relative sublimation of the conjugal bond (it should be kept 'back-stage', in Veena Das's apt formulation [1976]), and emphasis on the solidarity of the parent-child and fraternal bonds (the 'front-stage').

38. See papers in Uberoi 1996a; also Uberoi 2005.

39. I owe the conceptualization of the 'dual cultures of contemporary India' to Professor M.N. Srinivas (1977).

40. *B&H*, Mar–Apr 1998, p. 8. Readers were also interested in accounts of the management of 'fusion' weddings, inter-racial or inter-religious.

41. *B&H*, Oct–Nov 1997, p. 70.

42. *B&H*, Nov–Dec 1998, pp. 36-38.

43. *B&H*, Oct–Nov 1997, p. 84. Similarly, on a complaint regarding a husband's insistence on using 'really awful tiles in the bathroom', the wife was advised to be satisfied with designing another room: 'Remember that marriage is give and take, and sometimes one has to give more than the other does' (*B&H*, Jan–Feb 1998, p. 94).

44. *B&H*, Mar–Apr 1998, p. 90.

45. *B&H*, Jul–Aug 1998, p. 8.

46. *B&H*, Sept–Oct 1998, p. 32.

47. *B&H*, May–Jun 1998, p. 101.

48. The following issue contained suggestions for 'wedding night accessories' for him and her (*B&H*, Nov–Dec 1998, pp. 14, 16), including a Cartier gold bracelet for the groom to give the bride and Tiffany cuff links from bride to groom.

49. This assumption marks a major change of emphasis in a kinship culture where the young bride was traditionally expected to demonstrate her fertility at the earliest—

thereby also consolidating her position in her new family. The article concerned was most definitely *un-stylish*. Contrast Mary John's insightful deconstruction (1998) of the idiom of condom brands in post-liberalization India.

50. *B&H*, Sept–Oct 1998, pp. 35–38.

51. 'Wedding Gifts for the Perfect Wedding', *B&H*, Oct–Nov 1997, pp. 22–23.

52. For instance, the text of a De Beers advertisement for a diamond ring reads:

> My parents wanted to keep the occasion simple. His parents agreed... with one glittering exception. There we were, him and me and our closest ones. Out of the blue, he produced this beautiful diamond ring! *He said it was their joint decision—him and his parents—to let me know how special I was to them....* I look at my diamond all ablaze. And I understand how the simplest of occasions can come so memorably alive (*B&H*, Sept–Oct 1998, p. 11, emphasis added).

53. See, e.g., Dumont 1986: 237–58, 284–92; Fruzzetti 1990; Raheja 1988; and Vatuk 1975, to cite a handful of examples from a very extensive literature.

54. In the first year of *B&H*, the only mention of 'dowry' that I came across was in the personal column where a divorcée asked if she could prevent her ex-husband (who had harassed her for dowry) from getting a US 'green-card' (*B&H*, Jul–Aug 1998, p. 22).

55. An interesting parallel can be found in a photo-illustrated account of an otherwise 'traditional' wedding described in the *B&H* Album section (Mar–Apr 1998, p. 102):

> The mehendi ceremony, held at the bride's residence, was on Valentine's Day, and the groom arrived with a huge heart-shaped balloon and photographs of the couple in a heart frame. *Other than this romantic departure from the norm, the couple had a traditional wedding*, with the works (emphasis added).

56. Impression based on informal conversations with Chinese friends.

57. As remarked elsewhere (Uberoi 1996b: 147), in official discourse:

> the celebration of China's growing post-reform prosperity is often expressed in terms of the catalogue of consumer goods that young couples can now hope to purchase or expect to be gifted at the time of marriage, or of the variety of services that can now be availed of for facilitating the wedding celebrations or the planning of the honeymoon.

58. There is considerable feminist literature on this aspect of women's magazines, and also on romance fiction—both genres of the contemporary mass media, which are produced for a largely female audience and in which the woman is the narratival/visual focus and the presumed addressee. Summing up this work and the writings of historians of the family, sociologist Anthony Giddens has described romance fiction as 'the counter factual thinking of the deprived' (1992: 45).

59. Indeed, many of the costumes (saris and *lehenga*s) are bolder and more revealing than any I have actually seen at local weddings, and *B&H* is more conservative in this regard than several other bridal magazines now on sale. Apart from the bride herself, weddings are also an important occasion where young girls of the family are encouraged to dress up and, as it were, put themselves on display for the community matchmaking network.

60. The Chinese *Xinniang* that I looked at contained a feature on postures for photo-friendly and elegant kisses, a feature that I have not seen in any Indian bridal magazines (No. 40, Nov 2005, pp. 68–75). The models for this 'Passionate kiss' section were Caucasian.
61. I note that *Xinniang* (unlike *B&H*) does not cover real-life society weddings.
62. As a report of a recent high-society Delhi wedding comments:

> Inspired by Bollywood actress Raveena Tandon's wedding, the 23-year-old bride too wanted an equally spectacular ceremony. And so it was. A Rajasthani theme for the wedding made it a night to remember. Wedding planners...had transformed the wedding venue [in an 'affluent address' in Udaipur] into a Rajasthani village.... Music especially composed for the occasion regaled the guests while folk artistes performed traditional dances. The guests, too, had been instructed to dress in Rajasthani gear so as to blend with the theme (Trehan 2004).

References

Adrian, Bonnie. 2003. *Framing the Bride: Globalizing Beauty and Romance in Taiwan's Bridal Industry.* Berkeley: University of California Press.

Booth, Gregory D. 2005. *Brass Baja: Stories from the World of Indian Wedding Bands.* Delhi: Oxford University Press.

Bourdieu, Pierre. 1984 [1979]. *Distinction: A Social Critique of the Judgement of Taste.* London: Routledge & Kegan Paul.

Chen Xin. 2004. 'New Development of Consumerism in Chinese Society in the Late 1990s', *Asian Exchange,* 18(2) & 19(1): 163–75.

Currie, D.H. 1993. 'Here Comes the Bride': The Making of a 'Modern Traditional' Wedding in Western Culture, *Journal of Comparative Family Studies,* 24(3): 403–21.

Darling, Sir Malcolm. 1947 [First edn 1925]. *The Punjab Peasant in Prosperity and Debt.* Bombay: Oxford University Press.

Das, Veena. 1976. 'Masks and Faces: An Essay on Punjabi Kinship', *Contributions to Indian Sociology* (n.s.), 10(1): 1–30.

Davis, Deborah S. (ed.). 2000. *The Consumer Revolution in Urban China.* Berkeley: University of California Press.

Deshpande, Satish. 1997. 'From Development to Adjustment: Economic Ideologies, the Middle Class and 50 years of Independence', *Review of Development and Change,* 2(2): 294–318.

Dumont, Louis. 1986. *A South Indian Subcaste: Social Organization and Religion of the Pramalai Kallar.* Delhi: Oxford University Press.

Fruzzetti, Lina M. 1990 [1982]. *The Gift of a Virgin: Women, Marriage, and Ritual in a Bengali Society.* Delhi: Oxford University Press.

Giddens, Anthony. 1992. *The Transformation of Intimacy: Sexuality, Love and Eroticism in Modern Societies.* Cambridge: Polity Press.

Gillette, Maris. 2000. 'What's in a Dress? Brides in the Hui Quarter of Xi'an', in Deborah S. Davis (ed.), *The Consumer Revolution in Urban China.* Berkeley: University of California Press, pp. 80–106.

Hanchett, Suzanne. 1988. *Coloured Rice: Symbolic Structure in Hindu Family Festivals.* Delhi: Hindustan.

Ingraham, Chrys. 1999. *White Weddings: Romancing Heterosexuality in Popular Culture.* London: Routledge.

John, Mary. 1998. 'Globalization, Sexuality and the Visual Field: Issues and Non-issues for Cultural Critique', in Mary E. John and Janaki Nair (eds), *A Question of Silence? The Sexual Economies of Modern India.* New Delhi: Kali for Women, pp. 368–96.

Karve, Irawati. 1965. *Kinship Organization in India.* 2nd rev. edn. Bombay: Asia Publishing House.

Kaur, Kulwinder. 2004. 'Postmodernity and Popular Culture in Amritsar, *Indian Social Science Review,* 6(1): 107–34.

Munshi, Shoma. 1997. '"Women of Substance": Commodification and Fetishization in Contemporary Indian Advertising within the Indian "Urbanscape"', *Social Semiotics,* 7(1): 37–51.

Otnes, Cele C. and Elizabeth H. Pleck. 2003. *Cinderella Dreams: The Allure of the Lavish Wedding.* Berkeley: University of California Press.

Packard, Vance. 1959. *The Status Seekers: An Exploration of Class Behaviour in America.* Harmondsworth: Penguin Books.

Papanek, Hannah. 1990. 'To Each Less Than She Needs; For Each More Than She Can Do: Allocations, Entitlements and Value', in Irene Tinker (ed.), *Persistent Inequalities.* New York: Oxford University Press, pp. 162–81.

Raheja, Gloria G. 1988. *The Poison in the Gift: Ritual, Prestation, and the Dominant Caste in a North Indian Village.* Chicago: Chicago University Press.

Sengupta, Shuddhabrata. 1999. 'Vision Mixing: Marriage-video-film and the Video-*walla's* Images of Life', in Christiane Brosius and Melissa Butcher (eds), *Image Journeys: Audio-visual Media and Cultural Change in India.* New Delhi: Sage Publications, pp. 261–307.

Sharma, Ursula. 1986. *Women's Work, Class and the Urban Household.* London: Tavistock.

Sheel, Ranjana. 2005. 'Marriage, Money and Gender: A Case Study of the Migrant Community in Canada', *Indian Journal of Gender Studies,* 12(2 & 3): 335–56.

Singh, Amita Tyagi and Patricia Uberoi. 1994. 'Learning to "Adjust": Conjugal Relations in Indian Popular Fiction', *Indian Journal of Gender Studies,* 1(1): 93–120.

Singh, Supriya. 1997. *Marriage Money: The Social Shaping of Money in Marriage and Banking.* St. Leonards, NSW: Allen & Unwin.

Srinivas, M.N. 1977. 'The Dual Cultures of Independent India'. Gandhi Memorial Lecture, 1977. Bangalore: Raman Research Institute.

Trautmann, Thomas R. 1981. *Dravidian Kinship.* Cambridge: Cambridge University Press.

Trehan, Prerana. 2004. 'The Big Fat Indian Wedding', *The Sunday Tribune,* Spectrum Section, 29 August 2004. Available at http://www.tribuneindia.com/2004/20040829/spectrum/main1.htm, accessed on 6 September 2006.

Uberoi, Patricia (ed.). 1996a. *Social Reform, Sexuality and the State.* New Delhi: Sage Publications.

————. 1996b. 'The Family in Official Discourse', *India International Centre Quarterly,* Winter: 134–55.

Uberoi, Patricia. 1998. 'The Diaspora Comes Home: Disciplining Desire in *DDLJ*', *Contributions to Indian Sociology*, 32(2): 305–36.

————. 2001a. 'A Suitable Romance? Trajectories of Courtship in Indian Popular Fiction', in Shoma Munshi (ed.), *Images of the 'Modern Women' in Asia: Global Media/Local Meanings*. London: Curzon Press, pp. 169–87.

————. 2001b. 'Imagining the Family: An Ethnography of Viewing *Hum Aapke Hain Koun....!*', in Rachel Dwyer and Christopher Pinney (eds), *Pleasure and the Nation: The History and Politics of Popular Culture in India*. Delhi: Oxford University Press, pp. 309–51.

————. 2001c. 'Social Organization: Comparing Comparisons', in G.P. Deshpande and Alka Acharya (eds), *Crossing a Bridge of Dreams: Fifty Years of India and China*. New Delhi: Tulika.

————. 2003. 'The Family in India: Beyond the Nuclear versus Joint Debate', in Veena Das (ed.), *Oxford India Companion to Sociology and Social Anthropology*. Delhi: Oxford University Press, pp. 1061–1103.

————. (ed.). 2005. 'Legislating the Family in Post-Independence India', in Bharati Ray (ed.), *Women of India: Colonial and Post-colonial Periods*. History of Science, Philosophy and Culture in Indian Civilization (General Editor D.P. Chattopadhyaya), Volume 9, Part 3. New Delhi: Indian National Science Academy, pp. 26–52.

————. 2006. *Freedom and Destiny: Gender, Family, and Popular Culture in India*. Delhi: Oxford University Press.

Vatuk, Sylvia. 1975. 'Gifts and Affines in North India', *Contributions to Indian Sociology*, 9(2): 155–96.

Veblen, Thorstein. 1957 [1925]. *The Theory of the Leisure Class: An Economic Study of Institutions*. London: George Allen & Unwin. (First published, 1899).

13

Yeh Dil Maange More[1] ...Television and Consumer Choices in a Global City

SHOMA MUNSHI

India's conversion to a programme of economic liberalization, initiated in the 1980s, and which accelerated considerably after 1991, has
led to a widespread restructuring of the economy. An IMF Report of
September 2005 states that 'India's booming economy could have a
profound impact on the world economy at large if progress in boost-
ing regional and global trade links continues apace' (*The Economic
Times* 2005). Studies on the entertainment industry clearly indicate
that television is the fastest growing medium, recording a 20 per cent
growth annually. Presently, India has more than 100 million television
households, 50 million cable TV subscribers and over 100 cable TV
channels. Television reaches over 55 per cent of India's total population, estimated at around 1.1 billion, 85 per cent of the urban population and 45 per cent of the rural population (FICCI-Arthur Anderson
Report 2000, 2001, 2002; *The Economic Times* 2002).

It is well known that the Indian film industry is the largest in the
world; and the Indian media market—especially that of television—is
one of the biggest in the world today. These 'mediascapes' that

refer both to the electronic capabilities to produce and disseminate
information (newspapers, magazines, television stations, and
film-production studios)... are now available to a growing number
of private and public interests... what is most important about
these mediascapes is that they provide... large and complex reper-
toires of images, narratives and ethnoscapes to viewers.... (Appadurai
1996: 35)

Research on the Indian middle class and their lifestyles on the basis of
consumption include works like Appadurai and Breckenridge (1995),
Fernandes (2000), Scrase (2002), Varma (1998) and van Wessel (2004),
as well as some analyses of television reception such as Mankekar (1999)
and McMillin (2002, 2003).

This chapter focuses on the role of the media in general and television in particular in influencing consumer culture in the lives of women
who work as domestic help and as workers in beauty parlours in the
colonies of Sheikh Sarai and Navjivan Vihar in south Delhi. It investi-
gates how exposure to satellite TV, particularly advertising on TV,
affects the spending habits, behaviour and lifestyle choices of these
women and how, very importantly, this, in turn, allows the women to
feel part of a big city and global culture, and gives them a certain degree of autonomy and control over their lives (see McMillin 2003;
Munshi 1998, 2000). While McMillin's respondents are women factory labourers in Bangalore (2003: 497) and mine are urban workers
of a different kind, both studies stress the importance of recognizing
the 'critical agency' that these women possess.

RESEARCH CONTEXT AND METHOD

Saskia Sassen defines global cities as 'centers for the servicing and
financing of international trade, investment, and headquarter
operations... they are strategic production sites for today's leading
economic sectors' (1991). Contemporary Delhi, characterized by an
economic transition—which includes an increasing growth of financial and multinational industries, including media corporates
who are now beginning more and more to locate themselves in Delhi,

and governmental policies of economic liberalization which are actively seeking foreign investment—provides a striking instance of a new 'global city.'

Two important points of distinction, however, need to be made here. One, the women and minority service groups discussed in Sassen's global cities of New York, London, Tokyo, Buenos Aires, Bangkok and Mexico City—mainly immigrant, low paid service labourers who are exploited and employed for low wages to serve the top sectors and households (Sassen 1999) are, to some extent, different from the women in my study. The people involved in my research—female workers, both domestic help and workers in small businesses like beauty parlours—while also mainly immigrants to Delhi, denote a representative example of the rise of a 'new, aspiring middle class' in liberalizing India (cf. Fernandes 2000). The second point deals with an important difference. A study of the lower middle class in Calcutta and Siliguri in north Bengal computes the salary of this Bengali *bhadralok*[2] group ('white-collar, salaried persons') as ranging from Rs 2,000 to Rs 8,000[3] per month (Ganguly-Scrase and Scrase 1999). The women workers of my study, while not belonging to a *bhadralok* group as far as social status is concerned, earn higher salaries in New Delhi as compared to Calcutta.

Of the two areas I studied, Sheikh Sarai has a total of 1,112 three- and two-bedroom apartments built by the Delhi Development Authority (DDA) in the late 1970s in the first phase and later in the late 1980s. The first phase of building is called the Retiring Personnel Scheme (RPS) where mainly retired government officers own their apartments. The second phase of building called Self-Financing Scheme (SFS) also has people who own their apartments, but a larger number of younger professionals renting accommodation. Navjivan Vihar, on the other hand, is a residential colony of 160 houses, all privately owned one or two storied private bungalows with quarters allotted for domestic help.

Some of the women workers are married, some have children, while some are single. The average size of a family is four people. Aged 20–45, they are all, without exception, migrants from villages in Bengal and Bihar. Their families all own some farming land but due to large numbers of family members, pressure on land and inadequate earnings, they migrated to Delhi in search of a better life. They have, by now, lived and worked in Delhi for at least 10 years, and while they return home once or twice a year, not one of them has the intention of going back to her village permanently. Those working as domestic help in Sheikh Sarai live in the nearby Jagdamba Camp. Living quarters are cramped, mostly one or two rooms, with rents ranging from Rs 800 to Rs 1,200 per month. Some houses have their own small bathrooms, but mostly about 10 houses share a common bathroom. Residents of Jagdamba Camp mainly acquire their water and electricity illegally by diverting these from the main supply lines of the colony. In Navjivan Vihar, all the houses have quarters for domestic help where women workers live with their families. Their water and electricity supply is drawn from the supply of the main house and, in most cases, their employers pay for the use. The girls working in beauty parlours mainly live in shared, rented accommodation in Savitri Nagar, a colony adjoining Sheikh Sarai.

The women who work either as part-time domestic help in several houses in the colonies of Sheikh Sarai and Navjivan Vihar, from 6 a.m. till noon and at times for a couple of hours in the evenings as well, either as cooks or cleaners, earn between Rs 6,000 to Rs 7,000 per month. The girls in the neighbourhood beauty parlours earn more, anywhere between Rs 7,000 to 10,000 per month, plus the tips given to them by customers. The latter have the added advantage of availing free facilities provided by the parlours, such as waxing, threading, hair colouring, changes of nail varnish colour, and so on. Given that one can buy a cell phone today for as little as Rs 2,000, with monthly recharge costs of Rs 100, it is not surprising that most of them have cell phones with prepaid cards.

All of them have one TV set, and mostly, in colour. All the women watch about four hours of television every day, from 8 p.m. onwards till midnight. They see films and the popular prime time soaps on STAR, Sony and Zee, all of which are interspersed with advertising breaks, rather long ones at times. In Jagdamba Camp, as noted above, television lines are acquired illegally; in Navjivan Vihar, it is drawn from the employers' cable lines. Thus, none of these women pay cable subscription charges. It is only the single women, who stay in shared, rented accommodation in Savitri Nagar, who pay Rs 300 per month, again on a shared basis, as cable subscription. The cable distribution system in both the colonies—Sheikh Sarai and Navjivan Vihar, is the SitiCable network, supplied via the neighbourhood cable operators. A typical cable bouquet consists of the STAR, Zee and Sony channels, the two government-controlled Doordarshan channels and a variety of regional language channels based on viewer demand.

Scholars have focused on strategies used by women workers as forms of resistance and agency (see Fugelsang 1994, Hartsock 1993, Liechty 2002, McMillin 2003, Riano 1994, Sassen 1999). This chapter fills such a need by examining how women workers actively use television programmes and advertisements, both to adapt to the urban environment of Delhi and feel empowered in emulating a middle class lifestyle. Like all ethnographers, my position in researching this chapter is a multifaceted one, as a western-educated researcher, yet as someone who has spent a large amount of time 'at home' in India. The research for this chapter is based on fieldwork conducted in the two colonies of Delhi—Sheikh Sarai and Navjivan Vihar—in 2003–06, including ethnographic observations, published materials, and formal and informal in-depth interviews with 20 adult women workers. The three years spent in this ethnography were entirely spent living and working in Delhi. My informants, just like me, occupy multifaceted situations because of their identities as informants as well as their familial situations and increasing economic independence.

TELEVISION SOAPS AND ADVERTISEMENTS IN WOMEN WORKERS' LIVES

All my informants uniformly acknowledged that television is an important creator of needs, and supplies them with icons and images about lifestyles to copy. It also creates a demand for objects to buy.

Watching popular TV channels like STAR, Zee and Sony, one is reminded of Horkheimer and Adorno's observation that 'in the most influential American magazines, *Life* and *Fortune*, a quick glance can [now] scarcely distinguish advertising from editorial picture and text' (1998 [1946]: 163). Most television soaps are set in the rich-educated-urban class milieu. The images and stories woven around the themes of consumerist lifestyles create an '"ideal-form" of existence among viewers, which is marked by conspicuous consumption' (Gupta 1998; see also Varman and Vikas n.d.). This imagery sets up the discourse of consumption, and the desire by people to consume more and more. Such representations demonstrate a close nexus between advertising firms and television programmers increasingly portraying an urban, rich class with disposable incomes.

If consumer culture is characterized by a greater desire to procure objects of consumption, my participants repeatedly indicated that there was a substantial increase in the demand for consumption objects, foremost among which was the purchase of a colour television set. In one way or another, all of them have undergone economic hardships by cutting corners to acquire it. One reduced the consumption of milk and sugar to save up to buy the colour TV set; another reduced expenditure on clothing items to save the money; a third borrowed money. Several domestic workers said that they 'reduced their expenditure on food and did not buy clothes for themselves and their children for a year'. The single women, mainly beauty parlour workers—who, most times, shared a rented accommodation—pooled money to buy a colour television set. But, all of them said that in the end, the purchase of the TV set was 'worth it' for several reasons. One, it showed that they could afford to buy a colour TV set which served as a token of upward mobility. But much more important, they were all aware that it was the cheapest and most easily available form of entertainment, with daily soaps like *Kasautii Zindagi Kii, Kavyanjali, Kahani Ghar Ghar Ki* and *Kyunki Saas Bhi Kabhi Bahu Thi*, films and even popular game shows that gave contestants the chance of winning monetary prizes such as *Deal Ya No Deal*, and STAR TV's hugely popular *Kaun Banega Crorepati* (Who Wants to be a Millionaire), popularly called KBC, hosted by film star Amitabh Bachchan. Even talent shows like Zee TV's *Sa Re Ga Ma Pa* and Sony's *Indian Idol*, modelled on *American Idol*, bestow the winners with lucrative music contracts and a quick route to playback singing in Bollywood.

My interviews with several domestic workers in Sheikh Sarai highlights the issue of consumption and how television creates this demand. Asma lives with her daughter and son-in-law, another son lives with his wife and family in Gurgaon. She told me 'Didi (term used to refer to elder sister), now there is *showbaazi* (showing off) everywhere. Society has changed in the last few years. One person gets a cycle or scooter, and then my son also wants one.' Linking the issue of rising consumer culture to television, she said:

> I don't watch TV, but my children and grandchildren do. TV *bhookh badhati hai* (TV increases people's hunger [for material goods]). My grandson, who in any case, must eat meat daily or else he won't eat, now wants a bottle of Horlicks and Nestlé's Munch chocolate, and Pepsi—like Shah Rukh Khan has with the hamburger in the Pepsi ad. So I buy these things. My elder daughter-in-law is smart— she wants to copy TV stars and wear new saris, make-up and jewellery, long, dangling ear rings, bangles.

She goes on to say that grandchildren are meant to be spoilt, being 'the interest on one's capital sum'. But for herself, she will only buy what she needs. 'What are those?', I ask. She says 'coconut oil, soap and Colgate'. I ask, 'not toothpaste?' But I soon find out about the power of brands when for brushing teeth, the most commonly used sentence among most of my respondents was '*savere main Colgate karti hoon*' (I 'Colgate' in the mornings; as opposed to brushing one's teeth).

Highlighting the role of television and its impact on changing consumer demand, Yasmin, a mother of two young children, working as a domestic help in Navjivan Vihar says 'my children now ask for many more things. Whatever they see on TV, they want it…earlier *dal roti* (lentils and Indian bread) was sufficient, but now they want rice, chicken and vegetables … but mostly ask for Maggi 2-minute noodles and Coke or Pepsi.' For herself, Yasmin smiles and says 'I also buy the new style of *kurtis* (short, hip covering tunics) and my husband has just saved enough money from his salary as a driver (with overtime) to buy a second-hand scooter. She told me that if the people she works for can go from buying a small car to a medium size to a luxury sedan, then the trajectory from taking Delhi's buses (bad at any time) to a cycle and from thereon to a scooter is a natural trajectory.

Some of the women I interviewed who are in their 40s and have daughters of marriageable age, stressed the expenses associated with marriage. They are putting together money to buy TV sets, a cycle or scooter, fridge and other items like the new styles of *churidar-kurtas* (north Indian dress of loose pants and a long shirt), and so on. This comes not only from the fact of having to give dowry when their daughters get married, but also because their children wanted items they have seen advertised on TV, like the new non-stick frying pans, Hawkins pressure cookers that now come in different colours and shapes and Hero cycles. In different ways, they said 'Didi, samaj ka khayal toh rakhna parta hai...aur phir bachhe log bhi TV par dekhey huye cheezen maangtey hain. Ab shaadi ke waqt par bachchon ko thoda toh bigarna chahiye' (one has to pay heed to society's mores...and children always want the things they see advertised on TV. One should be able to spoil children, especially when they are getting married). One of them told me that her daughter wanted a few sets of the new style sequinned *kurtas* with slim pants like the character Prerna wears on STAR TV's popular soap *Kasautii Zindagi Kii*.

Since the women in their 40s, who are buying products for their children or for their daughters' weddings, are not necessarily spending money on themselves, my question to them was whether they objected to the media creating demands that they had to fulfil for the family. Interestingly, none of them had an objection. They felt that their increased levels of earnings now allowed them a greater freedom and increased control over their incomes which they willingly spent on their children. They felt proud that they were now able to 'spoil their children' like their employers did theirs.

All the women I interviewed said that TV advertisements influenced their and their family's choices in their eating habits. The most popular food items they buy are Maggi 2-minute noodles, health drinks like Horlicks and Complan, sodas like Coke, Pepsi, Limca and Sprite, as well as potato chips and chocolates. I have argued elsewhere that 'maternal angst over the children's and family's health and well-being is readily exploited by advertisers' and how '...ads locate the woman within dominant ideology as someone who bears the primary burden of responsibility of nurturing and caring for others' (Munshi 1998: 579, 580). 'Maggi' 2-minute noodles have recently started being advertised as made from 'atta' (whole grain), and their advertisement byline is 'taste bhi, health bhi' (both taste and health). Mothers are comforted by the food value of convenient 'Maggi' noodles. For the single women, they are easy to prepare, time-saving, as well as healthy. 'Horlicks' and 'Complan' are health drinks. As far as sodas, chips and chocolates are concerned, my respondents viewed them more as status symbols that their employers' consumed, rather than as unhealthy foods, saying 'ab hum bhi yeh sab khareed sakte hain' (now, we too can buy these things). Across the board, the fact that they are now able to buy the same products as their employers do is marked by pride and satisfaction.

Television impacts the lives of young single women by showing them the latest in fashion, make-up and grooming. Their earnings now allow them to indulge themselves, and the young women who work in the neighbourhood beauty parlours are focused on buying fashionable clothes like jeans and make-up items. One of them, Sarika, is in her 20s, unmarried, and shares a two-room rented accommodation in Savitri Nagar. She says that her earnings give her 'azadi' (independence)—she likes to buy good clothes and dress up like the film stars she sees on TV and magazines in the parlour. Dressed in hipster jeans, with streaked hair and painted nails, Sarika is well groomed and smart. She has a cell phone, is learning English and says that interaction with customers helps her see another world. The serial *Jassi Jaisi Koi Nahin* is popular with a number of the working girls. Jassi is a plain looking girl, with glasses and braces on her teeth, who has now metamorphosed into a beauty.

A striking feature among the young single women I interviewed was that they clearly expressed a desire not to get married at an early age, certainly not in their 20s. In fact, some of them do not want to get married at all. Sarika and a few of her friends expressly said that they do not want to get married because they have seen their sisters struggling with work, kids and husbands who are, at times, lazy. They prefer to 'spoil their nieces and nephews, buying jeans and toys for them and taking them out to McDonald's for treats.' The city is also a space of freedom for the young women, and all of them said that they would rather live and work here than return to oppressive, conservative familial structures in their village homes.

Television also greatly influences their choice of toiletry and make-up items. They buy popular face creams, such as Fair and Lovely, Tips' Elle range of nail polishes or Lakme's Street Wear range that cost Rs 20 compared to the higher end products of Revlon, and shampoos such as Sunsilk. Their preferred soap is Lux, almost always advertised by film stars. As far as clothes are concerned, they make their purchases from markets like Sarojini Nagar and Lajpat Nagar in Delhi where imitation Levis (and other branded) jeans are available for just Rs 50, and fashionable shoes with different coloured rhinestones can be purchased at Rs 100–120.

The media has also made young women very conscious of their bodies. My work elsewhere has dealt with the 'desirable' body now on display with the constant circulation of images in the media and helped along in no small measure by the numbers of beauty titles won by Indian women at international beauty pageants; and how in contemporary India:

> discourses of physical appearance and body care have shifted from the private to the public space...today the worked out, taut body has become a cultural icon in India: a statement to the world that the owner cares for herself and how she appears to others (Munshi 2004: 170).

All these women, without exception, are extremely figure-conscious and take care of their bodies. In order to wear hipster jeans, they said they exercise and wax their midriffs. When asked how they learnt about exercise, their replies were almost instantaneous. Television channels now have early morning shows on yoga and stretching and bending exercises, which they have the time to do before going to the parlours to start work at 10 a.m. They said:

> filmon mein ab Aishwarya Rai, Kareena Kapoor, Prerna (a TV character) kitne acchhe lagte hain—kitne slim hain, aur agar slim ho toh, sab kapre achhey lagte hain. Agar sardiyon (winter) mein moongfali kha kar thodey motey ho jaatey hain toh phir diet kar ke aur thoda aur exercise badaa kar phir se slim honey ki koshish kartey hain' (Filmstars like Aishwarya Rai and Kareena Kapoor, and TV stars like Prerna look so beautiful and slim. If one is slim, all clothes look good. If we eat peanuts during the winter [a favourite Delhi past time] and put on a little weight, then we diet and increase our exercising to become slim again).

Influenced by the circulation of media images of perfect bodies of their favourite heroines in both films and TV serials, these are now clearly important feminine preoccupations.

A New Space for Power and Empowerment

This chapter demonstrates how satellite television, with its film and entertainment based programmes and advertisements, exposes (lower middle class) working women to a new world—a global world—in a global city, and provides them with a space to emulate middle class identities through their purchase and use of products and emulation of middle class lifestyles.

A number of important findings have emerged from this ethnographic research. First, the fact that these women's increased earning and spending capacities do not grant them middle class social status is not as important as the fact that they can now afford some of the things that their employers consume and that their economic condition is vastly better than when they lived in villages. Second, none of the women I interviewed—even those who work as domestic help—feel 'exploited'. Indeed, all of them pointed to the fact of their monetary betterment in Delhi after leaving their economically deprived villages in Bengal and Bihar. Working in the jobs they do in Sheikh Sarai and Navjivan Vihar in south Delhi affords them a level of income sufficient to purchase many products that so far only their employers afforded. Those who live in shared rented accommodation and in quarters in Navjivan Vihar have more comfortable living conditions than those who live in cramped quarters in Jagdamba Camp. But this is not a matter of concern for these women working as domestic help. They have established kinship links with many of the others who live there, having come from the same villages or districts. They feel a sense of family and community (for a discussion on kinship links in India, see, for instance, Cohen 1998, Dube 1997, Harriss-White 2003, Moser 1993, Raheja 1994, Uberoi 1994). Third, drawn to a global city like Delhi for higher monetary gains, television is a medium of entertainment in their free time, with film stars and TV stars whose clothes and make-up they emulate. Television is also a medium of education on the range of products available, some of which they can now afford to buy. An important consequence of this is a sense of self-worth and empowerment.

The strategic nature of these dynamics for the women in my study 'signals the possibility of a variety of concrete politics of resistance, contestation and implementation by women' (Sassen, n.d.). As hardworking, courageous migrant women in a global city, the women in my study can, and do, 'buy membership and self-worth by following the lessons of consumerism dictated by television' (McMillin 2003: 509). The responses of the women in my study to television's role in their lives cannot, indeed, should not, be marginalized or ridiculed as unsuccessful attempts to emulate the middle class. 'To speak in an alternative voice is already to assert a subjectivity and be active in the creation of one's own world' (Kumar 1994: 19). The women respondents in this study are aware of their social position, but do not have any objections to their new lifestyle. Due to increased earnings and exposure to satellite television, they opt for products and lifestyles that give them a sense of optimism and empowerment. In my work on advertising and the 'new' Indian woman (Munshi 1998: 574), I have argued that 'in examining the larger socio-economic Indian context, even when it appears that women are subjugated and dominated, new spaces are constantly being opened up from where women create their own terms of resistance', and even if in small measure, *yeh dil maange more*, this is to be celebrated.

Notes

1. *Yeh dil maange more* (this heart wants more) is one of the most famous bylines used by Pepsi in their advertising campaign. This line was made even more famous when, during the Kargil War between India and Pakistan in 1999, Captain Vikram Batra of the Indian Army, after recapturing Point 5140 at an altitude of 17,000 feet, radioed his commanding officer and echoed this phrase victoriously. Captain Batra's heroics captured the imagination of a nation, made only more poignant by the fact that he was later killed while trying to rescue a junior officer. His cry of the Pepsi slogan became an iconic battle cry during the Kargil war, which was a televised war in India. Captain Batra was posthumously awarded the Param Vir Chakra, the highest award for gallantry in the Indian Armed Forces. The 2001 Hindi film *LOC Kargil* based on the entire Kargil conflict had Abhishek Bachchan playing the role of Captain Batra; and the 2004 Hindi film *Lakshya* (*Mission*), with Hrithik Roshan in the lead role, was a largely fictionalized film on Captain Batra's exploits and valour during the Kargil conflict.
2. *Bhadralok* can loosely be termed as the elite in Bengali society. For detailed discussions on the formation of social classes in West Bengal, and the complex linkages of economic status, social status and caste, see Bardhan 1982, Chatterjee 1979, Munshi 1996.
3. At the time of revising this chapter (June 2006), the exchange rate was Rs 45 = US$ 1.

References

Appadurai, A. 1996. *Modernity at Large: Cultural Dimensions of Globalization*. Minneapolis: University of Minnesota Press.

Appadurai, A. and C. Breckenridge. 1995. *Consuming Modernity: Public Culture in a South Asian World*. Minneapolis: University of Minnesota Press, pp. 1–20.

Bardhan, P. 1982. 'Agrarian Class Formation in India', *Journal of Peasant Studies*, 10(1): 73–94.

Chatterjee, P. 1993. *The Nation and Its Fragments: Colonial and Postcolonial Histories*. Princeton: Princeton University Press.

Chatterjee, T. 1979. 'Social Stratification and Dynamics of Political Power in the Village of Kurumba', *Journal of the Indian Anthropological Society*, 14(1): 1–31.

Cohen, L. 1998. *No Aging in India: Alzheimer's, the Bad Family, and Other Modern Things*. Berkeley and Los Angeles: University of California Press.

Dube, L. 1997. *Women and Kinship: Comparative Perspectives on Gender in South and South-East Asia*. Tokyo: United Nations University Press.

Fernandes, L. 2000. 'Restructuring the New Middle Class in Liberalizing India', *Comparative Studies of South Asia, Africa and the Middle East*, 20(1): 88–104.

FICCI-Arthur Anderson India Pvt. Ltd. 2000. *The Indian Entertainment Industry: Strategy and Vision*. New Delhi: FICCI-Arthur Anderson India Pvt. Ltd.

————. 2001. *Indian Entertainment Industry: Envisioning For Tomorrow*. New Delhi: FICCI-Arthur Anderson India Pvt. Ltd.

————. 2002. *Indian Entertainment Industry: The Show Goes On and On....* New Delhi: FICCI-Arthur Anderson India Pvt. Ltd.

Fugelsang, M. 1994. *Veils and Videos: Female Youth Culture on the Kenyan Coast*. Stockholm: Stockholm Studies in Social Anthropology.

Ganguly-Scrase, R. and T. Scrase. 1999. 'A Bitter Pill or Sweet Nectar? Contradictory Attitudes of Salaried Workers to Economic Liberalisation in India', *Development and Society*, 28(2): 259–83.

Gupta, N. 1998. *Switching Channels: Ideologies of Television in India*. Delhi: Oxford University Press.

Harriss-White, B. 2003. *India Working: Essays on Society and Economy*. Cambridge: Cambridge University Press.

Hartsock, N.C.M. 1993. *The Feminist Standpoint Revisited and Other Essays*. Colorado: Westview Press.

Horkheimer, M. and Adorno, T. 1946 (1998). *Dialectic of Enlightenment*. New York: Continuum.

Kumar. N. (ed.). 1994. *Women as Subjects: South Asian Histories*. New Delhi: Stree.

Liechty, M. 2002. *Suitably Modern: Making Middle-Class Culture in a New Consumer Society*. Princeton: Princeton University Press.

Mankekar, P. 1999. *Screening Culture, Viewing Politics*. Durham, N.C.: Duke University Press.

McMillin, D. 2002. 'Choosing Commercial Television's Identities in India: A Reception Analysis', *Continuum: Journal of Media and Cultural Studies*, 16: 135–48.

————. 2003. 'Television, Gender and Labor in the Global City', *Journal of Communication*, 53(3): 496–511.

Moser, C.O.N. 1993. *Gender Planning and Development: Theory, Practice and Training*. London: Routledge.

Munshi, S. 1996. 'Social Composition of the Nineteenth Century "Bhadralok" in Calcutta', *Bengal Past and Present*, 115(220–21): 28–48.

Munshi, S. 1998. 'Wife/Mother/Daughter-in-law: Multiple Avatars of Homemaker in 1990s Indian Advertising', *Media Culture & Society*, 20(4): 573–93.
————. 2000. 'Media, Consumers and Identity Politics in India: The New Globalization', *Asian Studies*, XXXVI(1): 183–212.
————. 2004. 'A Perfect 10: Modern and Traditional—Representations of the Body in Beauty Pageants, and the Visual Media in Contemporary India', in S. Sen and J.H. Mills (eds), *Confronting the Body: The Politics of Physicality in Colonial and Post-Colonial India*. London: Anthem Press, pp. 162–82.
Raheja, G.G. 1994. *Listen to the Heron's Words: Reimagining Gender and Kinship in North India*. Berkeley and Los Angeles: University of California Press.
Riano, P. (ed.). 1994. *Women in Grassroots Communication: Furthering Social Change*. Thousand Oaks, CA: Sage.
Sassen, S. 1991. *The Global City: New York, London, Tokyo*. Princeton: Princeton University Press.
————. 1999. *Globalization and its Discontents: Essays on the New Mobility of People and Money*. New York: The New Press.
————. n.d. 'Women in the Global City: Exploitation and Empowerment'. Available online at http://www.lolapress.org/elec1/artenglish/sass_e.htm, accessed on 16 June 2007.
Scrase, T.J. 2002. 'Television, the Middle Classes and the Transformation of Cultural Identities in West Bengal, India', *Gazette: The International Journal for Communication Studies*, 64(4): 323–42.
The Economic Times. 2002. 'Entertainment—2001–2002', The ET Knowledge Series.
————. 2005. 'Booming India to Have Global Impact', 22 September.
Uberoi, P. (ed.). 1994. *Family, Kinship and Marriage in India*. Delhi: Oxford University Press.
Varma, P.K. 1998. *The Great Indian Middle Class*. London: Viking.
Varman, R. and Ram Manohar Vikas. n.d. 'Media, Rising Consumer Culture and the Working Class', Conference Proceedings on 'Critical Marketing'. Available online at www.mngt.waikato.ac.nz/ejrot/cmsconference/2005/proceedings/criticalmarketing/Varman.pdf, accessed on 10 June 2007.
Van Wessel, M. 2004. 'Talking About Consumption: How an Indian Middle Class Dissociates from Middle Class Life', *Cultural Dynamics*, 16(1): 93–116.

14

Consuming Art in Middle Class China

Puay-peng Ho

Since the opening up of the Chinese economy in 1979 when the Great Helmsman Deng Xiaoping decreed that 'let some people first become rich', there has been no looking back for China. Chinese society, first along the coast and then the interior, was turned upside down and people became obsessed with the pursuit of money. A quarter of a century later, many people have made it rich or at least attained a comfortable standard of living. Today's metropoles, Guangzhou, Shanghai and Beijing, are nearly completely transformed into centres of insatiable consumption—what occupies the minds of most residents is probably making money and spending it. Jiang Shuo's sculptural group titled 'Looking forward, looking forward money' is a satirical sketch of the current situation. One figure (in the group of two figures) has a raised hand, holding a little red book; this figure symbolizes the days of the Cultural Revolution (1966–76) when the Red Guards ruled. The other figure has a mobile phone in his hand. The contrast between the little red book and the mobile phone is not intended to indicate how wealthy society has become, but the change in the fundamental orientation of society.

The pace of wealth creation continued unabated in the first five years of the new millennium. This period also ushered in a new spirit in urban China: the emergence of a middle class that is optimistic, liberated, fun-seeking and relatively well-off. Apart from making money, these small-time capitalists seek lifestyles consisting of good living, good food and a demand for luxury goods. Increasingly, a section of the middle class wanted a share of the burgeoning art market both for appreciation, as a status symbol and for investment. In return, artists responded with works that reflected the spirit of the age, suited to the taste of these newfound collectors. It was the same for designers and this had an impact on society in the form of new architectural creations. Houses and office blocks were designed to suit the taste and lifestyles of the nouveau rich. Cult status had been attained by artists, architects and developers who attracted attention both within China and internationally. At the same time, international architects have been engaged in designing many public buildings in China. This helped to create an ambience of globalization and set standards for outstanding design. Today, modern art and architecture have become subjects of public consumption through the promotion of the media.

This chapter studies the dynamics of local and international artists/ architects, played out in China in the last five years. The dialogue between local artists and their international audience takes place not only in the art galleries of Beijing and Shanghai, but also in Hong Kong, New York, London and at the Venice Biennale. Success at these international venues ensured success in the home market. As a result, the taste and hitherto unknown artistic orientations of these clients were shaped and nurtured by avant-garde artists and architects. This chapter also looks into the nature of art and architecture patronized by the middle class, which can be seen as expressions of their status, cultural orientations and self identity.

To understand what happened in this past five years, one must look back at the development of art and architecture in the last 20 years of the 20th century. Since the adoption of the open-door policy in 1979, artistic development was distinguished, according to Wu Hung (1999: 12), into five traditions or realms: (i) a highly politicized official art directly under the sponsorship of the Party, (ii) an academic art that struggles to separate itself from political propaganda by emphasizing technical training and higher aesthetic standards, (iii) a popular urban visual culture that eagerly absorbs fashionable images from Hong Kong, Taiwan and the West, (iv) a vanguard Chinese experimental art that consciously tries to link itself to various forms of western modernist and postmodernist art, and (v) an 'international' commercial art that, though often initially part of experimental art, eventually devotes itself to an international art market after finding sponsorship from Hong Kong, Taiwan or foreign galleries.

The situation with architectural development is similar. The right to design in China had always been in the control of state-owned design institutes. These large organizations existed at different levels of the government and were largely conservative—their works could be categorized as being a modernized version of beaux-art architecture. Some architects continued to search for the architecture of modern China by looking into its cultural roots, and expressed this in buildings with Chinese 'characteristics'.[1] Depending on the requirement of the clients, who might want a functional programme or a symbolic one, some architects began to experiment with architectural form, often resulting in amateurish outcomes. In the 1990s, when contacts with Hong Kong and the West strengthened, the architectural scene quickly changed by following the Hong Kong and western models in both commercial and residential developments. Many of these projects were developed by Hong Kong developers and designed by Hong Kong architects. Thus, parallel to the development of contemporary art, contemporary architecture in China came to a crossroad at the end of the 1990s—whether to follow the international style or develop its own indigenous characteristics. Although development in the art might be different from that of architecture, in a consumerist society, there could be many points of convergence between the two forms. How do art and architecture respond to the changing social reality in China? Or, more importantly, how can we understand the emerging consumer class through the art and architecture they patronize? To explore these issues, I shall look at three aspects of development in the last five years: commercialization, westernization and colonization.

COMMERCIALIZATION

One of the five modes of contemporary Chinese art suggested by Wu Hung is how avant-garde artists succumbed very quickly to commercial pressure by tailoring the art to market tastes. For these artists, to be famous in China, they had to go through a circuitous route, with dealers in Hong Kong being the first people to be contacted. Wu Hung summarizes:

> Chinese experimental art was 'discovered' in the early 1990s by curators and dealers in Hong Kong, Taiwan, and the West. A series of events, including the world tour of the *China's New Art, Post-1989* exhibition organized by Hong Kong's Hanart T.Z. Gallery, the appearance of young Chinese experimental artists in the 1993 *Venice Biennale*, and cover articles in Flash Art and the *New York Time Magazine*, introduced this art to a global audience (2000: 18).

Internationalization of Chinese art can be seen too through the first auction of contemporary art in 1998 when Christie's staged an auction entitled *Asian Avant-garde* (Liu Shuyong 2001: 1963). Many Chinese artists featured in the exhibition were already well regarded prior to the auction and many continued to be featured in recent auctions. The artists featured in this first international auction of contemporary Chinese art included Fang Lijun, Cai Guoqiang, Ma Liuming, Wang Guangyi and Xu Bing. These artists are the main draw of auctions even today. They now command very respectable prices, matching some of the well-established modern masters such as Lin Fengmian, Wu Guangzhong or Qi Baishi. The difference between the 1998 auction and the 2007 auctions was that not only had the artists become more expensive but also there was a change in the venue and the kind of people buying the art. It was no longer the foreign but mainland collectors who were buying this art. In the process, artists have gained acceptance at home, and the upper-middle classes have started collecting Chinese artists, whether they (the artists) are based in China or abroad.[2]

For the most successful artists, such as Fang Lijun and Yue Minjun, prices for their works continued to rise, whether sold at auctions or by commercial dealers. At Sotheby's Hong Kong, prices of works by these artists escalated in four consecutive sales alone. In the October 2004 sale, Zhang Xiaogang's *Big Family-Brother and Sister* fetched US$ 54,000; three smaller pieces of work along the same theme entitled *Bloodline Series* fetched US$ 69,400 in May 2005; and most recently, at the October 2005 auction, Zhang Xiaogang's *Yellow Baby Series* fetched a staggering

US$ 1,92,800. These prices were surpassed during the most international auction of contemporary art ever held, on 31 March 2006, in New York. The auction entitled *Contemporary Art Asia: China, Japan, Korea* attracted many bidders from the West and Asia. A painting in Zhang Xiaogang's *Yellow Baby Series* fetched US$ 4,19,200; another Zhang Xiaogang US$ 4,86,400; Yue Minjun's *Lion* US$ 5,64,800; and the scoop of the auction was a painting in Zhang Xiaogang's *Bloodline Series*, which fetched US$ 9,79,200, against an estimate of US$ 2,50,000–3,50,000 (*Artco* 2006: 280–83). In the most recent auctions, the prices for these artists' works took a great leap forward. Yue Minjun's *Life* was sold in the Christie's Hong Kong auction in November 2007 for US$ 28,08,975, three times the estimate. At the same auction, Zhang Xiaogang's *Portrait in Yellow* was sold for US$ 29,54,575, again slightly below three times the estimate. Of course, circumstances surrounding these auctions can be very unpredictable, but the escalation in prices seems unusually drastic. Although there is no clear evidence of who the buyers of these paintings might be, but for the Hong Kong auctions, the main bulk of the buyers were mainland Chinese collectors or investors, and for the New York auction, there were also Chinese buyers bidding with western galleries. The prices in 2007 indicate that the contemporary art market has entered into another phase of development, that of investment more than collection, boosted by the sustained economic boom in China. Alexander Ochs, a German gallery owner in Beijing, once said that: 'Chinese collectors would only collect expensive works. They do not know what they are buying. Asian galleries often bought these works in auctions and resell them to the collectors at exorbitant prices' (ibid.: 258).

For the Chinese, the international auction market is commercially significant. It is regarded as the venue for setting the artistic standards of works of art. A successful sale at an international auction is seen as achieving international recognition. The excellent results at the New York auction were commented on by Tobias Meyer, Deputy Chairman, Sotheby's Europe: 'the overwhelming passion shown during the auction is a clear indication of the international dimension of the market' (ibid.: 283). The auction result is also regarded as setting the price level for the artists in a fair and competitive way. For these two reasons, artists and commercial dealers test the market by offering their works on the auction market. Anthony Lin, the former Managing

Director of Christie's Asia, explains in a recent conversation that the auction market is an inseparable element of the commercial art market. Compared to the market for western contemporary art, Lin is of the opinion that the Chinese art market is still very young and that dealers have not done enough to systematically promote and nurture artists. Thus, it is the job of the auction market to help set the direction for art. However, it is clear that the driving force for these artists is the growing army of the Chinese middle class, whose taste has dictated the artistic directions of commercial art.

This trend prompted a mainland Chinese commentator to lament the shallowness of contemporary artists, summing up the performance of the market in 2005 as:

> The operation of the galleries, the demand of the market and even the creation of the artists tended to be homogenous and coarse.... Exhibitions were full of works produced clearly for the market, they lacked imagination and academic standard.... Like a factory production line, these art pieces were reproduced to satisfy the short-term and unrefined market demand, and at the same time, the artists could amass wealth in a short time. Although commercialization was not necessarily incompatible with intellectualism, the contemporary art situation was full of short-term commercial gain thereby lacking serious academic research and deep-rooted academic pursuits (Lu Yinghua 2006: 27).

The preference and action of these artists must have reflected the demands of the market and the aesthetics of the growing circle of Chinese collectors, as suggested by Lu. This is a clear sign of an art market that is immature and extremely commercialized.

In the area of architecture, since the liberalization of the housing market in the 1990s—the provision of housing not only by the work unit (*danwei*) but also by private developers—housing development started to mushroom at a feverish pitch. The model for development adopted to this day is still that of Hong Kong. It is clear that buildings are unnecessarily lavish and sales promoted not through good design but clever advertisements. The middle class lifestyle was featured in the promotion of chic urban apartments or spacious suburban villas. The end result has been continuous rising property prices, which do not match with the quality of the product. Commercial gain is clearly the objective of these housing developments.

WESTERNIZATION

The most important artistic achievement of the 1990s was experimental art of all shapes and expressions. Many artists worked hard to develop individual expressions. The artists selected for an exhibition curated by Wu Hung, all fall into this category. In Wu's words:

> The works of these artists are not mobilized by a shared political agenda, and these artists have shown little interest in affiliating themselves with any current political or ideological trend. Although most of them have shown works abroad, and some of them are represented by overseas galleries, their works do not follow the formulas provided by political pop or other recognizable styles. These artists' avoidance of an immediate stylistic or thematic identification signifies an effort to disassociate themselves from a prevailing consumer culture based on recognizable brand names. Instead, they have been working hard over the past four or five years to develop an individual artistic language (1999: 24).

The idea of West meets East was clearly demonstrated in a performance art staged by Xu Bing titled *A Case Study of Transference* in 1994. Two pigs were involved in the performance; the boar was stamped all over the body with invented words made up of alphabets, while the sow was stamped with made-up Chinese characters (an art form that brought international fame to Xu Bing). An artist audience was invited to witness the mating of the two pigs. This performance was interpreted as the domination of western influence over Chinese art.[3]

The entry of Chinese contemporary art into the international auction market is also seen by some as signifying the re-orientation of artistic concern to follow western trends. In a report published in the December 1998 issue of *Jiangsu huakan*, it is said that:

> These years, Chinese, Japanese and South Korean artists made frequent appearances in international art shows, their avant-garde art

has received the attention of Western people. Even though their art works are inclined towards the 'western taste', but because of the continued rise in Asian political and economic position, and coupled with the energy released by the [economic] transformation of these countries, art works of these countries become the most poignant expression [of these developments] (Liu Shuyong 2001: 1963).

Is westernization a form of artistic pursuit or a means for commercial success? Clearly, for some artists, the latter was the implicit goal. This is observed in an article in the April 1999 issue of *Jiangsu huakan* which suggests that contemporary Chinese art has entered into a post-colonial phase.

This post-colonial expression has arisen due to the lack of exhibition space in China and the entry of Chinese art into International post-colonial exhibition order in which the subject-matter of Chinese art was twisted. Under the influence of the foreign art market, [Chinese art] become more and more homogeneous in leaning towards the exotic stereotyping of Western culture. As a result, contemporary Chinese art cannot find a suitable road for self development (ibid.: 1983–84).

The works of Wang Guangyi, which mix Cultural Revolution iconic imageries with western consumer icons, such as the Andy Warholesque *Great Criticism Series* (1991–92),[4] can be seen as fitting examples of this observation.

In terms of architecture, it had long been felt that in order to sell housing development, it is necessary for the design to make references to the West. This trend was discerned as early as the mid-1990s. One classic example is the apartment designed with western classical motifs, seen in many housing developments in Beijing and Shanghai. Another example is the design of 1,000 villas planned for Beijing. These designs were possibly lifted from western pattern books. Obviously, the reason for the designs in western style is to increase sales. It is perceived that potential buyers, the middle class, would be more interested in the western form of house design.

However, there is now movement in the opposite direction, that is, using the Chinese courtyard house form as the basis for house design.

It is reported that a Beijing real estate company, Guantang, conducted a market research in 2003 before deciding on how to approach the design of a new development. The result of the survey suggests that more than 60 per cent of the respondents preferred houses built in the western style and only 30 per cent preferred the Chinese style. For this 30 per cent, Guantang went ahead with developing housing in the Chinese style. However, the interior was modelled after western interiors, suited to the lifestyle of the middle class.[5] In the case of architecture, the choice of style is more complex than what the simple East/West dichotomy suggests. Commercial consideration is definitely a strong motive; however, the idea of image and identity, and the suitability for modern living might be other factors at play in the decision on architectural styles.

COLONIZATION

Post-colonialism and western imperialism had been used by many critics to describe the 'invasion' of international architects into China in the last decade. To be sure, this criticism is not only seen in the professional circle, but also in popular media. A headline in *Xin Jinbao*, October 2004, reads 'Has China become the architecture colony of the West?'. Architects from Hong Kong, Singapore, Taiwan, Australia, Europe and North America all had a share in the design of commercial buildings that sprouted up during the fast-paced 1990s. These buildings are not regarded as controversial because they are architecturally generic and attract very little publicity. The first building to have come under the firing line and accused of being a symbol of 'western imperialism' was the National Grand Theatre, located to the west of the Great Hall of the People, a stone's throw from Tiananmen Square, and to the south of the former imperial palace.[6] The site is of crucial importance as it is right next to the centre of political power, past and present, that is, the imperial palace, Zhongnanhai, and the Great Hall of the People. An international competition was announced in 1999 and a shortlist produced in 2000. Juries from across the world were invited to select the winning design. In 2001, unexpectedly, the winner was announced without the knowledge of the juries. The award-winning scheme that was to be built was designed by the French architect Paul Andreu and was to consist of a gigantic oval dome clad with glass and titanium sheets. Under the dome, called the egg by the locals, there were to be four theatres. Access to the interior was to be through an underwater tunnel.

A huge outcry erupted and many letters and opinions were sent to the owner committee of the National Grand Theatre, including a letter signed by 123 fellows of the Academy of Science and the Academy of Engineering opposing Andreu's scheme. The objections included issues of compatibility with the surrounding environment, the appropriateness and meaning of the form, construction costs and future maintenance costs, and the safety of the structure. But the most vocal objections were about the form, which was described by some to be the great century egg, the stupid egg, and it was even said to resemble a gigantic tomb. Under pressure, the project was put on hold even when the site was starting to be excavated. Public consultations were organized but no one could satisfactorily explain the form and all other related questions, except to quote Andreu that the design was to break all tradition. This runs counter to the original brief of the competition that requires an appropriate form as a theatre and a national symbol. In the end, work resumed and the theatre was completed in 2007 and it is scheduled to open in 2008. Never had scholars and academicians joined force so powerfully to express opinions on an architectural project; never had public opinion been so strong as in this project; and never had both failed so miserably. What is important is the rhetoric of the objection: traditional form preferred over an ultra-modern design, local architect versus foreign architect, and even the *fengshui* issue—does Andreu know *fengshui*? In the final analysis, it is the idea of a national icon that is being debated—who is to design it, what form should it take and how can the sense of Chineseness be appropriately expressed?

Since the competition for the National Grand Theatre, international design competitions were organized for many landmark buildings in Beijing, Guangzhou and Shanghai. Some of the most important ones in recent years are the main indoor arena of the 2008 Beijing Olympics, won by Herzog and de Meuron; the Beijing airport extension by Lord Foster; and the headquarters of Chinese Central Television (CCTV) on the eastern fringe of Beijing by Rem Koolhaas. The stadium is designed to be aligned with the main axis of the city of Beijing, thus extending the 7 km long axis to the far north. The other building that attracts a lot of attention is the headquarters of CCTV, dubbed as the 'Titanic of Chinese architecture'. One of the most potent icons of totalitarian control over Communist China is the CCTV. Such a traditional bastion of state control will have a new building designed by a Dutch architect who thrives on theoretical exploration and postmodern posturing. The ground floor of this building is designed to be open so that the citizens of Beijing may stroll in and out of the void. With this new building, the urban space of Beijing is inverted. A new order has emerged where the form of individual building is no longer at the centre stage. It is the space, or the void, created around the buildings that has taken over and become the essential element of the 'liberated' city.

These buildings are more for public consumption; during the design and construction phase, they attract much media attention, and once complete, they are well used by the public. There are also architectural projects that are patronized by middle class consumers. One example is the *Commune by the Great Wall* project, started by a young Beijing entrepreneur Zhang Xin. She assembled 12 Asian architects to design a villa each on a piece of land next to the Great Wall. The project was enormously successful, winning for her a special prize at the 2002 Venice Biennale and the Montblanc de la Culture Arts Patronage Award 2004. The success of the project was seen not only as a real estate development, but also as the promotion of Asian design. Originally intended as a residential development to be sold off, due to the success, the development has now been turned into a hotel, attracting very high prices, with patrons coming from both inside and outside China. This success led to the rise of a number of residential developments around Beijing by Zhang Xin, the most notable one being Jianwai SOHO designed by Riken Yamamoto. This large scale development in downtown Beijing creates a new sense of urban space and is greatly welcomed by the new middle class, attracting high-end restaurant and retail outlets. Other projects by SOHO includes SOHO Shang Du, designed by Peter Davidson of LAB architecture studio, the architect for Federation Square in Melbourne, and Boao Canal village in Hainan island designed by Hong Kong architect Rocco Yim, one of the designers of the *Commune by the Great Wall*. With cutting-edge design by foreign architects, SOHO was able to create an image of modern sensitivity that appealed to the emerging middle class of Beijing.

The question of colonization does not seem to exist in the art world. Chinese collectors tend to buy Chinese art, perhaps due to a sense of patriotism, or perhaps because the prices of western art are too out-of-reach. Therefore, there is no question of colonization of Chinese art by foreign artists. Instead, contemporary Chinese art has been collected by international collectors. However, to ask a symmetrical question, why is it that no Chinese architect was commissioned with projects abroad? For comparison, Japanese architects have been sought internationally for many prestigious projects—the recently opened Museum of Modern Art in New York is designed by Yoshio Taniguchi, and the works of Tadao Ando, Arata Isozaki, Fuhimiko Maki and many more Japanese architects can be found in many cities throughout Europe and USA. Indian architects such as Charles Correa and the Sri Lankan architect Geoffrey Bawa are known worldwide and are beginning to receive international commissions. However, no Chinese architect is recognized in a similar way. One architect and educator who might be considered to have achieved international fame is Zhang Yonghe who is now the head of the department of architecture at MIT. However, his architecture does not attract the same amount of interest worldwide as the Japanese, Indian and Sri Lankan architects just mentioned. The reason for this is probably the lack of publicity and the quality of design work of Chinese architects in general.

SUMMARY

We have examined recent developments in art and architecture in contemporary China. The developments narrated demonstrate the mindset of the upper middle class of urban China and their aesthetic tastes. The accusation of commercialization, westernization and colonization in the production of art and architecture can be seen as a warning for the developing art world. The battle line seems to be drawn between commercialization and the purity of expression in art and architectural design; between westernization and those who advocate safeguarding of traditional values and forms; between colonization and self development and the preservation of indigenous efforts.

In developments in art, we see the flourishing of artistic talents push-
ing hard at the frontier, questioning society as it developed and expressing individualistic positions. One of the most promising centres
for presenting cutting edge artistic and architectural endeavours is the
site called Factory 798 (or Dashanzi). This is a disused factory district
which contains many buildings, some of which were designed in the
1950s by Soviet and German designers. The disused buildings are rented
to artists as studios and there are also exhibition spaces at the site.
Architecture is also an important aspect of Factory 798. Students and
faculty from SCI-Arc, Los Angeles, spent the summer of 2003 in map-
ping out a new Factory 798 according to artistic and visual experiences
(Huang 2004: 174–200). In return, students and faculty from the School
of Architecture, Central Academy of Fine Arts, Beijing, presented their
version of the reconfigured Factory 798 in 2004 (ibid.: 190–215). These
two attempts at remodelling district 798 are very instructional in
that they show different approaches to re-conceptualizing the factory,
based on different attitudes. The Beijing students attempted a post-
structuralist approach to the post-industry condition at the factory
while the Los Angeles students worked on the social programme for
the new 798:

Place/s of Production (21st century danwei—work unit): work and
production are to be preferenced in New Dashanzi [factory 798] at
all costs. Dashanzi was established as a *danwei* and as a place of production. If this critical aspect of Dashanzi's origin is lost, i.e. if total
'de-danweiisation' occurs, then the area will quickly evolve into a
vast consumption zone like New York's SOHO, and become nothing more than a hip shopping and restaurant zone for the ex-pats,
Eurotrash, and China's new 'small capitalists'. There is ample space
for already existing in Beijing. Work places are the foundation of
the new program for Dashanzi. In this way, its '*danwei-ness*' can be
preserved. If the *danwei* was originally a mechanism of social control, the reproduced 21st century *danwei* at Dashanzi is a space of
cultural growth, freedom, and production. Production runs the
gamut from cultural artifacts (art, file, design, architecture, literature, etc.) to energy production (the Power Plant and SHAC-Soft
Heating and Cooling Systems), to physical material production, to
the production of ideas (ibid.: 176–77).

This indeed had taken place at Dashanzi. One look at the exhibition, lecture and workshop schedule, as well as the roll call of artists living and working in the district would reveal a pulsating energy permeating the area. Indeed, it is a production unit capable of generating raw creative ideas that are not tainted by commercialization, westernization or colonization. Sites like Factory 798 in China, just like their predecessors in Xiamen, Chengdu, Guangzhou, Shanghai and Beijing East Village, are the incubating grounds for future artists with social consciousness, or those who might eventually gain international notice and turn commercial. The contemporary art world in China seems like a painful zero-sum game.

Notes

1. These include commercial buildings in Beijing and elsewhere in the country that are roofed with heavy glazed tiles used in traditional imperial architecture. In housing, the development in Ju'er Hutong, Beijing, expresses Beijing vernacular architecture with a modern language. However, when these buildings were built, there was no middle class in China.
2. In a gallery at 798 artist colony, prices for Yue Minjun or Fang Lijun are at the same level, if not higher than those in auctions or private overseas galleries.
3. For a description of the performance and a follow-up performance in which the texts were in reverse, see Erickson, pp. 85–87.
4. For a description of Wang's works, see Nuridsany 2004: 53–60. At the 2005 auction at Sotheby's Hong Kong, one of his *Great Criticism Series*—that of Campbell's soup executed in 2000—was sold for US$ 110,000.
5. See report in *Sanlian shenghuo zhoukan* 2005.
6. For an account of the controversy, see Rowe and Seng Kuan 2002: 192–95.

References

Artco. May 2006, pp. 280–83.

Erickson, Britta. 2004. *On the Edge: Contemporary Chinese Artists Encounter the West*. Stanford: Iris & B. Gerald Cantor Center for Visual Arts.

Gao Minglu (ed.). 1998. *Inside Out: New Chinese Art*. Berkeley: University of California Press.

Gao Qianhui. 2004. *After Origin: Topic on Contemporary Chinese Art in New Age*. Taipei: Artist Publishing Co.

Huang Rui (ed.). 2004. *Beijing 798: Reflection on Art, Architecture and Society in China*. Beijing: Timezone 8 Ltd. and Thinking Hands.

Liu Shuyong (ed.). 2001. *Museum for New China's Art Documents*, vol. 8. Harbin: Heilongjiang jiaoyu chubanshe.

Lu Yinghua. 2006. 'The "Expanding" Contemporary Art of China in 2005', *Contemporary Artists*, February 2006.

Nuridsany, Michel. 2004. *China Art Now*. Paris: Editions Flammarion.

Rowe, Peter G. and Seng Kuan. 2002. *Architectural Encounters with Essence and Form in Modern China*. Cambridge, Mass.: The MIT Press.

Sanlian shenghuo zhoukan. 2005. vol. 352, pp. 56–59.

Wu Hung. 1999. *Transience: Chinese Experimental Art at the End of the Twentieth Century*. Chicago: University of Chicago.

————. 2000. *Exhibiting Experimental Art in China*. Chicago: University of Chicago.

Yin Jinan. 2002. *Post-Motherism/Stepmotherism: A Close Look at Contemporary Chinese Culture and Art*. Beijing: Sanlian shuju.

About the Editors and Contributors

THE EDITORS

Christophe Jaffrelot is Director CERI (Centre d'Etudes et de Recherches Internationales) at Sciences Po (Paris) and Research Director at the CNRS (Centre National de la Recherche Scientifique). He teaches South Asian politics to doctoral students at Sciences Po. He has written extensively on political and regional issues of South Asia, particularly India and Pakistan. His most recent publications include *India's Silent Revolution: The Rise of Low Castes in North India* (2002) and *Dr Ambedkar and Untouchability: Analysing and Fighting Caste* (2004). His current research interests include theories of nationalism and democracy; the rise of lower castes and untouchables in north Indian politics; and ethnic conflicts in Pakistan.

Peter van der Veer is University Professor at Utrecht University, The Netherlands. He is also Chairman of the International Institute for Asian Studies and member of the Royal Netherlands Academy of Arts and Sciences. His research area is religion and nationalism in Asia and Europe and in 2001 he received the Hendrik Muller Award for his contribution to social science research on religion. His major works include *God on Earth* (1988), *Religious Nationalism* (1994) and *Imperial Encounters* (2001).

THE CONTRIBUTORS

Carol Upadhya is Fellow at the School of Social Sciences, National Institute of Advanced Studies, Bangalore.

Bertrand Lefebvre is a researcher at the University of Rouen and at the Centre de Sciences Humaines, Delhi.

Xiaohong Zhou is a Professor of Sociology at Nanjing University.

Jean-Louis Rocca is Research Fellow at CERI and Professor at Tsinghua University, Beijing.

Pál Nyíri is Professor of Anthropology at Macquarie University, Australia.

Anand V. Taneja is a researcher at SARAI, Delhi.

Xun Zhou is a Lecturer at SOAS, London.

Chua Beng Huat is a Professor of Sociology at the National University of Singapore.

Jacqueline Elfick is a researcher at Hong Kong Polytechnic University.

Patricia Uberoi is Honorary Director, Institute of Chinese Studies, Centre for the Study of Developing Societies, Delhi.

Shoma Munshi is Professor of Anthropology and Division Head-Social Sciences at the American University of Kuwait.

Puay-peng Ho is Professor of Architecture and Anthropology at the Chinese University of Hong Kong.

Index

I.E. 2008002198

1+23